MOTOR

AUTO TROUBLE SHOOTER

11th Edition

EDITOR	JOE OLDHAM
EDITORIAL ASSISTANT	LYNNE KANTER
CONTRIBUTING EDITOR	BOB BELL

Published by

MOTOR

1790 Broadway
New York, NY 10019
Printed in USA, © Copyright 1976 by The Hearst Corporation

ACKNOWLEDGMENTS

A book of this size and scope would be an impossibility were it not for the assistance of many different individuals and organizations. The editors of the Motor Auto Trouble Shooter would like to specially thank the following organizations whose cooperation has been invaluable in the preparation of this book.

AC Delco Division
General Motors Corporation

American Motors Corporation

Buick Division
General Motors Corporation

Cadillac Division
General Motors Corporation

Champion Spark Plug Company

Chevrolet Division
General Motors Corporation

Chrysler Corporation

Ford Division
Ford Motor Company

Lincoln-Mercury Division
Ford Motor Company

Oldsmobile Division
General Motors Corporation

Pontiac Division
General Motors Corporation

Books Published by MOTOR

> The nature of the automobile we know today makes it economically impractical to cover all phases of servicing in one book. A brief descriptive list of all titles is provided below for your convenience.

Auto Repair Manual

This most widely used and respected book of its kind covers 2300 car models of 37 series of American-make cars from 1969-76. Also includes tuneup and front end specs on models from 1946-68. The big 1976 edition has more than 1400 double-size pages featuring 55,000 essential service specifications and over 300 quick-check specification charts, 225,000 service and repair facts, and over 3000 how-to-do-it pictures.

Foreign Car Repair Manual

For the imported car owner who is interested in do-it-yourself car repairs, the maintenance of peak performance and in saving money. Also included is a section (not available elsewhere) on parts and tool availability that guides the car owner as to where he can buy the parts and special tools needed to keep his car in top running condition.

Truck Repair Manual

Service and repair is surprisingly easy with this new edition that covers 2800 truck models, 1962 through 1976. Over 1300 pages of step-by-step instructions, 2000 cutaway pictures, 3000 service and repair facts, specs and adjustments. Covers all popular makes of trucks. Manual also gives specs for gasoline and diesel engines used in off-highway equipment and farm tractors.

Auto Engines & Electrical Systems

Ideal basic book for car buffs, students, engineers, mechanics. Over 700 pages, 1300 pictures and diagrams explain the workings of engines, fuel and electrical systems. Special chapters on the rotary and turbine engines.

Hi-Performance Tuning Guide

Many car enthusiasts are getting back to the do-it-yourself thing simply because they want to tailor their cars looks, handling and performance to their own needs and desires. This book gives the basics of setting up a car to achieve the maximum performance from the carburetor . . . ignition . . . camshaft . . . exhaust system . . . gears . . . suspension . . . wheels . . . tires . . . plus hot street setups. Many photographs, diagrams, step-by-step instructions, compiled from authoritative sources, help to know the car better and describe the modifications necessary for peak performance. There are special Compression, Carburetor and Camshaft "Tips for Maximum Performance" and a chart of tire size designations and rim specifications.

Official Used Car Buyers Guide

This book is designed to help the reader become a shrewd used car buyer. It tells how to shop. It gives guidance every step of the way in the sometimes frightening world where cars are in limbo between owners. It reveals the tricks of the used car trade and shows how to see beyond the surface gloss of a car to size up its true mechanical worth. Contents include these chapters: So You Want To Buy A Used Car; Where To Find Used Cars; How To Shop For A Used Car; Checking Out A Used Car; Wheeling And Dealing; Financing Your Used Car; Selling Your Present Car.

101 Shop Secrets Of Master Mechanics

Revealed—the trade secrets master mechanics use to save lots of time, money and skinned knuckles. Simple instructions and detailed illustrations tell how to solve fuel, ignition and chassis problems exactly as the pros do it.
Explains how to: Check belt slippage and timing mark accuracy; Repair turn signals; Remove radiator hoses; Make an emergency fan belt; Easily remove shock absorber nuts; Install headlight springs; Test spark plugs and ignition wiring; Make emergency repairs; Make tools from junk parts; And much much more!

About This Book

The Auto Trouble Shooter is a unique publication among the vast array of books published by Motor. It is one of the only books in the line that doesn't tell you how to fix something.

Indeed, that is not its purpose. Motor publishes the most complete line of auto repair and maintenance manuals in the field. They cover the fix-it side of things very nicely.

The Auto Trouble Shooter is unique in that its sole purpose is to help you quickly spot a problem in an automobile, then give you comprehensive information on what could be causing the problem. This it does in spades.

This completely revised and updated 11th edition contains more than 2500 causes of passenger car and truck problems. Some of the areas you'll find covered are engines, electrical systems, fuel systems, clutches, manual transmissions, automatic transmissions, overdrives, rear axles, brakes, springs, shock absorbers, front suspension components, power steering units, power brake systems, windshield wiper systems, automatic level controls, concealed headlamps, cruise controls, and other systems.

If you're a veteran mechanic, many of the causes of problems listed here may seem simple or even just good common sense. We listed them anyway for a number of reasons. First, so that you'll always be able to rely on the Motor Auto Trouble Shooter as a *complete* guide. Second, because all of us need a little "memory jogging" once in a while, even to remember the obvious.

Novice mechanics will find the Auto Trouble Shooter an ideal helper on any job where diagnosis is involved. Sometimes, nothing is obvious to the novice and that's where this book can be invaluable.

Both expert and novice will find the information on automatic transmission troubleshooting perhaps the most comprehensive guide ever published on the subject.

We suggest that you keep the Auto Trouble Shooter handy for ready reference. If you're a professional mechanic, keep it on the shelf next to your other repair manuals. If you're a novice, your car's glovebox is a good place to keep this book so you'll have it should the need arise due to an on-road breakdown.

Whether you're a professional or a novice mechanic, the Auto Trouble Shooter will save you time and money every time you use it. So use it often.

—Joe Oldham

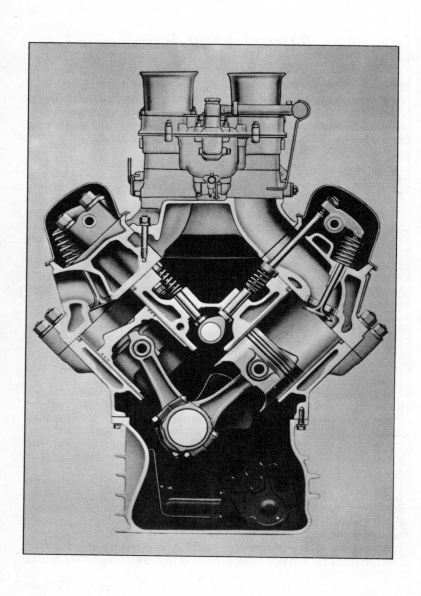

Index

Use this index to look up the specific problem you are trying to correct. If you cannot find the specific problem, then look up the component where the problem is occurring. For instance, if your automatic transmission won't downshift, look up the page number for the automatic transmission you are working on. You'll find specific problems listed there.

ENGINE PROBLEMS

ELECTRICAL PROBLEMS

CLUTCH PROBLEMS

MANUAL TRANSMISSION PROBLEMS

Overdrive Problems

Rambler E-Stick Problems

AUTOMATIC TRANSMISSION PROBLEMS

General Motors

Chrysler

Ford

Other Automatic Transmissions

REAR AXLE PROBLEMS

DRUM BRAKE PROBLEMS

DISC BRAKE PROBLEMS

POWER BRAKE PROBLEMS

FRONT END AND STEERING PROBLEMS

POWER STEERING PROBLEMS

ACCESSORIES

POWER TOP, WINDOW AND SEAT PROBLEMS

Hydro-Lectric Type

Electric Type For Windows And Seats

WINDSHIELD WIPER PROBLEMS

AIR CONDITIONING PROBLEMS

AUTOMATIC LEVEL CONTROL PROBLEMS
General Motors

Ford Motor Company

SPEED CONTROL PROBLEMS

SPEEDOMETER AND CABLE RELEASE
PROBLEMS

SPECIAL SITUATIONS SECTION

Engine Problems

Starting a Stalled Engine

When your car's engine fails to start, 90% of the time the fault will lie in the ignition system, rather than in the fuel system or other systems on the vehicle. If a systematic procedure is followed, the trouble can almost always be found without the use of special equipment.

To begin with, turn on the ignition switch. If the ammeter shows a slight discharge, or if the telltale lamp lights, it indicates that current is flowing. A glance at the gas gauge will indicate whether or not there is fuel in the tank.

Operate the starter. If the engine turns over freely, both the battery and starter are functioning properly. On the other hand, if the starter action is sluggish it may be due to a discharged or defective battery, loose, corroded or dirty battery terminals, mechanical failure in the starter, starter switch or starter drive. If the starter circuit is okay, skip this phase of the discussion and proceed to the ignition.

Starter Circuit Checkout

To determine which part of the starter circuit is at fault, turn on the light switch and again operate the starter. Should the lights go out or become dim, the trouble is either in the battery, its connections or cables. A hydrometer test of the battery should indicate better than 1.250 specific gravity, while a voltmeter placed across the positive and negative posts should indicate about 6 volts for a 6-volt battery and 12 volts for a 12-volt system. If either of these tests prove okay, clean and tighten the battery connections and cable terminals or replace any cable which seems doubtful.

17

If the lights remain bright when the starter is operated, the trouble lies between the battery and the starter. Or the starter switch may be at fault, since it is evident that there is no electrical connection between these points. If these connections are clean and tight, it is safe to assume that the starter or starter switch is defective.

Neutral Safety Switch

If the ammeter shows a slight discharge, or if the telltale lamp lights when the ignition is turned on, but the system goes dead when the starting circuit is closed, the neutral safety switch may be at fault. To check this out, bypass the switch with a suitable jumper. If the engine now starts, adjust or replace the switch.

CAUTION: With the safety switch bypassed, the car can be started in any gear. Be sure the transmission is in neutral or park and the parking brake is applied.

Primary Ignition Checkout

Let's assume that the battery and starter are doing their job and that fuel is reaching the carburetor, but the car does not start. Then the trouble must be somewhere in the ignition circuit. But first, before starting your diagnosis, it is advisable to give the whole system a visual inspection which might uncover obvious things such as broken or disconnected wires, etc.

The best way to start tracking down ignition troubles is to begin with the primary circuit since this is where troubles show up most frequently. First, remove the distributor cap and block the points open with a piece of cardboard. Then turn on the ignition and with a test bulb or voltmeter check to see if there is current at the terminal on the distributor. If you do not get a reading at this point, the current is cut off somewhere in the connections leading back to the ignition switch or it may be that the condenser has an internal short to the ground. The latter possibility can be eliminated if you can restore current at the distributor terminal by disconnecting the condenser from the distributor plate so that its outside shell is not grounded. With the possibility of a bad condenser out of the way, work toward the ignition switch and test for current at each connection until you get to one where you get a reading. Between this connection and the distributor lies the trouble.

18

On cars with 12-volt systems that have an external ignition coil ballast resistor, the foregoing steps in checking the primary circuit should include checking the ignition coil resistor for defects or loose connections. As this is done, bear in mind that while the starter cranks the engine, the resistor is bypassed by the starter switch on Ford and Delco-Remy systems. This means that while the circuit through the resistor may be satisfactory, a broken connection or high resistance between the starter switch bypass terminal and the coil would prevent starting. On the other hand, a satisfactory bypass circuit might start the engine while the engine would stall immediately upon releasing the starter switch if there was a defect in the coil resistance circuit.

If, to begin with, the test equipment shows a current reading at the distributor terminal, it is safe to assume that the trouble is in the unit itself, most likely burned or dirty breaker points. A final positive test for defective breaker points can be made very simply by removing the cardboard from between the points, and positioning the distributor cam by turning the engine to where the points are closed. With the points closed there should be no current at the distributor terminal. If there is current replace the points.

In an emergency, the points can be cleaned by using the sanded side of a match box, a knife blade, or the sharp edge of a screwdriver to scrape the scale from the contact faces. After cleaning the points, and a gauge is not available to set the gap, a quick adjustment can be made by using four layers of a piece of newspaper. The thickness of the paper is equivalent to about .020-inch, which is the approximate gap setting for most distributors. Of course, at the earliest opportunity, a precise point adjustment should be made.

If the procedure outlined under Primary Ignition Checkout does not uncover the trouble then it will be necessary to continue the tests into the secondary ignition circuit.

Secondary Ignition Checkout

First of all, remove the wire from one of the spark plugs, turn on the ignition and operate the starter. While the engine is cranking, hold the terminal of the spark plug wire about 1/4-inch away from the engine or spark plug base. If the spark is strong and jumps the gap, the trouble is confined to either the spark plugs or to a lack of fuel. Before going any further, wipe the outside of the plugs to remove any dirt or dampness which would create an easy path for the current to flow, then try to start the engine again. If it still fails to start, remove one of the spark plugs and if it is wet around the base it is an indication that the fuel system is okay. So it naturally follows that the spark plugs are at fault. Remove all the plugs, clean them and set the gaps. An emergency adjustment of spark plug gaps can be made by folding a piece of newspaper into five layers. When changing the gap, always bend the side (ground) electrode and never the center one as there is danger of breaking the insulation.

Fuel System Checkout

If the spark plug that was removed showed no indication of dampness on its base, check the fuel system. A quick check can be made by simply removing the carburetor air cleaner and looking down into the carburetor. Open and close the throttle manually and if fuel is present in the carburetor, the throttle will operate the accelerating pump, causing it to push gasoline through the pump jet. If it does, check the choke valve. If the engine is cold, the choke valve should be closed. If the choke won't close, the engine can be started by covering the carburetor throat with your hand while the engine is cranking, provided, of course, that fuel is reaching the carburetor.

Check the operation of the fuel pump by disconnecting the fuel lines from the pump to the carburetor. Crank the engine and if the pump is working, fuel will pulsate out of the line. If not, either the pump isn't working or the line from the tank to the pump is clogged. Before blaming the pump, however, disconnect the line at the inlet side of the pump which leads to the tank and, while a companion listens at the tank, blow through the line. If a gurgling sound is heard back in the tank, the line is open and the trouble is in the pump. Remove the sediment bowl and clean the screen. Then replace the bowl and screen, being sure that you have an airtight fit. If the pump still refuses to function, it should be removed and repaired.

The foregoing discussion will, in most cases, uncover the cause of why an engine won't start. However, if further diagnosis is necessary, the following list will undoubtedly provide the answer.

ENGINE WON'T START

Important—Alternator equipped cars cannot be push-started when the battery is completely dead because, unlike a generator, there is no residual magnetism in the rotor.

If the engine fires when the ignition switch is turned on but quits when the switch is released to its running position, it indicates that the ignition coil resistor has lost its continuity or there is a bad connection at the resistor terminals.

Due to Open Primary Ignition Circuit

1. Burned or oxidized ignition points.
2. Ignition coil resistance unit burned out or open (12-volt systems).
3. Starting switch ignition coil resistance bypass circuit open (12-volt systems).
4. Ignition points not closing.
5. Breaker arm binding on pivot post, preventing closing of points.
6. Breaker arm spring weak or broken.
7. Breaker arm distorted or bent.
8. Dirty ignition points.
9. Primary lead connection loose at distributor or coil.
10. Primary windings in coil broken.
11. Open ignition switch circuit.

Due to Grounded Primary Ignition Circuit

A grounded coil primary winding, a grounded ignition switch, or a grounded switch-to-coil primary lead will cause excessive current flow and will usually cause wires to burn.

1. Ignition points not opening or closing due to improper adjustment.
2. Ignition points not opening due to worn rubbing block on breaker arm.
3. Faulty insulating bushing in breaker arm.
4. Cracked or faulty insulator at distributor primary terminal.
5. Grounded condenser.
6. Distributor-to-coil lead grounded.
7. Primary coil winding grounded.

Due to Faulty Secondary Ignition Circuit

1. Corroded spark plug cable terminals.
2. Chafed or cracked insulation on cables.
3. Ignition coil weak or inoperative.

21

4. Moisture on ignition coil, terminals, distributor cover, spark plug porcelains, or in distributor.
5. Improper type of spark plugs.
6. Cracked distributor cap or a burned carbon track from distributor cap center terminal to distributor housing.
7. Improper installation of spark plug cable (not correct for engine firing order).
8. Spark plugs damaged, dirty or wet, porcelains cracked, or gaps improperly spaced.
9. Rotor contact spring bent or broken.
10. Distributor rotor grounded.
11. Distributor cap center terminal (inner) broken or missing.
12. Broken or burned out radio suppressor in distributor cap.

Due to Battery

1. Battery run down.
2. Terminals loose or badly corroded.
3. Improper ground.
4. Battery cables frayed or undersize.

Due to Starter Motor

1. Not operating properly.
2. Congealed engine oil due to use of too heavy a grade of oil or to the formation of sludge.
3. Starter gear binding in flywheel gear.
4. Defective starter switch.
5. Faulty neutral safety switch on cars with automatic transmission.

Due to Excessive Fuel Supply (Flooding)

The engine is said to be flooded with fuel when a quantity of liquid fuel collects in the intake manifold and perhaps also in the cylinders. This condition gives a mixture that is much too rich to ignite.

If the carburetor has a provision for opening the choke valve when the throttle is fully open, crank the engine with the throttle open until engine starts. It will start as soon as the extra fuel is pumped out.

If the choke valve is not designed to open when the throttle is fully opened, tie or block the choke valve open and crank the engine until it starts.

Flooding may also occur on the road. If the carburetor supplies too rich a mixture at full throttle, the intake manifold may be flooded with liquid fuel. The result is that when the engine is stopped, heat evaporates the fuel and thus provides an over-rich incombustible mixture. The engine won't start until the rich mixture is pumped out by cranking.

1. Choke not operating properly.
2. Automatic choke not properly set.
3. Carburetor unloader linkage (if equipped) not properly set.
4. Float level set too high.
5. Dirty, worn or faulty needle valve and seat.
6. Float sticking or rubbing against side of fuel bowl.
7. Leak in float, allowing fuel to get inside.
8. Fuel pump pressure too great.

Due to Insufficient Fuel Supply

1. Carburetor inlet needle stuck in its seat due to gum in fuel.
2. Float level too low.
3. Clogged inlet screen at carburetor.
4. Faulty fuel pump or one of insufficient capacity.
5. Fuel pump strainer clogged.
6. Faulty fuel pump bowl gasket.
7. Flexible line (if used) twisted, deteriorated or restricted.
8. Fuel line to tank clogged, kinked, restricted.
9. Vent in fuel tank filler cap clogged or restricted.
10. Worn fuel pump camshaft lobe.

HARD STARTING

When Engine is Hot

This condition is usually caused by an oversupply of fuel due to any of the items listed under *Engine Won't Start Due to Excessive Fuel Supply*. In rare cases, an ignition coil may lose its efficiency when it is hot and cause ignition failure.

When Engine is Cold

Many of the conditions enumerated under *Engine Won't Start*

23

also may cause hard starting in cold weather. Of particular import-
ance, however, are the following:
1. Choke setting too lean.
2. Fuel may have kerosene, water or ice in bottom of tank.
3. Ice in fuel filter bowl.
4. Ice in fuel lines.
5. Engine is cranked too slowly or won't turn over because:
   (a) engine oil is too thick in sub-zero weather, (b) battery
   weak due to extremely low temperature.
6. Another possibility, although remote, is that the water
   pump is jammed with ice, which will interfere with cranking
   engine if fan belt is tight.

Due to Vapor Lock

The term vapor lock means the flow of fuel to the mixing chamber
in the carburetor has been stopped (locked) by the formation of
vaporized fuel pockets or bubbles caused by overheating the fuel
by hot fuel pump, hot fuel lines or hot carburetor.

The more volatile the fuel the greater the tendency for it to vapor
lock. Vapor lock is encouraged by high atmospheric temperature,
hard driving, defective engine cooling and high altitude.

A mild case of vapor lock will cause missing and hard starting
when engine is warm. Somewhat more severe vapor lock will stop
the engine which cannot be started again until it has cooled off
enough so that any vaporized fuel has condensed to a liquid.

NOTE: Some cars equipped with air conditioning have a vapor
bypass system. These cars have a special fuel filter which has a
metering outlet in the top. Any vapor which forms is bled off and
returned to the fuel tank through a separate line alongside the fuel
supply line. This system greatly reduces the possibility of vapor
lock. However, if vapor lock is suspected examine the bypass valve
to see if it is functioning.

Due to Percolation

Percolation means simply that gasoline in the carburetor bowl is
boiling over into the intake manifold. This condition is most apt to
occur immediately after a hot engine is shut off. Most carburetors
have a provision for relieving the vapor pressure of overheated fuel

in the carburetor bowl by means of ports. If, however, percolation should take place, the engine may be started by allowing it to cool slightly and then holding the throttle wide open while cranking to clear the intake manifold of excess fuel.

After Long Storage

1. The more volatile components in the fuel have evaporated and those remaining are not sufficiently volatile to provide a combustible mixture.
2. Low or run-down battery.
3. Corrosion of engine parts may result in so much friction that starter cannot crank engine at proper speed, if at all.
4. Pistons, etc. may be stuck fast by gummy oil.
5. Engine valves may stick open due to gummy deposits.
6. There is the possibility that any small part essential to the running of the engine may be stuck due to gummy film or to corrosion.
7. Some of these troubles are most likely to occur in hot, humid climate and near salt water.

ENGINE STALLS

Many troubles which prevent smooth running at idle may cause stalling. The list includes almost everything that may cause hard starting or missing. Some of the more common causes are:

1. Engine idle speed set too low.
2. Large air leaks in intake manifold such as a disconnected windshield wiper vacuum line.
3. Ignition points need attention.
4. Vapor lock.
5. Oversupply of fuel (flooding).
6. Valves set too tight.
7. Carburetor seat and/or needle inoperative.
8. Contaminated fuel.
9. Choke sticking or improperly adjusted.
10. Faulty ignition system.
11. Spark plugs damp or dirty and/or gap incorrectly set.
12. Distributor advance inoperative.
13. Exhaust system restricted.
14. Burned, warped or sticking valves.

15. Low compression.
16. Engine overheating.
17. Loose or corroded wiring connections (bulkhead connector etc.).
18. Leaking exhaust gas recirculation valve.
19. Incorrect idle mixture adjustment.
20. Incorrect carburetor float setting.

If carburetor is equipped with a fast idle cam, which increases engine speed when the choke is in operation during the warm-up period, the engine may stall if the fast idle device fails to open the throttle due to sticking or need for adjustment.

On some cars equipped with a fluid coupling or torque converter, if the throttle is closed quickly the engine stalls. To avoid this trouble, most cars have a device which retards the speed of the throttle closing. This is called a throttle return check or dashpot and is usually mounted on the carburetor. It consists of a piston or diaphragm and a spring-closed check valve. If the linkage is out of adjustment or the check valve leaks, the engine will stall.

If the engine quits smoothly when car is in operation, the trouble is often caused by sudden lack of fuel due to:

1. Empty fuel tank.
2. Vapor lock.
3. Flooding.
4. Water in fuel.
5. Frozen fuel line.

Carburetor Icing

The carburetor discharges liquid fuel into the air stream in the form of an atomized spray which evaporates readily. The heat required to evaporate the gasoline is drawn from the entering air, thereby lowering its temperature. The cooler air chills the interior of the carburetor and may cause the moisture in the air to condense into droplets.

Under certain conditions of atmospheric temperature and humidity, the liberated moisture actually collects and freezes on the chilled carburetor surfaces, especially on the throttle plate and surrounding throttle body. When the throttle is almost completely closed for idling, this ice tends to bridge the gap between the throttle plate and throttle body, thereby cutting off the air supply and causing the engine to stall. Opening the throttle for re-starting breaks the ice bridge but does not eliminate the possibility of further stalling until the engine and carburetor have warmed up.

For carburetor icing to occur, the outside air must be cool enough so that the refrigerating effect of fuel evaporation in the carburetor will lower the temperatures of the throttle plate and body below both the dew point of moist air and the freezing point of water. The air must also contain sufficient moisture for appreciable condensation of water to occur when it is chilled in the carburetor.

Generally speaking, carburetor icing occurs when winter grade gasoline (more volatile than summer grade) is used and when the atmospheric temperature ranges from 30° to 50° F. at relative humidities in excess of 65%.

Carburetor icing problems can be reduced by the use of anti-icing additives, such as alcohol, in the fuel. Some fuel refiners use anti-stalling additives in their gasolines which have proved effective in combating carburetor icing.

Another form of carburetor icing has been observed in some engines during high-speed driving on cool, moist days. When certain cars are driven steadily at 60 to 80 mph, the large quantities of cool air passing through the carburetor may result in gradual ice formation within the carburetor's venturi. Since this ice restricts the venturi passage, the resultant increased vacuum in the venturi tends to increase the rate of fuel flow. The fuel-air mixture thus becomes excessively rich, causing loss of power and high fuel consumption.

ENGINE STARTS BUT WON'T DRIVE CAR

1. Broken part in the driveline anywhere from clutch to rear axle shaft.
2. No oil or not enough oil in fluid coupling or torque converter.
3. Some defect in automatic transmission causes binding or dragging of clutches or slipping bands.
4. Engine develops only enough power to run itself due to: (a) extremely lean or rich mixture, (b) excessive engine friction, (c) throttle does not open, (d) very dirty air cleaner, (e) clogged exhaust system.
5. Oil in fluid coupling or torque converter is semisolid due to zero temperature. This trouble is unlikely if the recommended oil is used.

ENGINE MISFIRES

At All Speeds

1. Fouled spark plug or broken porcelain.
2. Faulty spark plug cables.
3. Low battery voltage.
4. Low generator voltage.
5. Burned or pitted ignition points.
6. Incorrect ignition point gap.
7. Faulty condenser or coil.
8. Weak spark or no spark in one or more cylinders.
9. Faulty distributor cap or rotor.
10. Primary circuit restricted or open intermittently.
11. Primary circuit detoured by short intermittently.
12. Secondary circuit restricted or open intermittently.
13. Secondary circuit detoured by short intermittently.
14. Blown cylinder head gasket between cylinders. This can be noted when missing occurs in two adjacent cylinders.
15. Sticking valves.
16. Hydraulic tappet holds valve open slightly.
17. Broken valve spring.
18. Leak at intake manifold gaskets.
19. Mixture too rich or too lean.
20. Electronic ignition malfunction.
21. Engine valve leakage.
22. Exhaust Gas Recirculation malfunction.
23. Early Fuel Evaporation system malfunction (General Motors).
24. Heat control valve malfunction.
25. Malfunctioning fuel pump or fuel system.
26. Contaminated or substandard fuel.
27. Worn distributor cam.
28. Engine overheated.
29. Worn camshaft lobes.
30. Detonation or pre-ignition.
31. Incorrect firing order.

At High Speed

1. Hot spark plugs. Change to colder type but note that a hot plug may be due to loose installation or lack of a plug gasket—if gasket is called for.
2. Ignition point gap much too wide.
3. Breaker arm binding or sticking.
4. Breaker arm spring weak.
5. Sticking engine valves.
6. Valve springs too weak to close valves promptly.
7. Valve springs broken.
8. Valve springs shimmy.
9. Intermittent delivery of fuel to carburetor so that the mixture is momentarily too weak for combustion.
10. Mild vapor lock.
11. Weak spark.
12. Exhaust manifold clogged with carbon.
13. Exhaust manifold, muffler or tailpipe restricted.
14. Improper ignition timing.
15. Centrifugal advance not functioning properly.
16. Manifold heater valve held closed.
17. Dirty carburetor air cleaner.
18. Choke valve not completely open.
19. Carburetor throttle lever loose on shaft.
20. Improper fuel pump operation.
21. Pre-ignition.
22. Incorrect valve timing.
23. Spark plug(s) malfunctions.
24. Engine valve leakage.
25. Electronic ignition malfunction.
26. Ignition wires leaking, open or otherwise defective.
27. Malfunctioning fuel pump or fuel system.
28. Early Fuel Evaporation system malfunctioning.
29. PCV system malfunctioning.
30. Faulty carburetor inlet air temperature control.
31. Contaminated fuel.
32. Faulty coil or condenser.
33. Worn distributor cam.
34. Cracked distributor cap.
35. Incorrect firing order.

At Low or Idle Speeds

1. Faulty spark plugs.
2. Spark plug gaps too narrow.
3. Dirty or corroded secondary circuit connections or faulty ignition cables.
4. Cracked or faulty distributor cap. Radial contacts in cap burned or worn.
5. Dirty air cleaner.
6. Leaky valves.
7. Ignition point gap too narrow.
8. Faulty carburetion due to: (a) float level too high or too low, (b) float valve leaking, (c) incorrect or loose jets, (d) restricted or partially clogged idle air passage or jet, (e) air leak occurring between upper and lower carburetor body, (f) air leak occurring around carburetor throttle shaft.
9. Air leaks in intake manifold or carburetor resulting from: (a) loose manifold connections or leaks occurring in vacuum lines, (b) loose manifold nuts or capscrews, (c) broken or damaged intake manifold or carburetor gaskets, (d) cracked manifold, (e) warped or damaged manifold contacting surface.
10. Slight leaks occurring at fuel pump check valves.
11. Air leak occurring around intake valve stem because of excessive valve stem-to-guide clearance.
12. Engine vacuum leak.
13. Spark plug(s) malfunction.
14. Faulty ignition wires.
15. Electronic ignition system malfunction.
16. Exhaust Gas Recirculation malfunction.
17. PCV system malfunction.
18. Contaminated fuel.
19. Faulty coil or condenser.
20. Worn distributor cam.
21. Faulty or inoperative choke.
22. Faulty spark advance mechanism.
23. Burned, warped or pitted valves.
24. Incorrect valve lifter clearance.
25. Low compression.
26. Incorrect firing order.

When Car is Accelerated

If the engine misses when car is accelerated but does not miss when idling, the reason is that the spark plugs stop firing because of increased compression pressure caused by:
1. Weak spark.
2. Plug gaps too wide.
3. Plug fouled or damp.
4. Plug porcelain below par.
   Also see Flat Spot.
5. Incorrect ignition timing.
6. Incorrect firing order.
7. Faulty coil or condenser.

ENGINE LOPES WHILE IDLING

1. Air leaks between intake manifold and heads.
2. Blown head gasket.
3. Worn timing chain or sprockets.
4. Worn camshaft lobes.
5. Overheated engine.
6. Plugged crankcase vent valve.
7. Faulty fuel pump.
8. Leaking EGR valve.

LACK OF POWER OR HIGH SPEED PERFORMANCE

It should be noted that the altitude at which the car is operated has a decided effect on performance. A car adjusted for normal altitudes will lack performance at high altitudes. Whereas a car which operates normally at high altitudes may have a lean carburetor adjustment and show signs of pre-ignition when operated at sea level.
1. Ignition timing incorrect.
2. Centrifugal governor advance not operating properly.
3. Vacuum advance not operating properly.
4. Ignition points burned, pitted, sticking or bouncing (due to weak breaker arm spring).

5. Faulty spark plugs.
6. Faulty ignition cables.
7. Faulty ignition coil.
8. Faulty carburetion.
9. Lack of engine compression.
10. Pre-ignition.
11. Inoperative manifold heater valve (stuck in closed position).
12. Restricted carburetor inlet resulting from dirty air cleaner or choke valve not fully open.
13. Carburetor throttle lever loose on shaft.
14. Throttle linkage not properly adjusted.
15. Carburetor throttle valve not completely open.
16. Carburetor accelerating pump not functioning properly.
17. Improper fuel pump operation.
18. Partially restricted exhaust pipe, muffler or tailpipe.
19. Clutch slippage.
20. Excessive rolling resistance resulting from (a) dragging brakes, (b) tight wheel bearings, (c) misalignment of power transmitting units, (d) misalignment of rear axle, (e) underinflated tires.
21. Incorrect rear axle gear ratio.
22. Oversize tires.
23. Incorrect valve timing.
24. Inaccurate speedometer (gives impression of lack of performance).
25. Excessive play in distributor shaft or worn distributor cam.
26. Point dwell incorrectly set.
27. Carburetor float level incorrectly set.
28. Contaminated or substandard fuel.
29. Weak valve springs and/or valves sticking when hot.
30. Incorrect valve lifter clearance.
31. Worn camshaft lobes.
32. Pistons incorrectly fitted in engine.
33. Blown cylinder head gasket.
34. Flow control valve inoperative (power steering).
35. Engine overheating.
36. Transmission regulator valve sticking (automatic transmission).
37. Incorrect firing order.
38. Worn distributor rotor.
39. Defective electronic ignition.

ROUGH IDLE

The term rough idle means that the engine does not run smoothly when idling. The most likely cause is an over-rich mixture but any defect which produces uneven explosions or missing will cause a rough idle. The most common causes are:

1. Dirty idle jets and passages.
2. Improper idle adjustment.
3. Dirty air cleaner.
4. Improper float level.
5. Choke set too rich.
6. Air leak into intake manifold.
7. Clogged idle jets.
8. Improper ignition point gap.
9. Improper spark plug gap.
10. Weak spark.
11. Leaky engine valve.
12. Sticking valve or rocker arm.
13. Broken valve spring.
14. Insufficient tappet clearance.
15. Improper fuel pump pressure.
16. Sticking breaker arm.
17. Hydraulic tappet holds valve open.
18. Fuel volatility too high or too low.

SPARK KNOCK, PING, DETONATION

All three expressions mean the same thing. It is a sharp metallic knock caused by vibration of the cylinder head and block. The vibration is due to split-second high-pressure waves resulting from almost instantaneous abnormal combustion instead of the slower normal combustion.

The ping may be mild or loud. A mild ping does no harm but a severe ping will reduce power. A very severe ping may shatter spark plugs, break valves or crack pistons.

Pinging is most likely to occur on open throttle at low or moderate engine speed. Pinging is encouraged by:

1. Overheated engine.
2. Low octane fuel.
3. Too high compression.

33

4. Spark advanced too far.
5. Hot mixture due to hot engine or hot weather.
6. Heavy carbon deposit which increases the compression pressure.

Tendency to ping increases with mixture temperature including high atmospheric temperature, intake manifold heater valve on when engine is warm, hot cooling water, hot interior engine surfaces due to sluggish water circulation, or water jackets clogged with rust or dirt—especially around exhaust valves. Some of these troubles may be confined to one or two cylinders.

If an engine pings objectionably because of too low octane fuel, retard the spark setting. But first be sure that the cooling system is in good condition, the mixture not too lean and the combustion chambers free of carbon deposit.

PRE-IGNITION

Pre-ignition means that the mixture is set on fire before the spark occurs, being ignited by a red hot spot in the combustion chamber such as an incandescent particle of carbon, a thin piece of protruding metal, an overheated spark plug, or a bright red hot exhaust valve. The result is reduction of power and overheating accompanied by pinging. The bright red hot exhaust valve may be due to a leak, to lack of tappet clearance, to valve sticking, or to a weak or broken spring.

Pre-ignition may not be noticed if it is not severe. Severe pre-ignition results in severe pinging. The commonest cause of pre-ignition is a badly overheated engine.

When the engine won't stop when the ignition is shut off, the cause is often due to red hot carbon particles resting on a heavy carbon deposit in a very hot engine.

ENGINE KICKBACK

If ignition is set too far advanced, spark may occur before top dead center when engine is cranked. The first (and only) explosion runs the engine backward. A kickback may jam the starter or break the starter drive housing.

BACKFIRE

Backfiring is a subdued explosion in the intake manifold. Causes are:

1. Lean mixture (often due to dirt or water in fuel).
2. Engine cold and choke too lean.
3. Leaky or sticking intake valve or weak or broken intake valve spring.
4. Leakage of current across distributor cap may cause backfire by enabling spark to occur in a cylinder which is on its intake stroke. Two mixed-up spark plug wires may also cause this trouble.
5. Popping back is same as backfire.

MUFFLER EXPLOSION

1. Late ignition timing.
2. Late valve timing.
3. Burned exhaust valve(s).
4. Weak or broken exhaust valve spring(s).
5. Tight exhaust valve(s).
6. Intermittent open circuit in primary (ammeter needle springs further away from zero when generator is charging).
7. Intermittent short in primary (ammeter swings toward zero when generator is charging).
8. Short in coil or secondary coil wire.
9. If just a couple of explosions are heard and then no more for a time (even for days), the trouble may be due to a gradually failing condenser.

AFTERBURNING

A subdued put-putting at the exhaust tailpipe may be due to leaky exhaust valves which permit the mixture to finish combustion in the muffler. If the exhaust pipe or the muffler is red hot, let it cool, as there is some danger of setting the car on fire. This is most likely to occur when the mixture is lean.

35

FLAT SPOT

If an engine does not respond promptly when the throttle is opened quickly it, or the carburetor, is said to have a flat spot. This is usually caused by any of the following:

1. Accelerator pump piston (or diaphragm) leaks.
2. Accelerator pump valves leak.
3. Accelerator pump stroke too short.
4. Accelerator pump passages restricted.
5. Fuel volatility too low or too high.
6. Float level too low.
7. Fuel pump pressure too low.
8. The anti-percolating valve on some carburetors may open too soon when throttle is closed. If so, carburetor may have flat spot next time throttle is opened when engine is hot.
9. Fuel too hot due to hot engine and hot weather (see Vapor Lock).
10. If carburetor has a metering pin operated by the throttle linkage and also a vacuum piston linked to the throttle to give a rich mixture at part throttle and moderate engine speed, a flat spot will be noted if the device fails to function properly because of a stuck piston, vacuum leakage or restricted vacuum passage.
11. If the carburetor has a vacuum piston which provides a richer mixture at part throttle and moderate engine speed by opening an additional passage or jet within carburetor, a flat spot will occur if the fuel valves fail to work, or the fuel passages are restricted, or if the piston does not function because it is sticking, vacuum leakage or restricted vacuum passages.
12. Late ignition timing.

ENGINE FAILS TO REACH OPERATING TEMPERATURE

1. Defective thermostat.
2. Thermostat stuck open.

3. Thermostat removed from vehicle (during flushing of cooling system and not replaced).
4. Defective temperature sending unit or dash unit.

ENGINE CONTINUES TO RUN AFTER IGNITION IS TURNED OFF

This condition, known as dieseling, run-on, or after running, is caused by improper idle speed and/or high temperature. Idle speed and engine temperature are affected by:

Carburetor adjustment: High idle speed will increase the tendency to diesel because of the inertia of the engine crankshaft and flywheel. Too low an idle speed, particularly with a lean mixture, will result in an increase in engine temperature, especially if the engine is allowed to idle for long periods of time.

Ignition timing: Because advanced ignition timing causes a corresponding increase in idle speed and retarded timing reduces idle speed, ignition timing influences the tendency to diesel in the same manner as carburetor adjustment.

Fuel mixture: Enriching the idle fuel mixture decreases the tendency to diesel by causing the engine to run cooler.

Fuel content: High octane fuels tend to reduce dieseling. Increased fuel content of lead alkyl increases the tendency to diesel. Phosphates and nickel fuel additives help prevent dieseling.

Spark plugs: Plugs of too high a heat range for the engine in question can cause dieseling.

Throttle plates: If the throttle plates are not properly aligned in the carburetor bore, a resulting leanness in fuel mixture occurs, contributing to dieseling.

Electrical system: Normally, during dieseling, ignition is self-supplied by a hot spot, self-igniting fuel, etc. However, there is a possibility of the vehicle's electrical system supplying the necessary ignition. When the ignition switch is turned off, a small amount of current can flow from the generator into the primary of the ignition coil through the generator telltale light. This is particularly true when the warning light bulb has been changed for one of increased wattage.

NOTE: Run-on is more prevalent in an engine when the ignition is turned off before the engine is allowed to return to idle. Therefore, it can be reduced by letting the engine return to idle before shutting

off the ignition. Run-on incidence can be reduced on automatic transmission units by turning off the engine when in gear.
A certain amount of run-on can be expected from any gasoline engine regardless of make, size or configuration. Diesel engines operate on this principle. However, if the above suggestions are correctly employed, run-on will be reduced to an unnoticeable level.

ENGINE OVERHEATS: WATER COOLED

Water is used to cool the engine and air is used to cool the water. Anything which prevents this water-air system from working properly will cause overheating. Oil or grease in the water will reduce the ability of the water to absorb heat from the block and to transfer heat in the water to the radiator. There are six basic causes of overheating:

1. Water does not cool engine.
2. Air does not cool water.
3. Pre-ignition.
4. Pinging.
5. Excessive friction in engine or elsewhere in power transmitting units.
6. Excessive back pressure in exhaust system.

Water Too Hot

1. Slipping fan belt.
2. Not enough water in system.
3. Carburetor mixture too lean.
4. Clogged exhaust system.
5. Late ignition timing.
6. Centrifugal advance fails to advance spark as engine speed increases because weights stick or because of sticking elsewhere in mechanism.
7. Pre-ignition.
8. Detonation.
9. Water circulation impeded by installation of wrong cylinder head gasket.
10. Cylinder head gasket installed incorrectly, blocking off water holes.

11. Leaky cylinder head gasket permits exhaust gas to enter water. The gas bubbles interfere with the ability of the water to cool the engine.
12. Water circulation slowed down by rust, scale or dirt in water jackets.
13. Water distributing tube (when used) within cylinder block rusted out, dented or improperly installed so that not enough water reaches some cylinders, thus causing local overheating.
14. Local overheating at one cylinder (or more) due to heavy deposit of rust, scale or dirt in water jacket around cylinder or exhaust valve port.
15. Water circulation impeded by thermostat which fails to open fully or sticks closed.
16. Water temperature increased by thermostat which fails to open at correct temperature, or the installation of a thermostat which opens at too high a temperature.
17. Any water hose which has rotted on inside, allowing loosened strips of rubber to impede water circulation.
18. The baffle in top tank may be bent in such a way as to interfere with free discharge of water from the hose.
19. Water passages in radiator are partially clogged with dirt, rust, corrosion or scale (mineral salts in hard water).
20. Exterior of radiator clogged with dirt, leaves or insects.
21. Rotting of water hose may weaken it so that pump suction causes it to collapse when engine is running fast, thus throttling the water flow.
22. If water pump seal leaks, air may be drawn into the water. Air bubbles in cooling water reduce the cooling ability of the water.
23. Water pump impeller loose on its shaft or impeller blades badly corroded.
24. Overheats due to alcohol type antifreeze during mild weather.
25. Faulty radiator cap.
26. Car overloaded.
27. Idle speed too low.
28. Air trapped in cooling system.
29. Car in heavy traffic.
30. Incorrect cooling system components installed.
31. Cooling system clogged.
32. Casting flash in cooling passages.

33. Car working beyond cooling system capacity.
34. Antifreeze concentration over specification.
35. Defective fan clutch.

WATER LEAKAGE

Cylinder Head

1. Loose attaching bolts.
2. Dirty, corroded or burred surface prevents tight fit.
3. Warped surface does not fit tight against gasket.
4. Cracked due to freezing or excessive heat.
5. On overhead valve head, exhaust valve seats may be cracked, allowing water to leak into cylinders and crankcase.

Cylinder Block

1. Dirty, corroded or burred surface prevents tight fit.
2. Warped surface does not fit tight against gasket.
3. Cracked due to freezing or excessive heat.
4. Excessive heat may crack exhaust valve seats, allowing water to leak into crankcase.
5. Block cracked due to use of cylinder head bolt which is too long.
6. Leaky expansion plugs or pipe plugs in water jacket.

Cylinder Head Gasket

1. Dirty, corroded or broken.
2. Loose because cylinder head bolts are loose.
3. Leaks because it cannot make tight contact between head and block.

Water Pump

1. Loose pump.
2. Faulty gasket.
3. Improper installation.
4. Warped pump body or dirty metal surfaces.
5. Hole or crack in pump body.

6. Worn seal.
7. Seal improperly installed.
8. Bent pump shaft.
9. Loose bearings or bushings or worn pump shaft.

Radiator

1. Leaks due to freezing or corrosion.
2. Strain due to improper attachment to car.
3. Fan striking radiator.
4. Drain plug or petcock leaks.
5. Radiator baffle bent so that water is directed into overflow pipe.
6. Clogged radiator causing water to pile up in upper tank which causes coolant to flow out overflow pipe.

Hose

1. Hose clamps loose.
2. Hose improperly installed.
3. Hose rotted through.

NOTE: See that all heater connections are tight and that heater core does not leak.

Coolant Recovery System Inoperative

1. Coolant level low.
2. Leak in system.
3. Pressure cap not tight or gasket missing or leaking.
4. Pressure cap defective.
5. Overflow tube clogged or leaking.
6. Recovery bottle vent plugged.

No Coolant Flow Through Heater Core

1. Plugged return pipe in water pump.
2. Heater hose collapsed or plugged.
3. Plugged heater core.
4. Plugged outlet in thermostat housing.
5. Heater bypass hole in cylinder head plugged (six-cylinder).

Loss of Coolant

1. Leaking radiator.
2. Leaking coolant reservoir or hose.
3. Loose or damaged hoses or connections.
4. Water pump seal leaking.
5. Water pump gasket leaking.
6. Radiator cap damaged, or filler neck distorted.
7. Cylinder head gasket leaking.
8. Improper cylinder head screw torque.
9. Cylinder block core plug leaking.
10. Cracked cylinder head or block or warped cylinder head or block gasket surface.
11. Leaking heater core.
12. Leaking heater water control valve.
13. Overfilled cooling system.
14. Quick shutdown after a long run.
15. Air in system causing an occasional burping in system.
16. Insufficient antifreeze allowing coolant boiling point to be too low.
17. Antifreeze deteriorated allowing coolant point to be too low.

ENGINE OVERHEATS: AIR COOLED

These engines run at a higher operating temperature and depend on circulation of air across the cooling fins to keep temperature at a safe level. Overheating can be caused by:
1. Broken fan belt.
2. Seized blower bearing.
3. Jammed or maladjusted damper doors.
4. Defective damper door thermostats.
5. Engine cooling fins clogged with leaves, dirt, etc.
6. Oil cooler fins clogged.
7. Lean carburetor mixture.
8. Incorrect ignition timing.
9. Pre-ignition.
10. Detonation.

ENGINE OIL LEAKAGE

NOTE: If engine is equipped with a positive crankcase vent valve, check the valve for proper operation before checking causes of leak. A clogged crankcase vent valve can build up pressure in the crankcase which will cause seals and gaskets to leak.

1. Oil pan drain plug loose or gasket missing.
2. Crack or hole in oil pan.
3. Oil pan gasket leaks due to: (a) loose screws, (b) damaged gasket, (c) improperly installed gasket, (d) bent oil pan flange.
4. Timing case cover gasket leaks due to: (a) loose screws, (b) damaged gasket, (c) improperly installed gasket, (d) bent cover flange, (e) leakage at engine support plate.
5. Front crankshaft oil seal leaks due to: (a) worn oil seal, (b) seal not properly installed, (c) rough surface on crankshaft, or fan pulley or damper, (d) damper or pulley loose, (e) seal or cover not centered on crankshaft, (f) oil return passage to crankcase clogged up (if provided).
6. Rear main bearing oil seal leaks due to: (a) worn oil seal, (b) improper oil seal installation, (c) worn rear main bearing, (d) rough crankshaft surface.
7. Oil return passage to crankcase clogged.
8. Expansion plug in block at rear of camshaft leaks due to poor fit, careless installation, or corrosion.
9. Leakage at any external piping.
10. Plugs at ends of oil passages in cylinder block leak.
11. Oil filter leaks.
12. Leakage at distributor housing.
13. Valve cover leaks due to loose screws, defective gasket, improperly installed gasket or bent cover flange.
14. Rocker arm cover or push rod cover leaks because of loose screws, defective gasket, improper gasket installation or bent cover flange.
15. Pipe connections loose on oil gauge or oil filter lines.
16. Loose oil pump or faulty gasket (if pump is on outside of block).
17. Clogged breather and/or crankcase ventilating discharge pipe, permits increase in pressure within engine. This causes oil to be forced out past any oil seals or gaskets.
18. If oil pressure relief valve is mounted on outside of block, leakage may occur if unit is loose or its gaskets defective.

HIGH OIL CONSUMPTION

1. External oil leaks.
2. Leaky piston rings due to wear.
3. Leaky piston rings due to sticking caused by gummy deposit. Try to free up with suitable solvent poured in fuel tank. Blue smoke at tailpipe indicates badly leaking rings.
4. Worn pistons and cylinders.
5. Cylinder block distorted by tightening cylinder head bolts unevenly.
6. Excessive clearance between intake valve stems and guides allows oil mist to be sucked into cylinders.
7. Punctured vacuum pump diaphragm permits oil from crankcase to be sucked into intake manifold.
8. Worn main or rod bearings allow excessive leakage from bearings. Result is cylinder walls are flooded with oil.
9. Oil pressure too high due to faulty action of oil pressure relief valve, or clogged relief passage.
10. If pressure lubricated, loose piston pins may permit excessive leakage to cylinder walls.
11. Grade of oil used is too light. A poor quality oil may become far too thin when engine is hot. Hard driving on hot days will also consume more oil.
12. Clogged crankcase ventilator system.
13. Intake valve seals missing or damaged.
14. Plugged drain back holes in cylinder head.
15. Intake manifold leak in conjunction with valve cover gasket leak.
16. Oil level too high.
17. Piston ring gaps not staggered.
18. Incorrect ring size installed.
19. Piston rings out of round, broken or scored.
20. Insufficient piston ring tension due to engine overheating.
21. Ring grooves or return slots clogged.
22. Piston rings stuck in piston grooves.
23. Piston ring grooves worn excessively.
24. Compression rings installed upside down.

OIL PRESSURE RELIEF VALVE LEAKS

1. Relief valve needs tighter adjustment.

2. Relief valve spring weak or broken.
3. Valve seat worn or distorted.
4. Plunger type valve face worn.
5. Plunger type valve stuck open.
6. Ball type valve damaged.
7. Pump discharge pipe or passages leak.

ENGINE OIL DILUTION

1. Oil contains foam caused by presence of water in oil. Water may be due to condensation within crankcase or to a leaky cylinder head gasket.
2. Extreme dilution of oil by fuel may add enough liquid to oil to mislead. In extreme cases, oil level may increase. Dilution is greatest when frequent stops are made in cold weather.

NO OIL PRESSURE

1. Oil pressure gauge defective.
2. Pipe to oil pressure gauge stopped up.
3. Not enough oil in crankcase.
4. Oil pump inoperative.
5. Oil pressure relief valve stuck open.
6. Oil passages on discharge side of pump stopped up.
7. Oil screen or passages on intake side of pump stopped up.

LOW OIL PRESSURE

1. Oil pressure gauge inaccurate.
2. Pipe to pressure gauge restricted.
3. Oil too thin due to dilution, poor quality, or too light a grade used.
4. Oil pressure relief valve adjustment too light.
5. Relief valve spring weak.
6. Oil pump gears worn.
7. Oil pump cover worn.
8. Oil pump body or cover loose.

9. Oil pump gasket damaged, improperly installed or too thick.
10. Air leak in oil intake pipe (if oil level is low).
11. Air leak in top of floating screen (if used).
12. Oil intake pipe or screen clogged with water, sludge, gummy oil, dirt or ice.
13. Oil leak in discharge pipe.
14. Loose connections in oil lines.
15. Worn main, rod or camshaft bearings.
16. Loose camshaft bearings.
17. Leakage at internal oil passages.

HIGH OIL PRESSURE

1. Oil pressure gauge defective.
2. Oil too heavy.
3. Oil pressure relief valve adjustment too heavy.
4. Relief valve spring too stiff.
5. Oil pressure relief passage clogged.
6. Plunger type relief valve stuck by gummy oil or plunger is too tight a fit.
7. Main oil passages on pressure side of pump clogged.

ENGINE NOISES

Loose Main Bearing

A loose main bearing is indicated by a powerful but dull thud or knock when the engine is pulling. If all main bearings are loose, a noticeable clatter will be audible.

The thud occurs regularly every other revolution. The knock can be confirmed by shorting spark plugs on cylinders adjacent to the bearing. The knock will disappear or be lessened when the plugs are shorted. This test should be made at a fast idle equivalent to 15 mph in high gear. If the bearing is not quite loose enough to produce a knock by itself, the bearing may knock if the oil is too thin or if there is no oil at the bearing.

Loose Flywheel

This is evidenced by a thud or click which is usually irregular. To test, idle the engine at about 20 mph and shut off the ignition. If thud is heard, the flywheel may be loose.

Loose Rod Bearing

This is evidenced by a metallic knock which is usually loudest at about 30 mph with the throttle closed. The knock can be reduced or even eliminated by shorting the spark plug. If the bearing is not loose enough to produce a knock by itself, the bearing may knock if the oil is too thin or if there is no oil at the bearing.

Piston Pin

Piston pin, piston and connecting rod noises are difficult to tell apart.

A loose piston pin causes a sharp double knock which is usually heard when the engine is idling. The severity of the knock should increase when the spark plug to this cylinder is short-circuited. However, on some engines the knock becomes more noticeable at 25 to 35 mph on the road.

The piston pin rubs against the cylinder wall, caused by a loose piston pin or a broken snap ring.

Piston and Rings

1. Excessive clearance between pistons and cylinders (piston slap).
2. Out-of-round or tapered bores.
3. Top piston ring strikes ridge at top of cylinder bore.
4. Carbon deposit on top of piston strikes cylinder head.
5. Piston rubs against cylinder head gasket.
6. Broken piston ring.
7. Excessive side clearance of ring in groove.
8. Worn or broken piston ring lands.
9. Broken piston.

NOTE: Exhaust gas leaks may cause spitting or ticking sounds easily mistaken for valve or valve lifter noise. When investigating noises of this type, the following areas should be checked for exhaust gas leaks.
1. EGR valve gaskets.

2. EGR back pressure transducers.
3. EGR back pressure transducer gasket.
4. Choke stove gaskets.
5. Intake manifold gaskets.
6. Exhaust manifold gaskets.

Any such leaks should be corrected prior to doing any mechanical work related to such noise complaints.

Valves

1. Valve click due to too much tappet clearance, hydraulic tappet not working properly, warped valve, sticking valve, binding rocker arm.
2. Insufficient oil to valve mechanism, especially overhead valves.
3. Worn or scored parts anywhere in valve mechanism.
4. Broken valve springs.
5. Weak valve springs.
6. Cocked valve springs.
7. Excessive tappet guide clearance.
8. Lower end of tappet scored, chipped, rough, worn or broken.
9. Very rough surface on cams.
10. Excessive valve stem-to-guide clearance.
11. Valve face not concentric with valve stem.
12. Valve seat face not concentric with valve stem.
13. Valve covers on overhead valve engines tightened excessively will amplify normal valve noise.
14. Dirt in tappets.
15. Low oil pressure.
16. Bent or excessively worn pushrods.
17. Sticking or excessively worn rocker arms.
18. Worn valve guides.
19. Excessive run-out of valve face or seat.
20. Thin or diluted oil.
21. Oil level excessively high or low.
22. Rocker arm retaining nut installed upside down.

Main Bearing Noise

1. Insufficient oil supply.

2. Low oil pressure.
3. Thin or diluted oil.
4. Excessive bearing clearance.
5. Excessive end play.
6. Crankshaft jounal out-of-round, worn.
7. Loose flywheel or torque converter.
8. Loose or damaged vibration dampener.
9. Sprung crankshaft.
10. Excessive belt tension.

Connecting Rod Noise

1. Insufficient oil supply.
2. Low oil pressure.
3. Thin or diluted oil.
4. Excessive bearing clearance.
5. Connecting rod journals out-of-round.
6. Misaligned connecting rods.
7. Connecting rod bolts tightened improperly.
8. Piston-to-cylinder wall clearance excessive.
9. Cylinder walls excessively tapered or out-of-round.
10. Piston ring broken.
11. Loose or seized piston pin.
12. Connecting rods misaligned.
13. Piston ring side clearance excessively loose or tight.
14. Carbon build-up on piston is excessive.

Hydraulic Lifters

The malfunctioning of a hydraulic valve lifter is almost always accompanied by a clicking or tapping noise. Some hydraulic lifter noise may be noticeable when the engine is cold. But if lifters are functioning properly, the noise should disappear when the engine warms up.

If all, or nearly all, lifters are noisy, they may be stuck because of dirty or gummy oil.

If all lifters are noisy, the oil pressure to them may be inadequate. Foaming oil may also cause this trouble. If the oil foams, there will be bubbles on the oil level dipstick. Foaming may be caused by water in the oil, by too high an oil level, or by a very low oil level.

If the hydraulic plungers require an initial adjustment, they will be noisy if this adjustment is incorrect.

If one lifter is noisy the cause may be:
1. Plunger too tight in lifter body.
2. Weak or broken plunger spring.
3. Ball valve leaks.
4. Plunger worn.
5. Lock ring (if any) improperly installed or missing.
6. Lack of oil pressure to this plunger.

If the ball valve leaks, clean the plunger in special solvent such as acetone and reinstall. Too often, plungers are condemned as faulty when all they need is a thorough cleaning.

Gum and dirty oil are the most common causes of hydraulic valve lifter trouble. Engine oil must be free of dirt. Select a standard brand of engine oil and use no other. Mixing up one standard brand with another may cause gummy oil or sticking plungers. Do not use any special oils unless recommended by the car manufacturer and change oil filter or element at recommended intervals.

Timing Gears

1. Gears loose on hubs or shafts.
2. Gears misaligned.
3. Excessive gear backlash.
4. Eccentric gear, usually due to high key.
5. Teeth meshed too tight (new oversize gear).
6. Too much end play in camshaft or crankshaft.
7. Front crankshaft bearing clearance excessive.
8. Chipped tooth—usually on camshaft gear.

Timing Chain

1. Chain loose due to wear.
2. Sprocket teeth worn.
3. Sprockets loose on hubs or shafts.
4. Sprockets misaligned.
5. Front camshaft bearing clearance excessive.
6. Front main bearing clearance excessive.
7. Loose vibration damper or drive pulley.

Loose Engine Mountings

This may be detected by the presence of an occasional thud with the car in operation. It is most likely to be noticed at the moment the throttle is opened or closed.

Excessive Crankshaft End Play

A rather sharp rap which occurs at idling speed but may be heard at higher speeds also may be due to excessive crankshaft end play. The noise should disappear when the clutch is disengaged.

Water Pump

1. Water pump shaft pulley loose.
2. Impeller loose on shaft.
3. Too much end play in pump shaft.
4. Too much clearance between shaft and bearings.
5. Impeller blades rubbing against pump housing.
6. Impeller pin sheared off or impeller broken.
7. Rough bearing.
8. Pump seal too hard.

Fan Belt

1. Belt worn or burned.
2. Wrong belt. Does not fit pulley grooves properly.
3. Belt too tight. Squeaks.
4. Belt or pulley dirty or sticky with gummy oil.
5. Pulley bent, cracked or broken.
6. Belt pulleys misaligned.
7. Belt loose—squeaks when engine is accelerated.

Fan

1. Fan blades bent.
2. Fan blades loose on hub.
3. Fan out of balance when made.
4. Fan blades strike radiator.
5. Fan shaft end play excessive.
6. Fan shaft loose on its bearings.
7. Defective fan bearings.
8. Bearings need lubrication.

Engine Vibration

1. Unequal compression in cylinders.
2. Missing at high speed.
3. Unbalanced fan or loose fan blade.
4. Incorrect adjustment of engine mounts, or damaged mounts.
5. Loose engine mounts.
6. Engine support loose on frame or cylinder block.
7. Unbalanced or sprung crankshaft.
8. Excessive engine friction due to tight pistons, etc.
9. Defective vibration damper.

Fuel Pump Noise

The diagnosis of a fuel pump suspected of being noisy requires that some form of sounding device be used. Judgment by ear alone is not sufficient. In this way, a fuel pump may be needlessly replaced in attempting to correct noise contributed by some other component. Use of a stethoscope, a long screwdriver, or a sounding rod is recommended to locate the area or component causing the noise. The sounding rod can easily be made from a length of copper tubing $1/4$- to $3/8$-inch in diameter.

If the noise has been isolated to the fuel pump, remove the pump and run the engine with the fuel remaining in the carburetor bowl. If the noise level does not change, the source of the noise is elsewhere and the original fuel pump should be reinstalled. On models using a fuel pump push rod, check for excessive wear and/or galling of the push rod.

Electrical Problems

NOTE: Ignition problems, both conventional and electronic, are included in the *Engine Problems* section under the various operating difficulties these problems could cause.

BATTERY REQUIRES FREQUENT RECHARGING

Insufficient Current Flow to Battery

1. Defective generator or alternator.
2. Incorrect voltage regulator setting.
3. Regulator contacts oxidized or burned.
4. Sulphated battery.
5. Corroded battery terminals.
6. Regulator not grounded.
7. Loose connections or grounds in lighting or ignition circuits.
8. Slipping fan belt.
9. Blown regulator fuse.
10. Wrong size generator drive pulley.
11. Shorted or open alternator rectifiers.
12. Grounded stator windings in alternator.

Excessive Starting Load Causing Abnormal Current Flow from Battery

1. Frequent use of starting motor.
2. Excessive use of starting motor due to difficulty in starting.
3. Faulty starting motor.
4. Excessive engine friction due to tight pistons, etc., or heavy engine oil.

Excessive Lighting Load

1. Car operation confined largely to night driving.
2. Tail and stop light wires reversed.
3. Stop light switch inoperative (closed at all times).
4. Unnecessary use of head lamps while parking.
5. Ground or short in lighting circuit.

Abnormal Accessory Load

1. Radio.
2. Heater.
3. Windshield defroster.
4. Cigar lighter.
5. Spotlights.

Internal Discharge of Battery

1. Plates badly sulphated.
2. Cell leak due to cracked jar or sealing compound.
3. Water level not maintained at proper height.
4. Plate separators ineffective.
5. Exterior of battery covered with corrosion and acid-soaked dirt which forms a path to ground for current.

Miscellaneous

Radio suppressor is connected to the generator or regulator field terminal.

STARTER WON'T ROTATE
OR ROTATES SLOWLY

If the lights become dim or go out when the starter switch is closed, the battery may be too weak to operate the starter. In this case, the engine may be started by pushing the car.

NOTE: Some engines cannot be started by pushing the car because these transmissions have no rear oil pump to drive the engine through the transmission. In such cases, a fully charged battery should be installed or a jumper circuit should be used from another charged battery.

Cars equipped with alternators cannot be push started if the battery is completely dead because alternators retain no residual magnetism.

Due to Starter Circuit

1. Low battery. Lights grow very dim or go out when starter switch is closed.
2. Connections loose, dirty, corroded or broken at battery terminals, starter switch terminal, battery ground strap.
3. Short circuit across starter terminal.
4. Neutral start switch out of adjustment or defective.

Due to Starter Switch

1. Starter pedal (if any) stuck.
2. Starter switch stuck.
3. Pedal linkage fails to close starter switch (older cars).
4. Defective solenoid.
5. Neutral safety switch on cars with automatic transmissions out of adjustment or defective.
6. Starter switch makes poor contact due to dirt, corrosion, bent parts, weak contact spring.
7. Starter switch fails to close circuit because of sticking or broken contact parts.

Due to Armature and Field Circuits

1. Armature windings burned out, shorted, grounded or open-circuited.
2. Short circuit in armature winding or brush pigtail lead.
3. Broken wire in armature winding or brush pigtail lead.
4. Loose, dirty or corroded connections in armature circuit, including ground.
5. Field coils burned out, shorted or grounded.
6. Broken wire in field winding or broken lead.
7. Loose, dirty or corroded connections in field circuit.

Due to Commutator and Brushes

1. Brush pigtail leads loose or broken.
2. Starter brushes cracked crosswire (prevents flow of current).
3. Arm type brush holder sticks.
4. Brush sticks in sliding brush holder.
5. Bent brush holder misaligns brush and causes poor contact.
6. Starter brushes badly worn.
7. Brush leads shorted or have loose, dirty, corroded or broken connections.
8. Poor brush contact due to weak or broken springs.
9. Brushes coated with oil.
10. High mica between commutator segments prevents brush contact.
11. Commutator bars loose and/or solder melted.
12. Commutator dirty, corroded or burned.

Due to Engine Resistance

1. Piston sticking to cylinders in overheated engine.
2. Pistons stuck to cylinders because of gummy oil.
3. Pistons binding in cylinders because of corrosion after long layup.
4. Jammed generator armature.
5. Combustion chamber full of water.
6. Solid ice in water pump.
7. Broken part in engine causes jamming.
8. Excessive engine friction, due to cold weather and too heavy oil.

Due to Improper Engine Repairs

1. New rings too tight.
2. New pistons too tight.
3. Main or rod bearings too tight.
4. New camshaft bearings too tight.

Due to Armature Binding

1. Loose field poles.

2. Armature shaft frozen in bearings.
3. Loose end plates.
4. Windings thrown out of armature slots.
5. Armature locked magnetically to field poles because of loose bearings or worn or bent armature shaft.
6. Bendix spring retaining screws loose (jammed against housing).
7. Cracked or distorted drive housing.
8. Starter misaligned.
9. Starter jams because of burred teeth on drive pinion or flywheel gear.
10. Starter pinion (sliding gear type) jams because of incorrect endwise clearance.

STARTER SPINS BUT WON'T ENGAGE FLYWHEEL GEAR

Bendix Type

1. Bendix pinion stuck on shaft due to dirty, gummy, or bent shaft.
2. Bendix spring broken.
3. Bendix spring bolt broken.
4. Pinion housing cracked.
5. Drive key sheared.
6. Pinion teeth broken off.
7. Starter ring gear has several teeth missing.
8. Armature shaft broken.

Sliding Gear Type

1. Weak or broken meshing spring.
2. Fault in sliding gear linkage.
3. Fault in solenoid.
4. Overrunning clutch worn out or lubricant caked or gummy.
5. Drive key sheared.
6. Pinion teeth broken off.
7. Flywheel ring gear has several teeth missing.
8. Armature shaft broken, dirty or dry.
9. Wrong starter pinion clearance.

STARTER PINION
JAMMED INTO FLYWHEEL GEAR

1. Burred teeth on pinion or ring gear.
2. Misalignment of starter or armature shaft.
3. If engine kicks back when being started, Bendix pinion may jam. Loosen starter to free pinion.

STARTER PINION DISENGAGES SLOWLY

Bendix Type

The most probable cause of the above problem is a dirty Bendix drive shaft. Or the pinion may bind on its shaft because it is bent or there is too tight a fit between the pinion and the splines.

When a Bendix Folo-Thru starter drive stays in mesh too long it is probably due to a sticking release pin which is designed to be released by centrifugal force at a certain engine rpm. In such an instance the drive should be replaced.

Sliding Gear Type

1. Pinion binds on its shaft due to too tight a fit or due to bent or burred shaft.
2. Pinion shaft sticky or dirty.
3. Sliding gear operating linkage sticking or binding.
4. Solenoid does not operate properly.

STARTER PINION WON'T RELEASE

Bendix Folo-Thru Drive

A failure to disengage would most probably be caused by a stuck release pin which is designed to be released by centrifugal force at a given engine rpm. If this is the case, replace the drive unit.

Sliding Gear Type

If solenoid operated, the solenoid may be defective. If pedal operated, the shift linkage may be binding or sticking. This problem may also be caused by a defective starter switch on cars with a key-starter switch or by improper starter pinion clearance.

STARTER NOISE

1. Loose pole pieces rubbing against armature.
2. Gear noise due to defective teeth.
3. Flywheel ring gear untrue.
4. Starter drive housing loose on flywheel housing.
5. Starter loose on drive housing.
6. Commutator end plate loose.
7. Armature shaft bent.
8. Worn armature shaft, bearings or bushings.
9. Drive pinion shaft bent.
10. Worn drive pinion shaft, bearings or bushings.
11. Misalignment caused by dirt or burrs on mating surfaces.

GENERATOR DOES NOT CHARGE

1. Fan belt broken or slips badly.
2. Belt pulley slips on armature shaft.
3. Cutout relay fails to close.
4. Armature won't rotate because of seized bearing, etc.
5. External wiring from generator to starter switch terminal short-circuited or circuit is open because of detached wire or very dirty or corroded connection.
6. Voltage regulator inoperative.
7. Open circuit or short circuit in armature
8. Brushes stick.
9. Brushes coated with oil.
10. Brush lead connections dirty or disconnected.
11. Improperly seated brushes.
12. Weak brush springs.
13. Very dirty commutator.
14. Burned or corroded commutator.
15. Commutator bars short-circuited.
16. High mica on commutator.
17. Solder melted at commutator bar connections.

GENERATOR NOISE

1. Generator loose on engine.
2. Generator end plates loose.
3. Armature shaft bent.
4. Armature shaft worn.
5. Bushing or bearing worn or needs lubrication.
6. Armature shaft end play excessive.
7. Generator pulley loose on its shaft.
8. Generator or pulley misaligned.
9. Bent, cracked or broken pulley.
10. Generator fan rubs on generator.

GENERATOR BRUSH NOISE

1. High mica between commutator bars.
2. Sprung armature shaft.
3. Rough, dirty or glazed commutator.
4. Worn or loose brushes.
5. Commutator out of round.
6. Brushes not seating properly.
7. Too little or too much brush spring tension.

ALTERNATORS

Alternator Fails to Charge

1. Drive belt loose.
2. Brushes sticking.
3. Open charging circuit.
4. Break in stator winding circuit.
5. Faulty soldered connections at output terminal stud.
6. Rectifiers open circuited.

Low Unsteady Charging Rate

1. Drive belt loose.
2. High resistance at battery terminal posts.
3. Loose connections.
4. Poor ground between engine and body ground wire.

5. Resistance in charging circuit.
6. Open stator windings.

Low Output

1. Grounded stator.
2. Shorted rectifier.
3. Voltage regulator faulty.

Excessive Charging Rate

1. Voltage regulator faulty.
2. Open circuited rectifier.

Noisy Alternator

1. Misaligned belt or pulley, or loose pulley.
2. Shorted rectifier.
3. Worn bearings.
4. Rotor shaft sprung.

Regulator Points Oxidized

1. Poor ground connections.
2. Improper voltage regulator air gap setting.
3. Shorted field in alternator.
4. Voltage regulator setting too high.

Burned Points or Coil Windings in Regulator

1. Voltage regulator setting too high.

Voltage Regulator Points Stuck

1. Poor ground connections between alternator and regulator.

LOCATING ELECTRICAL SHORTS WITH TEST LAMP

Due to the complexity of locating electrical short circuits where several circuits are protected by the same fuse, it is recommended that you fabricate a test lamp from the material shown in the accompanying illustration. Fig 1. By substituting the test lamp for the blown fuse, the short circuit can be isolated.

When the test lamp is inserted into the fuse panel, the bulb will light and continue to glow until the short circuit is removed. Determining which circuit is at fault can be accomplished by disconnecting the affected circuits one at a time until the test lamp goes out. Then trace the circuit to find the cause of the short (wire contacting sharp sheet metal edges, wire pinched between two metal objects, etc.).

For circuits that are not connected to the fuse panel but are protected by an in-line fuse cartridge, use a test lamp having two needle point probes in place of the blown fuse. Insert one probe through the insulation and into the wire on each side of the blown in-line fuse and follow the same testing procedure outlined above.

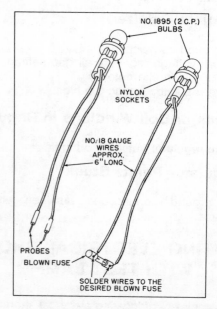

Fig. 1.   Test lamp for locating shorts.

FUSIBLE LINKS

Some cars, starting with 1965 models, have fusible links located between the battery and the lower ends of the main supply wires. These links are the weakest point in the electrical supply system for the entire car and, as such, will act as a fuse for every wiring harness in the car. Every electrical accessory is still protected by a fuse or circuit breaker, of course. But fusible links have been added to protect the wiring harnesses *before* the fuses.

In the past, if a wire became grounded in the portion between the battery and the fuse block, a long section of the wire would burn out, making replacement of a complete wiring harness necessary. Now, with the fusible links, a short or ground in any unfused wire will cause only a short link to burn out. Because of its location, the possibility of a fire, such as was sometimes caused by a burned-out wiring harness, is very remote.

A fusible link is simply a short section of wire that is several sizes smaller in gauge than the wire in the circuit which it protects. If a short or ground occurs, the fusible link will melt before the insulation is damaged elsewhere in the circuit. Replace the burned-out fusible link as directed in the illustration, Fig. 2

LIGHTS FLICKER

Circuit Breaker Vibrates

When the circuit breaker vibrates and causes the lights to flicker, it indicates a short in one of the lighting circuits, which may be traced as follows:

1. Pull switch successively to each lighting position. If circuit breaker vibrates in all positions except OFF, the trouble should be found in the tail lamp and license lamp circuit, or instrument, map light, or clock light circuits.
2. If circuit breaker vibrates in parking lamp position only, look for a short in the parking lamp circuit.
3. If circuit breaker vibrates in headlamp position only, inspect headlamp wiring circuit and lamp assemblies. If both filaments in headlamps burn at the same time, check dimmer switch.

63

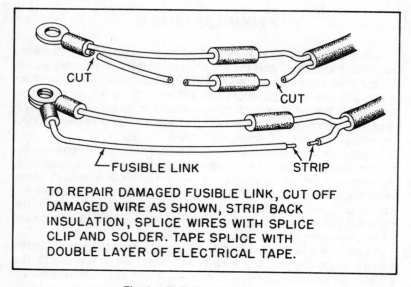

CUT

CUT

FUSIBLE LINK   STRIP

TO REPAIR DAMAGED FUSIBLE LINK, CUT OFF
DAMAGED WIRE AS SHOWN, STRIP BACK
INSULATION, SPLICE WIRES WITH SPLICE
CLIP AND SOLDER. TAPE SPLICE WITH
DOUBLE LAYER OF ELECTRICAL TAPE.

Fig. 2.   Repairing fusible links.

LAMPS FAIL TO BURN

1. Burned out bulb.
2. An open circuit in wiring.
3. A defective switch.
4. Burned out fuse.

LIGHTS FLARE UP WHEN ENGINE IS SPEEDED UP

This condition is caused by high voltage in the electrical system
due to one or more of the following:
1. Electrolyte in battery low or weak.
2. High resistance in circuit between generator and battery
   due to loose or dirty connections.
3. Poor ground between generator and engine.
4. Voltage regulator adjusted too high.

5. Voltage regulator inoperative.
6. Ground or short in generator field circuit.

One Bulb Inoperative

1. Bulb burned out.

One Side Inoperative

1. Loose connection, open wiring or defective bulbs.
2. Defective directional signal switch or cancelling cam.

All Inoperative

1. Stop-hazard fuse blown.
2. Stop-switch maladjusted or defective.

Will Not Turn Off

1. Stop switch maladjusted or defective.

STOP LIGHTS

1. Check stop light switch.
2. Check brake pedal clearance.
3. Check for dragging brakes.

NOTE: If the compensating port in the brake master cylinder is plugged by foreign material or is covered by the piston primary cup when the brake pedal is released, high pressure will be maintained in the hydraulic system and the stop light switch will remain closed.

BACKUP LAMPS

One Lamp Inoperative or Intermittent

1. Loose or burned out bulb.
2. Loose connection.
3. Open ground connections.

Both Lamps Inoperative or Intermittent

1. Neutral start switch misadjusted. (Open when shift lever is in reverse position.)
2. Loose connection or open circuit.
3. Blown fuse.
4. Defective neutral start switch.
5. Defective ignition switch.

Lamp Will Not Turn Off

1. Neutral start switch maladjusted. (Closed when shift lever is not in reverse position.)

SIDE MARKER LAMPS

One Lamp Inoperative

1. Turn signal bulb burned out (front lamp).
2. Side marker bulb burned out.
3. Loose connection or broken wiring.

Front or Rear Lamps Inoperative.

1. Loose connection or open ground connection.
2. Multiple bulbs burned out.

All Lamps Inoperative

1. Blown fuse.
2. Loose connection.
3. Broken wiring

TAIL, PARK AND LICENSE LAMPS

One Side Inoperative

1. Bulb burned out.
2. Open ground connection at bulb socket or ground wire terminal.

Both Sides Inoperative

1. Tail lamp fuse blown.
2. Loose connection.
3. Open wiring.
4. Multiple bulb burnout.
5. Defective light switch.

TURN SIGNALS

1. If signals are inoperative on both turns, look for a blown fuse or a defective flasher.
2. If stop lights burn, the fuse and rear signal lamp bulbs are okay.
3. An inoperative right signal light may be caused by a burned out bulb at the right indicator or a right signal lamp. The opposite applies for an inoperative left signal light.
4. If bulbs are okay, look for an open circuit or defective switch.
5. If indicator light on dash burns steadily when lever is placed in a turn position, check for burned out bulb in park or stop light. If park and stop light bulbs are okay, check for faulty flasher.
6. If indicator light on dash does not burn when lever is in a turn position, check for burned out bulb, faulty flasher, high resistance to bulb at socket, breaks or grounds in wiring harness from front turn signal bulb socket to indicator lights.
7. If switch fails to cancel after completion of turn, remove steering wheel and check for worn or broken mechanism.
8. If turn signal lever is difficult to operate, check for loose actuator rod, distorted or broken yoke, loose or misplaced springs, foreign parts and/or material, or a loosely mounted switch.
9. If turn signal lights flash very slowly, check for inoperative turn signal flasher, low charging voltage, high resistance ground at light sockets, loose connections.
10. If turn signal will not remain in turn position, check for foreign material or loose parts in turn signal.
11. If hazard switch cannot be turned off, check for foreign material between hard support cancelling leg and yoke.
12. If hazard switch will not remain on or is difficult to turn off,

check for loose switch mounting screws, interference with other components, foreign material or improperly installed actuating lever.

13. If hazard signal lights will not flash but turn signal functions properly, check for blown fuse, inoperative hazard warning flasher, loose connections.

KEY BUZZER PROBLEMS

Buzzer Does Not Sound With Key Fully Inserted in Lock Cylinder With the Driver's Door Open

1. Defective buzzer.
2. Bad connection at buzzer.
3. Power not available to buzzer.
4. Horn relay inoperative. (Some models.)
5. Door jamb switch on driver's side maladjusted or inoperative.
6. Short in chassis wiring.
7. Short or fault in signal switch wiring.
8. Chips, burrs, foreign material preventing actuator tip function.
9. Defective lock cylinder.
10. Chips, foreign material affecting buzzer switch operation.
11. Damaged or broken buzzer switch.
12. Switch appears good but will not make contact.
13. Buzzer switch contact gap too large.

Buzzer Continues to Operate With Key in the Lock Cylinder With the Driver's Door Either Opened or Closed and Ceases When Key is Removed

1. Door jamb switch on driver's side maladjusted or inoperative.
2. Wire from signal switch to door jamb switch shorted.

Buzzer Continues To Operate With Key Out, But Stops When Driver's Door is Closed

1. Turn lock towards start position. If buzzer stops in Run position or when turned past Run towards Start, the problem is a sticky lock cylinder actuator.
2. Chips, foreign material in lock cylinder bore.
3. Sticky lock cylinder actuator tip.
4. Damaged or broken buzzer switch.
5. Buzzer switch contact gap too close.

ELECTRIC CLOCK

If the clock does not run, check for a blown clock fuse. If the fuse is blown, check for a short in the wiring. If the fuse is not blown, check for an open circuit.

With an electric clock, the most frequent cause of a blown fuse is low voltage at the clock which will prevent a complete wind and allow the clock contacts to remain closed. This may be caused by any of the following: a discharged battery, corrosion on contact surface of battery terminals, loose connections at battery terminals, at junction block, at fuse clips, or at terminal connection of clock. Therefore, if in reconnecting the battery or the clock, it is noted that the clock is not ticking, always check for a blown fuse, or examine the circuits at the points indicated above to determine and correct the cause.

HAZARD WARNING FLASHERS

To make a quick check of the system, pull the hazard warning switch to ON position. The rear turn signal bulbs should flash as well as the front turn signal bulbs, turn signal indicator bulbs and pilot bulb. All lights will burn continuously when the brake pedal is depressed. This is normal.

Pilot Bulb Fails to Flash

Check for burned out bulb and loose or defective ground wire. Replace bulb, repair ground wire or tighten ground wire screw. If

69

this does not correct the condition, replace flasher switch and harness assembly. Then repeat quick check procedure.

All Bulbs Fail to Flash

1. Check for loose harness connections at hazard warning connectors and secure connectors if necessary.
2. Check for a burned out tail- and stop light fuse and replace if necessary.
3. Check for a defective hazard warning flasher or switch. This may be done by removing the flasher and installing a new flasher.
4. Pull switch to ON position. If flasher does not operate properly, replace flasher switch and harness assembly, installing old flasher. If system still does not operate properly, install new flasher along with new switch.

Some Bulbs Fail to Flash While Others are Operative

1. Turn on ignition switch and turn off hazard warning switch.
2. Place turn signal lever first to right and then to left turn position. If turn signal circuits operate properly, the hazard warning switch and harness assembly should be replaced.
3. If the same bulbs fail to flash, the cause is most likely a burned out bulb. In the case of turn signal indicator bulbs, a loose or defective ground wire can also cause this condition. Repair as necessary.

NOTE: If any turn signal bulb fails to flash when the turn signal circuit is actuated, the reduced current in the circuit will cause the remaining signals on that side of the car to burn steadily. If the hazard warning flasher is energized, however, all turn signal bulbs and indicator bulbs will flash except those that have a circuit defect. They will flash at a constant rate unless the battery is completely run down. This is because the hazard warning flasher overrides the turn signal circuit flasher.

4. If the condition is still not resolved, disconnect the hazard warning connectors and again check the operation of the

turn signal circuits. If the affected bulbs now flash, replace flasher switch and harness assembly.
5. If the condition is still not resolved, look for defects in the connectors to the affected bulb.
6. Repeat quick check test.

Turn Signals Inoperative One Side

1. Bulb(s) burned out (flasher cannot be heard).
2. Open wiring or ground connection.
3. Improper bulb or defective turn signal switch.
4. Short to ground. (Flasher can be heard, no bulbs operate.)

Turn Signals Inoperative

1. Blown turn signal fuse.
2. Defective flasher.
3. Loose connection.

Hazard Warning Lamps Inoperative

1. Blown stop-hazard fuse.
2. Defective hazard warning flasher. (Located on fuse panel.)
3. Open in wiring or defective turn signal switch.

HEADLAMPS

One Headlamp Inoperative or Intermittent

1. Loose connection.
2. Defective sealed beam.

One or More Headlights Are Dim

1. Open ground connection at headlight.
2. Black ground wire mislocated in headlight connector (type 2 sealed beam).

One or More Headlights Have Short Life

1. Voltage regulator misadjusted.

All Headlights Inoperative or Intermittent

1. Loose connection.
2. Defective dimmer switch.
3. Open wiring—light switch to dimmer switch.
4. Open wiring—light switch to battery.
5. Shorted ground circuit.
6. Defective light switch.

Upper or Lower Beam Will Not Light Or is Intermittent

1. Open connection or defective dimmer switch.
2. Short circuit to ground.

HORN

Horn Will Not Operate

1. Loose connections in circuit.
2. Defective horn switch.
3. Defective horn relay.
4. Defects within horn.

Horn Has Poor Tone

1. Low available voltage at horn.
2. Defects within horn.

Horn Operates Intermittently

1. Loose or intermittent connections in horn relay or horn circuit.
2. Defective horn switch.
3. Defective relay.
4. Defects within horn.

Horn Operates Constantly

1. Sticking horn relay.

2. Horn relay energized by grounded or shorted wiring.
3. Horn button can be grounded by sticking closed.

CHARGING SYSTEM INDICATOR

Light On, Ignition Off

1. Shorted positive diode.

Light Not On, Ignition On And Engine Not Running

1. Bulb burned out.
2. Open in light circuit.
3. Open in field.

Light On, Engine Running Above Idle Speed

1. No generator output.
2. Shorted negative diode.
3. Loose or broken generator belt.

COOLANT TEMPERATURE INDICATOR

Hot Indicator Light Not Lit When Cranking Engine

1. Bulb burned out.
2. Open in light circuit.
3. Defective ignition switch.

Light On, Engine Running

1. Wiring grounded between light and switch.
2. Defective temperature switch.
3. Defective ignition switch.
4. Coolant temperature above 258° F.

OIL PRESSURE INDICATOR

Light Not Lit, Ignition On and Engine Not Running

1. Bulb burned out.

2. Open in light circuit.
3. Defective oil pressure switch.

Light On, Engine Running Above Idle Speed

1. Grounded wiring between light and switch.
2. Defective oil pressure switch.
3. Low oil pressure.

RADIO

Radio Inoperative

1. Blown fuse.
2. Antenna open or shorted.
3. Faulty radio power connections.
4. Faulty speaker connections.
5. Faulty speaker.
6. Faulty radio.

Radio Noise, Varies With Engine Speed

1. Insufficient or faulty engine ignition and engine accessory radio frequency suppression devices.

Radio Noise, Does Not Vary With Engine Speed

1. Outside electrical interference.
2. Interference caused by electrical motors, solenoids and/or switches located in vehicle.
3. Faulty radio.

Weak Reception

1. Antenna trimmer misadjusted.
2. Shorted antenna lead.
3. Open antenna lead.
4. Faulty radio.

Distorted Reception

1. Faulty speaker.
2. Faulty radio.

Intermittent Reception

1. Open or shorted antenna lead.
2. Loose power or antenna connections.
3. Loose radio mounting causing poor ground.
4. Faulty speaker.
5. Faulty radio.

CONCEALED HEADLAMPS

Vacuum Type

Examine all hoses for splits. These splits occur most often around connections. Also look for kinked or pinched hoses, a condition which often occurs when retaining clips are too tight, thus blocking off vacuum flow.

If inspection reveals that all the hoses are satisfactory, check each vacuum actuator by disconnecting the actuator hoses one at a time and hooking a vacuum gauge to the hose(s). With the engine running, if the gauge indicates at least 14 inches of vacuum, the problem is either in the actuator, which must be replaced, or because of jammed covers or linkage.

If the gauge shows less than 14 inches of vacuum, check the vacuum at the storage tank, distribution valve, check valve vacuum relay, if used, and at each hose connection.

Electrical Type

Connect a jumper wire directly from the battery to the motor(s). If the system operates, check the headlight or motor control switch. If the switch is eliminated as the cause of trouble, check the wiring. Look for loose connections, broken wires or terminals.

If the system fails to operate with the jumper wire, remove the motor for repair or install a new or rebuilt unit.

Clutch Problems

Clutch Drags

Clutch drag means that when the clutch pedal is depressed fully, the clutch disc is not completely released. Consequently, it does not come to rest, but continues to rotate, being dragged around by the rotation of the engine. Clutch dragging causes clashing of gears, especially when shifting from Neutral to Low or Reverse.

1. Pedal cannot disengage clutch because of excessive free pedal travel. Pedal linkage should be adjusted so that the pedal shank is about 1 inch from the underside of the toe-board.
2. Worn clutch linkage.
3. Release levers need adjustment.
4. Clutch disc warped out of true.
5. High spot on clutch facing.
6. Broken or loose facings.
7. Loose rivet in facing.
8. Clutch disc hub binds on splined clutch shaft due to bent shaft, tight fit, burred splines or splines covered with gummy oil or dirt.
9. Clutch disc wobbles because of broken springs in hub.
10. Clutch disc hub out of true.
11. Clutch shaft bent.
12. Clutch shaft out of true because of worn bearings.
13. Transmission is not in alignment with flywheel housing.
14. Clutch pressure plate warped, thus throwing release levers out of adjustment.
15. Flange of clutch cover not in alignment with flywheel because of loose attaching screws, bent flange, dirt between flange and flywheel.
16. Grease on clutch facings.
17. Engine misaligned due to deteriorated or broken engine mounts.
18. Loose flywheel housing-to-engine attaching bolts.
19. Release fork pivot worn.

Clutch Slips

The clutch disc slips whenever the clutch pressure plate fails to hold it tight against the face of the flywheel. If clutch slippage is severe, the engine speed will rise above normal on full throttle in high gear. Slight but continuous slippage may go unnoticed until the clutch facings are ruined by excessive temperature caused by friction.

In a very high percentage of cases, clutch slippage is due to less than zero clearance between the shank of the pedal and the toe-board because of failure to have the pedal adjusted in time. The consequence is worn and burned clutch facings. Before the clutch starts slipping, the normal wear of the facings causes a gradual reduction in clutch pedal free play. When there is no free play of the pedal, the clutch starts slipping.

Other causes of clutch slippage are:
1. Driving with foot resting on pedal.
2. Binding or sticking of pedal or its linkage.
3. Binding or sticking of clutch disc hub on clutch shaft.
4. Binding of release levers.
5. Release bearing sleeve sticks.
6. Weak or broken clutch pressure springs.
7. Worn clutch facings.
8. Facings covered with grease or oil.
9. Facings burned.
10. Release levers improperly adjusted.
11. Pressure plate sticks.

Clutch Grabs

A clutch is said to grab when it engages too abruptly. The usual causes are:
1. Loss of tension in cushioning plates in the rim of the steel clutch disc. These plates cause the clutch facings to bulge outward slightly. The resulting springy action of the facings aids in producing a smooth, gentle clutch engagement.
2. Use of wrong type of clutch facing.
3. Grease or oil on facings.
4. Clutch springs too stiff.
5. Momentary binding in clutch linkage while clutch is being engaged.

6. Exposed rivet heads due to excessively worn facing or loose rivets.

Clutch Chatters

If a clutch chatters while it is being engaged, the trouble is caused by rapid gripping and slipping. The usual causes are:
1. Somewhat sticky clutch friction surfaces due to gummy lubricant.
2. Clutch friction surfaces damp or wet.
3. Weak clutch springs.
4. Slight binding in clutch linkage during engagement.
5. Slight binding of pressure plate during engagement.
6. Loose engine mounts.

Clutch Pedal Pulsates

Clutch pedal pulsation has often been termed a nervous pedal. When a slight pressure is applied on the pedal, with the engine running, the pedal will vibrate or bounce with every revolution of the engine. As the pressure on the pedal is increased, the pulsation will cease.
1. Loose or improperly adjusted engine mounts.
2. Collar on clutch release sleeve does not run true due to a bent clutch shaft. Or the clutch shaft may be misaligned between crankshaft and transmission.
3. Clutch release levers not adjusted to uniform height.

Clutch Rattles

This condition will occur when the engine is idling with transmission in Neutral.
1. Excessive clearance at pressure plate driving lugs.
2. Anti-rattle springs or retractor springs on release levers (or release bearing) weak, broken or disconnected.
3. Looseness in clutch pedal operating linkage.
4. Loose flywheel.

Noise When Pedal is Depressed

1. Clutch release bearing worn, dirty, damaged, broken or inadequately lubricated.
2. Clutch shaft bearing or bushing in crankshaft worn, damaged, broken or inadequately lubricated.
3. Clutch shaft rear bearing at front end of transmission, worn, dirty or lacks lubricant.

Noise When Pedal Is Released

1. Misalignment of transmission with engine causing slight wobble of clutch disc hub. Noticeable with engine idling or at low road speed.
2. Disc hub loose fit on splined clutch shaft.
3. Disc damper springs weak or broken.
4. No pedal play.
5. Weak or broken pedal return spring.
6. Weak or broken release sleeve spring.
7. Clutch linkage sticks.
8. Clutch pedal sticks.
9. Clutch release sleeve sticks.
10. Clutch release fork binds.
11. Bad clutch release bearing.
12. Loose flywheel.

BEARING NOISE

Clutch Release Bearing

With the engine idling, there is a high-pitched rubbing noise when the foot rests on the clutch pedal.

Clutch Pilot Bearing

A fairly high-pitched noise is evident when the clutch pedal is fully depressed with the engine idling.

Manual Transmission Problems

THREE-SPEED TRANSMISSION

General Motors Transmission With Second Speed Gear Located At Rear Of Mainshaft Non Synchronized First Gear

Slips Out of High and/or Second Gear

1. Transmission mounting bolts loose.
2. Control rods interfere with engine mounts or clutch release lever.
3. Control linkage does not work freely.
4. Gear does not fully engage.
5. Damaged mainshaft pilot bearing.
6. Clutch gear bearing retainer broken or loose.
7. Dirt between transmission case and clutch housing (front mounted), or between transmission case and differential carrier (rear mounted).
8. Misalignment of transmission.
9. Worn or broken synchronizer assembly.
10. Weak springs in transmission cover.

Slips Out of Low and/or Reverse

1. First and/or Reverse gears damaged from operating at part engagement.
2. Improperly mated splines on inside of First and Reverse gear and/or external splines on Second and Third synchronizer sleeve.

Sticking in Gear

1. Clutch not releasing completely.
2. Low lubricant level.
3. Corroded transmission levers.
4. Tight main drive gear pilot bushing.
5. Defective synchronizer sleeve or blocking ring.

Forward Gears Clash

1. Clutch not releasing completely.
2. Weak or broken springs in synchronizer assembly.
3. Worn blocking rings and/or cone surfaces.
4. Broken blocking ring.

Noisy In Forward Speeds

1. Insufficient or incorrect lubricant.
2. Transmission misaligned or loose.
3. Main drive gear or bearings worn or damaged.
4. Countergear bearings worn or damaged.
5. Synchronizers worn or damaged.

Noisy In Reverse

1. Reverse idler gear or shaft worn or broken.
2. Reverse gear worn or broken.
3. Improperly adjusted linkage.
4. Weak spring in transmission cover.

Hard Shifting

1. Improper clutch or adjustment.
2. Worn or damaged shift linkage.
3. Incorrect lubricant.
4. Synchronizers worn or broken.

Jumping Out Of Gear

1. Maladjusted, worn or loose shift linkage.
2. Transmission loose or misaligned.
3. Worn pilot bearing.

4. Excessive end play in main drive gear.
5. Weak detent cam spring.
6. Detent cam notches worn.
7. Worn clutch teeth on main drive gear or synchronizer sleeve.
8. Worn or broken synchronizer.
9. Bent output shaft.

Noisy in All Gears

1. Not enough lubricant.
2. Worn countergear bearings.
3. Worn or damaged clutch gear and countershaft drive gear.
4. Damaged clutch gear or mainshaft ball bearings.
5. Damaged speedometer gears.

Noisy in High Gear

1. Damaged clutch gear bearing.
2. Damaged mainshaft bearing.
3. Damaged speedometer gears.

Noisy in Neutral with Engine Running

1. Damaged clutch gear bearing.
2. Damaged mainshaft pilot bearing roller.

Noisy in All Reduction Gears

1. Not enough lubricant.
2. Worn or damaged clutch gear or countershaft drive gear.

Noisy in Second Only

1. Damaged or worn Second gear.
2. Worn or damaged countergear rear bearings.

Noisy in Low and Reverse Only

1. Worn or damaged First and Reverse sliding gear.
2. Damaged or worn Low and Reverse countergear.

Noisy in Reverse Only

1. Worn or damaged Reverse idler.
2. Worn Reverse idler bushings.
3. Damaged or worn Reverse countergear.

Excessive Backlash in Second Only

1. Second gear thrust washer worn.
2. Mainshaft rear bearing improperly installed in case.
3. Worn countergear rear bearing.

Excessive Backlash in Reduction Gears

1. Worn countergear bushings.
2. Excessive end play in countergear.

Leaks Lubricant

1. Too much lube in transmission.
2. Loose or broken clutch gear bearing retainer.
3. Clutch gear bearing retainer damaged.
4. Cover loose or gasket damaged.
5. Operating shaft seal leaks.
6. Idler shaft expansion plugs loose.
7. Countershaft loose in case.
8. Lack of sealant on bolts.

FULLY SYNCHRONIZED TRANSMISSION

Noises

When diagnosing transmission noise, note the gear position in which the noise occurs. Noise present in all gear positions may be due to worn or damaged constant mesh gears or bearings. Noise present in only one gear can usually be traced to the particular gear

involved. Other causes of noise are as follows:
1. Misalignment due to loose mounting bolts.
2. Clutch housing misalignment.
3. Dirt or metal chips in lubricant.
4. Not enough lube in transmission.
5. Improper lubricant.

FOUR-SPEED TRANSMISSION

Noisy in All Speeds

1. Incorrect lubricant level.
2. Incorrect type lubricant.
3. Countergear bearings worn or damaged.
4. Countergear worn or damaged.
5. Clutch gear bearing worn or damaged.
6. Mainshaft bearing worn or damaged.
7. Clutch gear worn or damaged.
8. Transmission misaligned or loose.

Noisy in First Gear

1. First gear worn or damaged.
2. Countergear worn or damaged.
3. Countergear bearings worn or damaged.
4. Synchronizers worn or broken.
5. Countershaft worn or damaged.

Noisy in Second Gear

1. Second gear worn or damaged.
2. Countergear worn or damaged.
3. Countergear bearings worn or damaged.
4. Synchronizers worn or broken.
5. Countershaft worn or damaged.

Noisy in Third Gear

1. Third gear worn or damaged.
2. Countergear worn or damaged.
3. Countergear bearings worn or damaged.

4. Synchronizers worn or broken.
5. Countershaft worn or damaged.

Noisy in Fourth Gear

1. Clutch shaft bearing worn or damaged.
2. Mainshaft bearing worn or damaged.
3. Synchronizers worn or broken.

Noisy in Reverse

1. Reverse idler gear or shaft worn or damaged.
2. Reverse sliding gear worn or damaged.
3. Shift linkage out of adjustment.
4. Shift linkage bent or damaged.
5. Shift linkage parts loose.
6. Shift levers, shafts or forks worn.

Shifts Hard

1. Clutch pedal free travel incorrect.
2. Clutch parts worn or damaged.
3. Shift linkage out of adjustment.
4. Shift linkage bent or damaged.
5. Shift linkage parts loose.
6. Shift levers, shafts or forks worn.
7. Lubricant type incorrect.
8. Lubricant level incorrect.

Jumps Out of Gear

1. Shift linkage out of adjustment.
2. Shift linkage bent or damaged.
3. Shift linkage parts loose.
4. Shift levers, shafts or forks worn.
5. Shift cover loose or gasket damaged.
6. Transmission misaligned or loose.
7. Synchronizers worn or broken.
8. Clutch gear bearing retainer broken.
9. Clutch gear bearing worn or damaged.
10. Clutch pilot bearing worn or broken.
11. Mainshaft and/or pilot worn or damaged.
12. Mainshaft bearing worn or damaged.

Sticking In Gear

1. Clutch not releasing fully.
2. Low lubricant level.
3. Incorrect lubrication.
4. Corroded transmission levers (shaft).
5. Tight main drive gear pilot bearing.
6. Frozen synchronizing blocking ring on main drive gear cone.
7. Burred or battered teeth on synchronizer sleeve and/or main drive gear.

Forward Gears Clash

1. Clutch not releasing fully.
2. Weak or broken springs in the synchronizer assembly.
3. Worn blocking rings and/or cone surfaces.
4. Broken blocking rings.
5. Excessive rock of synchronizer assembly on mainshaft.

Gears Spinning When Shifting Into Gear From Neutral

1. Clutch not fully releasing.
2. Binding main drive gear pilot bearing.
3. Synchronizers not functioning.

Reverse Gear Clash

1. Allow approximately 3/4 seconds after the clutch pedal has been depressed before shifting into Reverse.
2. If gear clash continues after allowing proper time for the clutch plate to stop, check the clutch adjustment to make sure that it is within specifications.
3. Make sure that the engine idle speed is set to specifications.
4. Dragging clutch driven plate.
5. Distorted clutch driven plate.
6. Tight or frozen main drive gear bearing.

Scored or Broken Gear Teeth

1. Insufficient lubricant.
2. Failure of the car operator to fully engage the gears on every shift before engaging the clutch and applying engine power.

Leaks Lubricant

1. Lubricant level incorrect.
2. Lubricant type incorrect.
3. Vent plugged.
4. Clutch gear bearing retainer or gasket loose.
5. Clutch gear bearing retainer broken.
6. Shift cover loose or gasket damaged.
7. Shifter shaft seals leaking.
8. Shift cover bolts not sealed.
9. Countershaft loose in case bore.

OVERDRIVE PROBLEMS

1975 American Motors

Overdrive Will Not Engage

1. Low lubricant level.
2. Open wire or switch in electrical control circuit.
3. Plugged oil pan or pressure filters, plugged or sticking pump non-return valve assembly.
4. Sticking relief valve piston.
5. Broken relief valve assembly or piston springs.
6. Plugged control orifice.
7. Solenoid valve sticking, grounded or open.
8. Sticking or worn sliding clutch.
9. Broken or weak clutch return springs.
10. Leaking clutch or internal case leaks.
11. Damaged or worn gear components.
12. Pump body misaligned with oil feed slot in case bore.
13. Pump plunger of body worn excessively.

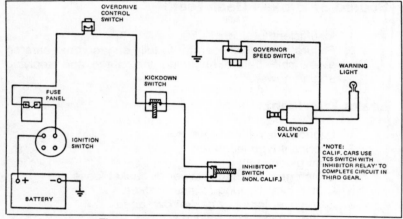

Fig. 3.   Overdrive electrical control circuit.

Overdrive Will Not Disengage

CAUTION: This condition requires immediate correction, as extensive damage may result if vehicle is moved in Reverse.

1. Closed switch or short in electrical circuit.
2. Solenoid valve stuck or shorted.
3. Relief valve piston stuck or spring broken.
4. Control orifice plugged.
5. Sliding clutch sticking.
6. Damaged or seized gear components.

Slow Disengagement and/or Overdrive Freewheels On Overrun

1. Solenoid valve oil feed holes plugged or valve sticking.
2. Control orifice plugged.
3. Overrunning clutch worn or seized.
4. Worn or damaged sun gear or sliding clutch hub.
5. Worn or damaged friction material on sliding clutch.
6. Worn or damaged brake ring.
7. Relief valve piston sticking.

Overdrive Slips When Engaging

1. Low lubricant level.

2. Plugged oil pan or pressure filter.
3. Sticking or plugged non-return valve.
4. Broken spring on relief valve assembly.
5. Control orifice stuck.
6. Solenoid valve sticking.
7. Oil feed holes plugged.
8. Loose wire at solenoid terminal.
9. Worn clutch or worn friction material on sliding clutch.
10. Internal leak in case.
11. Worn pump plunger or body.
12. Damaged or worn gear components.
13. Pump body not aligned with oil feed slot in case bore.
14. Annulus gear clutch surface worn, burned, or galled.

Shudders, Chatters When Backing Up (Overdrive Disengaged)

1. Loose or defective engine and transmission support cushions.
2. Transmission clutch slipping, incorrectly adjusted.
3. Weak clutch return springs.
4. Worn or damaged friction material on sliding clutch.
5. Burned or galled annulus gear clutch surface.

Noisy When Engaged

1. Sliding clutch slipping.
2. Worn, galled or pitted bearings or rear bushing.
3. Pinion gears or mainshaft annulus gear teeth chipped or broken.
4. Worn or chipped overrunning clutch rollers, or clutch race in annulus gear.
5. Mainshaft thrust washer worn, broken or missing.
6. Sun gear chipped or missing.

Light Knocking Sound

1. Pump body installed improperly (flat not aligned with oil hole).

All Other Models

Figs. 4 to 7 illustrate the overdrive circuit diagrams in use. Since

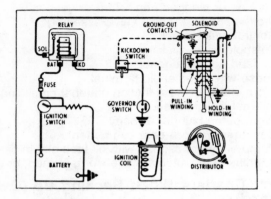

Fig. 4.   Overdrive circuit diagram with relay.

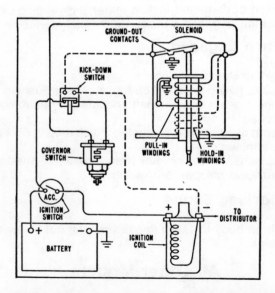

Fig. 5.   Overdrive circuit diagram without relay. Beginning with 1964.

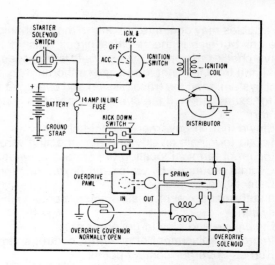

Fig. 6. Overdrive circuit diagram without relay. 1958–63.

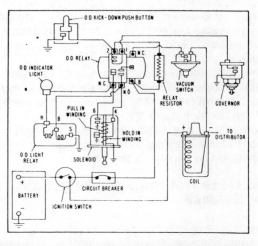

Fig. 7. Rambler twin stick overdrive circuit diagram. Beginning with 1964.

91

overdrive troubles may originate not only in the mechanical operation of the unit but also in the electrical circuit which controls that unit, always check the control system before disassembling the overdrive. If the trouble is not found after a thorough inspection of the control system, then the transmission and overdrive should be removed for examination. If the overdrive operation is unsatisfactory, look for:

1. Blown fuse in governor-solenoid circuit.
2. Loose terminals on any of the connecting wires.
3. Incorrect terminal location of connecting wires.
4. Circuits grounded by water, dirt or deformation.
5. Defective solenoid points.
6. Insufficient travel or unsatisfactory contacts in kickdown switch.
7. Excessive end play in governor shaft.
8. Improper adjustment of governor control springs.
9. Burned governor contact points.
10. Damage to governor cap and contacts.
11. Absence of rubber cover to exclude water and dirt.
12. Insufficient travel of shift rod (adjust control cable).

Overdrive Won't Drive Unless Locked Up Manually

1. Occasionally the unit may not drive the car forward in direct drive unless locked up by pulling the dash control. This may be caused by one or more broken rollers in the roller clutch. The remedy is to replace the entire set of rollers.
2. This condition may also be caused by sticking of the roller retainer upon the cam. This retainer must move freely to push the rollers into engaging position under the pressure of the two actuating springs.
3. Sometimes this condition is due to slight indentations worn in the cam faces by the spinning rollers. This is remedied by replacing the cam.

Overdrive Does Not Engage or Lockup Does Not Release

1. Dash control improperly connected.
2. Transmission and overdrive improperly aligned.
3. Kickdown switch improperly adjusted.

4. Improper installation of solenoid.
5. Improper positioning of blocker ring.
6. Broken or slipping governor drive pinion.
7. Too much end play in mainshaft.

Overdrive Engages with Severe Jolt or Noise

Insufficient blocker ring friction may cause the ring to lose its grip on the hub of the sun gear control plate.

Freewheels At Speeds Over 30 mph

If cam roller retainer spring tension is weak, the unit will freewheel at all times.

RAMBLER E-STICK PROBLEMS

NOTE: In addition to the problems listed below, the clutch is subject to the same problems, such as chatter, grabbing, etc., as the conventional type clutch. For clutch problems, refer to the Clutch Problems section.

Excessive Slip

1. Low servo oil pressure.
2. Release lever improperly adjusted or release fork not installed on release bearing guide pins.
3. Low engine oil level.
4. Air valve solenoid inoperative or leaking excessively.
5. Check valve orifice blocked in servo.
6. Diaphragm push rod stuck in valve and diaphragm assembly.
7. Diaphragm vent plugged.

Excessive Creep

1. Retractor spring too light or broken.
2. Servo oil pressure too high.
3. Broken retractor straps.

No Clutch Release

1. Bent or damaged diaphragm cover.

2. Vacuum lines leaking.
3. Control valve stuck in valve body.
4. Actuating switch not operating properly.
5. Actuating switch cam out of adjustment.
6. Faulty wiring circuit to air valve solenoid.
7. Air valve solenoid not functioning.
8. Servo piston binding in its bore.
9. Diaphragm push rod sticking.
10. Air vent in servo body plugged.
11. Vacuum diaphragm leaking.

Engine Overspeeds on Clutch Engagement

1. Clutch release lever out of adjustment.
2. Servo piston binding in its bore.
3. Servo body vent hole plugged.
4. Oil regulator valve not seating.
5. Servo check valve sticking on shaft.
6. Check valve orifice in servo restricted.

No Clutch Engagement

1. Actuating switch not operating properly.
2. Actuating switch cam out of adjustment.
3. Faulty wiring circuit to air valve solenoid.
4. Air valve solenoid not functioning.
5. Lube valve stuck closed.
6. Servo piston binding in its bore.
7. Broken spring in dump diaphragm.
8. Oil pressure regulator valve stuck open.
9. Low engine oil level.

Automatic Transmission Problems

BUICK SPECIAL DUAL-PATH DRIVE, Fig. 8

With the linkage properly adjusted and the engine warmed up, make a road test and observe the general performance of the transmission. Check for abnormal noises. Accelerate from a stop

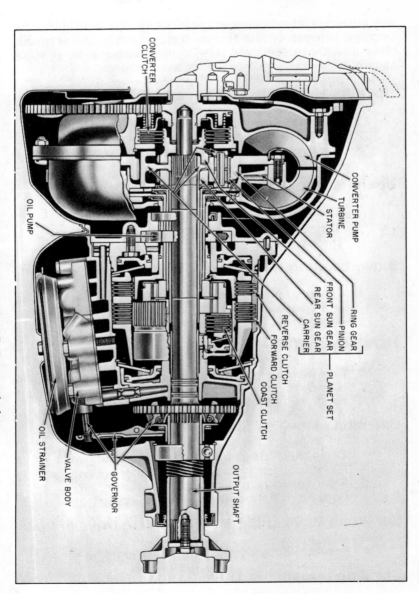

CONVERTER
CLUTCH

CONVERTER PUMP

TURBINE

STATOR

RING GEAR

PINION

FRONT SUN GEAR

REAR SUN GEAR

CARRIER

PLANET SET

OIL PUMP

REVERSE CLUTCH

FORWARD CLUTCH

COAST CLUTCH

OIL STRAINER

VALVE BODY

GOVERNOR

OUTPUT SHAFT

Fig. 8.   Cutaway of Dual Path transmission.

95

with the accelerator depressed just to detent. Upshift should occur smoothly between 40 and 45 mph. If the upshift occurs at speeds other than those specified, refer to the text below for possible causes.

Upshifts Below Normal Speed

1. Governor valve not adjusted properly or sticking.
2. Shift valve or shift regulator valve sticking.
3. Throttle valve pressure too low. Could be worn or broken spring, or sticking valve.

Upshifts Above Normal Speed

1. Governor valve not adjusted properly or sticking.
2. Shift valve or shift regulator sticking.
3. Throttle valve pressure too high, valve sticking.

Slow, Lagging Upshift

1. Converter pressure regulator valve sticking. This results in a slower lowering of converter pressure and a slow engagement of converter clutch.

Harsh Upshift

1. Converter pressure regulator valve sticking and creating a low converter pressure at all times. This results in a harsh, fast engagement of the converter clutch.

Car Won't Move or Slips in Reverse

1. Coast clutch slipping, burned out or not engaged.
2. Reverse clutch slipping, burned out or not engaged.
3. Front overrunning clutch slipping.
4. Forward clutch locked up or not releasing.

Car Won't Move or Slips on Takeoff in Drive or Low

1. Forward clutch slipping, burned out or not engaged.

Car Won't Upshift in Drive Range

1. Throttle valve stuck in high pressure position or throttle

valve linkage may be binding, holding throttle valve open.
2. Converter clutch slipping, burned out or not engaged.
3. Converter pressure regulator valve stuck, keeping converter pressure high at all times.
4. Governor valve stuck in OFF position or improperly adjusted.
5. Shift valve stuck in OFF position or shift regulator valve stuck.

Car Coasts on Deceleration in Low

1. Coast clutch slipping, burned out or not engaged.

Car Locks Up When it Upshifts in Drive Range

1. Coast clutch locked up or not releasing.
2. Rear overrunning clutch locked up.

Car Backs Up in Neutral

1. Reverse clutch locked up or not releasing.

Car Pulls Forward in Neutral

1. Forward clutch locked up or not releasing.
2. Converter clutch locked up or not releasing.

Car Labors on Takeoff or Stalls

1. Converter clutch locked up or not releasing.

Car Slips on Takeoff in Drive or Low

1. Front overrunning clutch slipping.

Engine Labors When Approaching Cruising Speed

1. Front overrunning clutch locked up.

Car Won't Move in Drive

1. Rear overruning clutch slipping.

Car Labors on Takeoff in Drive—Cruises Normally but Will Not Downshift

1. Governor valve stuck in OPEN position.
2. Shift valve stuck in converter clutch ON position.

Upshifts Early but Will Not Downshift

1. Throttle valve stuck in OFF position.

Upshifts Only at High Speed

1. Throttle pressure regulator valve stuck, causing throttle pressure to be too high.
2. Throttle detent valve stuck wide open.

Upshifts Early except at Wide Open Throttle

1. Shift regulator stuck.

TURBO HYDRA-MATIC 200

No Drive in Drive Range

1. Low oil level.
2. Manual linkage maladjusted.
3. Low oil pressure due to restricted or plugged oil screen, oil screen gasket improperly installed, oil pump pressure regulator, pump drive gear tangs damaged by converter, case porosity in intake bore.
4. Forward clutch malfunctioning due to forward clutch not applying due to cracked piston, damaged or missing seals, burned clutch plates, snap ring not in groove.
5. Forward clutch malfunctioning due to seal rings damaged or missing on turbine shaft, leaking feed circuits due to damaged or mispositioned gasket.
6. Clutch housing check ball stuck or missing.
7. Cup plug leaking or missing from rear of turbine shaft in clutch apply passage.
8. Incorrect forward clutch piston assembly or incorrect number of clutch plates.

9. Roller clutch malfunctioning due to missing rollers or springs or possibly galled rollers.

Oil Pressure High Or Low

1. Throttle valve cable maladjusted, binding, disconnected or broken.
2. Throttle lever and bracket improperly installed, disconnected or binding.
3. Throttle valve shift valve, throttle valve or plunger binding.
4. Pressure regulator valve and spring malfunctioning due to binding valve, incorrect spring, oil pressure control orifice in pump cover plugged, causing high oil pressure, or pressure regulator bore plug leaking.
5. Manual valve disconnected.
6. Intermediate boost valve binding, causing oil pressures to be incorrect in Second and Low.
7. Orifice in spacer plate at end of intermediate boost valve plugged.
8. Reverse boost valve binding, causing pressure to be incorrect in reverse only.
9. Orifice in spacer plate at end of reverse boost valve plugged.

1-2 Shift At Full Throttle Only

1. Throttle valve cable maladjusted, binding, disconnected or broken.
2. Throttle lever and bracket assembly binding or disconnected.
3. Throttle valve exhaust ball lifter or number 5 check ball binding, mispositioned or disconnected.

NOTE: If number 5 ball is fully seated, it will cause full throttle valve pressure regardless of throttle valve position.

4. Throttle valve and plunger binding.
5. Valve body gaskets leaking, damaged or incorrectly installed.
6. Porous control valve assembly.

First Gear Only, No 1-2 Shift

1. Plugged governor oil feed orifice in spacer plate.

2. Plugged orifice in spacer plate that feeds governor oil to the shift valves.
3. Balls missing in governor assembly.
4. Governor cover O-ring missing or leaking. If governor cover O-ring leaks, an external oil leak will be present and there will be no upshift.
5. Governor shaft seal missing or damaged.
6. Governor driven gear stripped.
7. Governor assembly missing.
8. Control valve assembly 1-2 shift valve or 1-2 throttle valve stuck in downshift position.
9. Porosity in case channels or undrilled Second gear feed holes.
10. Excessive leakage between case bore and intermediate band apply ring.
11. Intermediate band anchor pin missing or disconnected from band.
12. Missing or broken intermediate band.
13. Servo to cover oil seal ring damaged or missing.
14. Porous servo cover or piston.
15. Incorrect intermediate band apply pin.
16. Incorrect cover and piston.

First and Second Only, No 2-3 Shift

1. 2-3 shift valve or 2-3 throttle valve stuck in downshift position.
2. Direct clutch feed orifice in spacer plate plugged.
3. Valve body gaskets leaking, damaged or incorrectly installed.
4. Porosity between case passages.
5. Pump passages plugged or leaking.
6. Pump gasket incorrectly installed.
7. Rear seal on pump cover leaking or missing.
8. Direct clutch oil seals missing or damaged.
9. Direct clutch piston or housing cracked.
10. Direct clutch plates damaged or missing.
11. Direct clutch backing plate snap ringout of groove.
12. Intermediate servo to case oil seal broken or missing on intermediate servo piston.
13. Intermediate servo exhaust hole in case between servo piston seals plugged or undrilled.

Moves Forward in Neutral

1. Manual linkage maladjusted.
2. Forward clutch does not release.
3. Cross leakage between pump passages.
4. Cross leakage to forward clutch through clutch passages.

No Drive in Reverse or Slips in Reverse

1. Throttle valve cable binding or maladjusted.
2. Manual linkage maladjusted.
3. Throttle valve binding.
4. Reverse boost valve binding in bore.
5. Low overrun clutch valve binding in bore.
6. Reverse clutch piston cracked, broken or has missing seals.
7. Reverse clutch plates burned.
8. Reverse clutch has incorrect selective spacer ring.
9. Porosity in passages to direct clutch.
10. Pump to case gasket improperly installed or missing.
11. Pump passages cross leaking or restricted.
12. Pump cover seals damaged or missing.
13. Direct clutch piston or housing cracked.
14. Direct clutch piston seals cut or missing.
15. Direct clutch housing ball check, stuck, leaking or missing.
16. Direct clutch plates burned.
17. Incorrect direct clutch piston.
18. Direct clutch orifices plugged in spacer plate.
19. Intermediate servo to case seal cut or missing.

Slips 1-2 Shift

1. Aerated oil due to low level.
2. Second gear feed orifice in spacer plate partially blocked.
3. Improperly installed or missing spacer plate gasket.
4. 1-2 accumulator valve stuck, causing low 1-2 accumulator pressure.
5. Weak or missing 1-2 accumulator valve spring.
6. 1-2 accumulator piston seal leaking or spring missing or broken.
7. Leakage between 1-2 accumulator piston and pin.
8. Incorrect intermediate band apply pin.

101

9. Excessive leakage between intermediate band apply pin and case.
10. Porous intermediate servo piston.
11. Servo cover to servo seal damaged or missing.
12. Incorrect servo and cover.
13. Throttle valve cable improperly adjusted.
14. Shift throttle valve or throttle valve binding.
15. Intermediate band worn or burned.
16. Case porosity in Second clutch passages.

Rough 1-2 Shift

1. Throttle valve cable improperly adjusted or binding.
2. Throttle valve or plunger binding.
3. Shift throttle or 1-2 accumulator valve binding.
4. Incorrect intermediate servo pin.
5. Intermediate servo piston to case seal damaged or missing.
6. 1-2 accumulator oil ring damaged, piston stuck, bore damaged or spring broken or missing.

Slips 2-3 Shift

1. Low oil level.
2. Throttle valve cable improperly adjusted.
3. Throttle valve binding.
4. Direct clutch orifice in spacer plate partially blocked.
5. Spacer plate gaskets improperly installed or missing.
6. Intermediate servo to case seal damaged.
7. Porous direct clutch feed passages in case.
8. Pump to case gasket improperly installed or missing.
9. Pump passages cross feeding, leaking or restricted.
10. Pump cover oil seal rings damaged or missing.
11. Direct clutch piston or housing cracked.
12. Direct clutch piston seals cut or missing.
13. Direct clutch plates burned.

Rough 2-3 Shift

1. Throttle valve cable improperly installed or missing.
2. Throttle valve or throttle valve plunger binding.
3. Shift throttle valve binding.
4. Intermediate servo exhaust hole undrilled or plugged be-

tween intermediate servo piston seals.
5. Direct clutch exhaust valve number 4 check ball missing or improperly installed.

No Engine Braking in Second Gear

1. Intermediate boost valve binding in valve body.
2. Intermediate-Reverse number 3 check ball improperly installed or missing.
3. Shift throttle valve number 3 check ball improperly installed or missing.
4. Intermediate servo to cover seal missing or damaged.
5. Intermediate band off anchor pin, broken or burned.

No Engine Braking In First Gear

1. Low overrun clutch valve binding in valve body.

NOTE: The following conditions will also cause no Reverse.

2. Low-Reverse clutch piston seals broken or missing.
3. Porosity in Low-Reverse piston or housing.
4. Low-Reverse clutch housing snap ring out of case.
5. Cup plug or rubber seal missing or damaged between case and Low-Reverse clutch housing.

No Part Throttle Downshift

1. Throttle plunger bushing passages obstructed.
2. 2-3 throttle valve bushing passages obstructed.
3. Valve body gaskets improperly installed or damaged.
4. Spacer plate hole obstructed or undrilled.
5. Throttle valve cable maladjusted.
6. Throttle valve or shift throttle valve binding.

Low or High Shift Points

1. Throttle valve cable binding or disconnected.
2. Throttle valve or shift throttle valve binding.
3. Number 1 throttle shift check ball improperly installed or missing.
4. Throttle valve plunger, 1-2 or 2-3 throttle valves binding.

103

5. Valve body gaskets improperly installed or missing.
6. Pressure regulator valve binding.
7. Throttle valve exhaust number 5 check ball and lifter, improperly installed, disconnected or missing.
8. Throttle lever binding, disconnected or loose at valve body mounting bolt or not positioned at the throttle valve plunger bushing pin locator.
9. Governor shaft to cover seal broken or missing.
10. Governor cover 0-rings broken or missing.

NOTE: Outer ring will leak externally and the inner ring will leak internally.

11. Case porosity.

Will Not Hold In Park

1. Manual linkage maladjusted.
2. Parking pawl binding in case.
3. Actuator rod or plunger damaged.
4. Parking pawl damaged.
5. Parking bracket loose or damaged.
6. Detent lever nut loose.
7. Detent lever hole worn or damaged.
8. Detent roller to valve body bolt loose.
9. Detent roller or pin damaged, incorrectly installed or missing.

SUPER TURBINE 400 AND TURBO HYDRA-MATIC 375 AND 400, Fig. 9

Oil Pressure High or Low

1. Vacuum line or fittings clogged or leaking.
2. Vacuum modulator.
3. Modulator valve.
4. Pressure regulator.
5. Oil pump.
6. Governor.

No Drive in Drive Range

1. Low oil level (check for leaks).

104

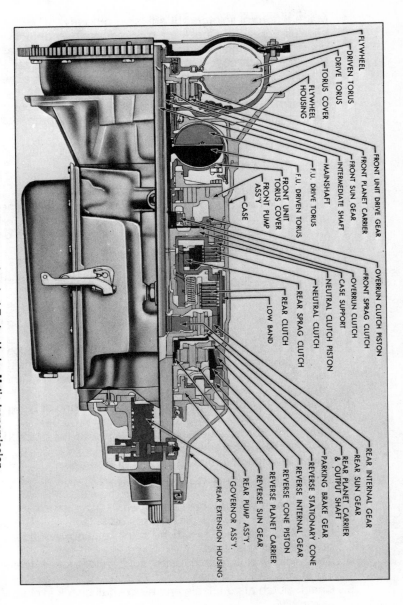

FLYWHEEL
DRIVEN TORUS
DRIVE TORUS
TORUS COVER
FLYWHEEL HOUSING
FRONT PLANET CARRIER
FRONT SUN GEAR
INTERMEDIATE SHAFT
MAINSHAFT
F.U. DRIVEN TORUS
FRONT UNIT TORUS COVER
FRONT PUMP ASS'Y
CASE
FRONT UNIT DRIVE GEAR
OVERRUN CLUTCH PISTON
FRONT SPRAG CLUTCH
OVERRUN CLUTCH
CASE SUPPORT
NEUTRAL CLUTCH PISTON
NEUTRAL CLUTCH
REAR SPRAG CLUTCH
REAR CLUTCH
LOW BAND
REAR INTERNAL GEAR
REAR SUN GEAR
REAR PLANET CARRIER & OUTPUT SHAFT
PARKING BRAKE GEAR
REVERSE STATIONARY CONE
REVERSE INTERNAL GEAR
REVERSE CONE PISTON
REVERSE PLANET CARRIER
REVERSE SUN GEAR
REAR PUMP ASS'Y.
GOVERNOR ASS'Y.
REAR EXTENSION HOUSING

Fig. 9. Cutaway of typical Turbo Hydra-Matic transmission.

105

2. Manual control linkage not adjusted properly.
3. Low oil pressure. Check for blocked strainer, defective pressure regulator, pump assembly or pump drive gear. See that tangs have not been damaged by converter.
4. Check control valve assembly to see if manual valve has been disconnected from manual lever pin.
5. Forward clutch may be stuck or damaged. Check pump feed circuits to forward clutch, including clutch drum ball check.
6. Sprag or roller clutch assembled incorrectly.

1-2 Shift at Full Throttle Only

1. Detent switch may be sticking or defective.
2. Detent solenoid may be stuck open, loose or have leaking gasket.
3. Control valve assembly may be leaking, damaged or incorrectly installed.
4. Porous transmission case.

First Gear Only—No 1-2 Shift

1. Governor valve may be sticking.
2. Driven gear in governor assembly loose, worn or damaged.
3. The 1-2 shift valve in control valve assembly stuck closed. Check governor feed channels for blocks, leaks, and position. Also check control valve body gaskets for leaks and damage.
4. Intermediate clutch plug in case may be leaking or blown out.
5. Check for porosity between channels and for blocked governor feed channels in case.
6. Check intermediate clutch for proper operation.

No 2-3 Shift—First and Second Only

1. Detent solenoid may be stuck open.
2. Detent switch may not be properly adjusted.
3. Control valve assembly may be stuck, leaking, damaged, or incorrectly installed.
4. Check direct clutch case center support for broken, leaking or missing oil rings.
5. Check clutch piston seals and piston ball check in clutch assembly.

Moves Forward in Neutral

1. Manual control linkage improperly adjusted.
2. Forward clutch does not release.
3. Oil pump.
4. Internal leakage.

No Drive in Reverse or Slips in Reverse

1. Check oil level.
2. Manual control linkage improperly adjusted.
3. Vacuum modulator assembly may be defective.
4. Vacuum modulator valve sticking.
5. Strainer may be restricted or leaking at intake.
6. Regulator or boost valve in pump assembly may be sticking.
7. Control valve assembly may be stuck, leaking or damaged.
8. Rear servo and accumulator may have damaged or missing servo piston seal ring.
9. Reverse band burned out or damaged. Determine that apply pin or anchor pins engage properly.
10. Direct clutch may be damaged or may have stuck ball check in piston.
11. Forward clutch does not release.
12. Low-Reverse ball check missing from case.

Slips in All Ranges and on Starts

1. Check oil level.
2. Vacuum modulator defective.
3. Modulator valve sticking.
4. Strainer assembly plugged or leaking at neck.
5. Pump assembly regulator or boost valve sticking.
6. Leaks from damaged gaskets or cross leaks from porosity of case.
7. Forward and direct clutches burned.

Slips 1-2 Shift

1. Incorrect oil level.
2. Vacuum modulator valve sticking.
3. Vacuum modulator defective.

4. Pump pressure regulator valve defective.
5. Porosity between channels in case.
6. Control valve assembly.
7. Pump-to-case gasket may be mispositioned.
8. Intermediate clutch plug in case may be missing or leaking excessively.
9. Intermediate clutch piston seal missing or damaged.
10. Intermediate clutch plates burned.
11. Front or rear accumulator oil ring may be damaged.

Slips 2-3 Shift

1. Items 1 through 6 under Slips 1-2 Shift will also cause 2-3 shift slips.
2. Direct clutch plates burned.
3. Oil seal rings on direct clutch may be damaged, permitting excessive leaking between tower and bushing.

Rough 1-2 Shift

1. Modulator valve sticking.
2. Modulator assembly defective.
3. Pump pressure regulator or boost valve stuck or inoperative.
4. Control valve assembly loosened from case, damaged or mounted with wrong gaskets.
5. Intermediate clutch ball missing or not sealing.
6. Porosity between channels in case.
7. Rear servo accumulator assembly may have oil rings damaged, stuck piston, broken or missing spring or damaged bore.

Rough 2-3 Shift

1. Items 1, 2 and 3 under Rough 1-2 Shift will also cause rough 2-3 shift.
2. Front servo accumulator spring broken or missing. Accumulator piston may be sticking.

No Engine Braking in Second Speed

1. Front servo or accumulator oil rings may be leaking.

2. Front band may be broken or burned out.
3. Front band not engaged on anchor pin and/or servo pin.

No Engine Braking in Low Range

1. Low-Reverse check ball may be missing from control valve assembly.
2. Rear servo may have damaged oil seal ring, bore or piston; leaking pressure.
3. Rear band broken, burned out or not engaged on anchor pins or servo pin.

No Part Throttle Downshifts

1. Vacuum modulator assembly.
2. Modulator valve.
3. Regulator valvetrain.
4. Control valve assembly has stuck 3-2 valve or broken spring.

No Detent Downshifts

1. Detent switch needs fuse, connections tightened or adjustment.
2. Detent solenoid may be inoperative.
3. Detent valvetrain in control valve assembly malfunctioning.

Low or High Shift Points

1. Oil pressure. Check vacuum modulator assembly, vacuum line connections, modulator valve, and pressure regulator valvetrain.
2. Governor may have sticking valve or feed holes that are leaking, plugged or damaged.
3. Detent solenoid may be stuck open or loose.
4. Control valve assembly. Check detent, 3-2, and 1-2 shift valvetrains, and check spacer plate gaskets for positioning.
5. Check case for porosity, missing or leaking intermediate plug.

Won't Hold in Park

1. Manual control linkage improperly adjusted.

2. Internal linkage defective. Check for chamfer on actuator rod sleeve.
3. Parking pawl broken or inoperative.

Excessive Creep at Idle

NOTE: Transmissions having the variable pitch stator.
1. High idle speed.
2. Stator switch inoperative or defective.
3. Stator solenoid defective.
4. Pump may have stator valvetrain stuck.
5. Pump lead wires disconnected or grounded out.
6. Pump feed circuit to stator may be restricted or blocked.
7. Converter out. Check valve may be broken or stuck.
8. Turbine shaft may have defective oil seal ring.
9. Stator orifice plug in case may be blocked.
10. Converter assembly defective.

Poor Performance—³/₄ Throttle

NOTE: Transmissions having the variable pitch stator.
1. Stator and detent switch inoperative.
2. Items 3 through 10 above will also cause poor performance at ³/₄ throttle.

Noisy Transmission

1. Pump noises caused by high or low oil level.
2. Cavitation due to plugged strainer, porosity in intake circuit or water in oil.
3. Pump gears may be damaged.
4. Gear noise in Low gear of Drive range; transmission grounded to body.
5. Defective planetary gear set.
6. Clutch noises during application can be worn or burned clutch plates.

Forward Clutch Plates Burned

1. Check ball in clutch housing may be damaged, stuck or missing.
2. Clutch piston cracked, seals damaged or missing.

3. Low line pressure.
4. Manual valve mispositioned.
5. Restricted oil feed to forward clutch.
6. Pump cover oil seal rings missing, broken or undersize. Ring grooved oversize.
7. Case valve body face not flat or porosity between channels.
8. Manual valve bent and center land not properly ground.

Intermediate Clutch Plates Burned

1. Constant bleed orifice in center support missing.
2. Rear accumulator piston oil ring damaged or missing.
3. 1-2 accumulator valve stuck in control valve assembly.
4. Intermediate clutch piston seal damaged or missing.
5. Center support bolt loose.
6. Low line pressure.
7. Intermediate clutch plug in case missing.
8. Case valve body face not flat or porosity between channels.
9. Manual valve bent and center land not ground properly.

Direct Clutch Plates Burned

1. Restricted orifice in vacuum line to modulator.
2. Check ball in direct clutch piston damaged, stuck or missing.
3. Defective modulator bellows.
4. Center support bolt loose.
5. Center support oil rings or grooves damaged or missing.
6. Clutch piston seals damaged or missing.
7. Front and rear servo pistons and seals damaged.
8. Manual valve bent and center land not cleaned up.
9. Case valve body face not flat or porosity between channels.
10. Intermediate sprag clutch installed backwards.
11. 3-2 valve, 3-2 spring or 3-2 spacer pin installed in wrong location in 3-2 valve bore.

GM FRONT WHEEL DRIVE
TURBO HYDRA-MATIC 200

No Drive in Drive Range

1. Low oil level. Check for external leaks or vacuum mod-

111

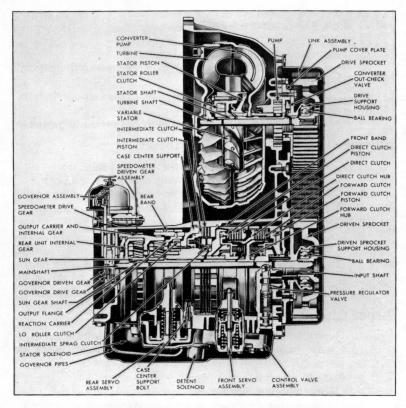

Fig. 10. Cutaway of Front Drive Turbo Hydra-Matic.

ulator diaphragm leaking.

2. Manual linkage maladjusted. Correct alignment in manual lever shift quadrant.

3. Low oil pressure.

4. Oil strainer O-ring seal missing or damaged, neck weld leaking, strainer blocked.

5. Oil pump pressure regulator stuck or inoperative. Pump drive gear tangs damaged by converter.

6. Case porosity in intake bore.

7. Control valve. Manual valve disconnected from manual lever pin. (Other shift lever positions would also be affected.)

112

8. Forward clutch does not apply. Piston cracked, seals missing or damaged. These defects can be checked by removing the valve body and applying air pressure to the drive cavity in the case valve body face. Missing, damaged or worn oil rings on driven support housing can also cause the forward clutch not to apply. Clutch plates burned.
9. Roller clutch inoperative. Rollers worn, damaged springs, or damaged races. May be checked by placing selector lever in L range.

No Drive in Reverse or Slips in Reverse

1. Low oil level.
2. Manual linkage.
3. Oil pressure. Vacuum modulator defective, modulator valve sticking. Restricted strainer, leak at intake pipe or O-ring seal. Pressure regulator or boost valve sticking.
4. Control valve body gaskets leaking or damaged (other malfunctions may also be indicated). Low-reverse check ball missing from case (this will cause no overrun braking in low range). The 2-3 valvetrain stuck open (this will also cause 1-3 upshifts in drive range). Reverse feed passage not drilled; also check case passages. Apply air to reverse passage in case valve body face.
5. Rear servo and accumulator. Servo piston seal ring broken or missing. Apply air pressure to drilled hole in intermediate clutch passage of case valve body face to check for piston operation and excessive leakage. Band apply pin too short (this may also cause no overrun braking or slip in overrun braking in low range).
6. Rear band burned, loose lining, apply pin or anchor pin not engaged; band broken.
7. Direct clutch outer seal damaged or missing. Clutch plates burned. May be caused by stuck ball check in piston.
8. Forward clutch does not release (will also cause drive in neutral range).

Drive in Neutral

1. Manual linkage maladjusted.

113

2. Forward clutch does not release (this condition will also cause no reverse)

First Gear Only—No 1-2 Upshift

1. Governor valve sticking, driven gear loose, damaged or worn. If driven gear shows signs of wear or damage, check output flange drive gear for nicks or rough finish.
2. Control valve. The 1-2 shift valvetrain stuck closed. Dirt, chips or damaged valve in 1-2 shift valvetrain. Governor feed channels blocked or leaking; pipes out of position. Valve body gaskets leaking or damaged. Case porosity between oil channels. Governor feed passage blocked.
3. Intermediate clutch. Case center support oil rings missing, broken or defective. Clutch piston seals missing, improperly assembled, cut or damaged. Apply air to intermediate clutch passage located in case valve body face to check for these defects.

1-2 Shift Obtained Only at Full Throttle

1. Detent switch sticking or defective.
2. Detent solenoid loose, gasket leaking, sticks open, electrical wire pinched between cover and casting.
3. Control valve body gasket leaking or damaged. Detent valvetrain stuck.

First and Second Gears Only No 2-3 Shift

1. Detent solenoid stuck open (the 2-3 shift would occur at very high speeds) may be diagnosed as no 2-3 shift.
2. Detent switch sticking or defective.
3. Control valve body. The 2-3 valvetrain stuck with dirt or foreign material. Valve body gaskets leaking or damaged.
4. Direct clutch. Case center support oil rings missing or broken. Clutch piston seals missing, improperly assembled, cut or damaged; piston ball check stuck or missing. Apply air to direct clutch passage in case valve body face to check these conditions.

Slips in All Ranges

1. Oil level incorrect.

2. Low oil pressure. Vacuum modulator defective or valve sticking. Oil strainer plugged or leaks at neck; O-ring (case to strainer) missing or damaged. Pressure regulator or boost valve sticking.
3. Case cross channel leaks; porosity.
4. Forward, intermediate and direct clutches slipping. Clutch plates burned. Always look for a primary defect that would cause clutch plates to burn (missing feed holes, seals and oil rings, etc., are primary defects).
5. Roller clutch rollers worn; springs or cage damaged, and worn or damaged races. Operates normally in low and reverse ranges.

Slips 1-2 Shift

1. Oil level incorrect.
2. Low oil pressure. Look for defective vacuum modulator or valve sticking. Pump pressure regulator valve stuck.
3. Front servo accumulator piston cracked or porous, oil ring damaged or missing.
4. Control valve. The 1-2 accumulator valvetrain may cause a slip-bump shift. Porous valve body or case valve body face.
5. Rear servo accumulator oil ring missing or damaged; case bore damaged; piston cracked or damaged.
6. Case porous between oil passages.
7. Intermediate clutch lip seals missing, cut or damaged. Apply air pressure to intermediate clutch passage in case valve body face to check. Clutch plates burned. Case center support leaks in feed circuits (oil rings damaged or grooves damaged) or excessive leak between tower and bushing.

Rough 1-2 Shift

1. Oil pressure. Check vacuum modulator for loose fittings, restrictions in line; defective vacuum modulator. Modulator valve stuck. Pressure regulator boost valve stuck.
2. Control valve. 1-2 accumulator valvetrain; valve body-to-case bolts loose; gaskets inverted, off location, or damaged.
3. Case. Intermediate clutch passage check ball missing or

not seating. Case porous between channels.
4. Rear servo accumulator piston stuck. Apply air pressure to 1-2 accumulator passage in case valve body face (you should hear the servo piston move). Broken or missing spring; bore scored or damaged.

Slips 2-3 Shift

1. Oil level high or low.
2. Low oil pressure. Modulator defective or valve sticking. Pump pressure regulator valve or boost valve sticking.
3. Control valve. Accumulator piston pin leak at valve body end.
4. Direct clutch piston seals leaking. Case center support oil seal rings damaged or excessive leak between tower and bushing. Apply air to direct clutch passage, center support is defective.

Rough 2-3 Shift

1. Oil pressure high. Vacuum modulator defective or valve sticking. Pump pressure regulator valve or boost valve stuck or inoperative.
2. Front servo accumulator spring missing or broken; accumulator piston stuck.

Shifts Occur at Too High or Too Low Car Speed

1. Oil pressure. Vacuum modulator defective or valve sticking. Leak in vacuum line (engine to transmission). Vacuum modulator line fitting on carburetor blocked. Pump pressure regulator valve or boost valvetrain stuck.
2. Governor valve stuck or sticking. Feed holes restricted or leaking; pipes damaged or mispositioned.
3. Detent solenoid stuck open or loose on valve body (will cause late shifts).
4. Control valve. Detent valvetrain sticking; 3-2 valvetrain sticking; 1-2 shift valve stuck; 1-2 detent valve sticking open (will probably cause early 2-3 shift).
5. Spacer plate gaskets inverted or mispositioned; orifice holes missing or blocked; check balls missing or mislocated.
6. Case porous in channels or foreign material blocking channels.

No Detent Downshift

1. Detent switch mispositioned or electrical connections loose.
2. Solenoid defective or electrical connections loose.
3. Control valve detent valvetrain stuck.

No Engine Braking—Super Range (Second Gear)

1. Front servo or accumulator piston rings broken or missing. Case or valve body bores worn oversize, causing excessive leakage.
2. Front band worn or burned (check for cause); band end lugs broken or damaged; band lugs not engaged on anchor pins or servo apply pin (check for cause).

No Engine Braking—Low Range (First Gear)

1. Control valve Low-Reverse check ball missing from case.
2. Rear servo oil ring damaged or missing. Piston damaged or porous, causing a leak in apply pressure.
3. Rear band lining worn or burned (check for cause); band end lugs broken; band ends not engaged on anchor pin or servo apply pin. These items will also cause slip in Reverse or no Reverse.

Will Not Hold Car in Park Position

1. Manual linkage maladjusted (external).
2. Parking brake lever and actuator rod assembly defective (check for proper actuator spring action). Parking pawl broken or inoperative.

Poor Performance or Rough Idle

1. Stator switch defective or maladjusted.
2. Stator solenoid defective or wire ground to solenoid housing; electrical connection loose; stator valvetrain stuck (located in valve body); oil feed circuit to stator restricted or blocked (check feed hole in stator shaft); converter-out check valve broken or missing (reed valve located in cover plate under drive support housing).
3. Turbine shaft converter return passage not drilled; oil seal

rings broken, worn or missing.
4. Case porous in feed circuit channels or foreign material blocking feed circuit.
5. Converter assembly defective.

Transmission Noise

1. Pump noise. Oil level high or low; water in oil, driving gear assembled upside down; driving or driven gear teeth damaged.
2. Gear noise (first gear drive range). Check planetary pinions for tooth damage. Check sun gear and front and rear internal gears for tooth finish or damage.
3. Clutch noise during application. Check clutch plates.
4. Sprocket and chain link assembly. Chain link too long (sounds similar to popcorn popping). There will be a rough burr along teeth of drive sprocket if chain link is too long; replace chain link and drive sprocket. Drive or driven sprocket teeth damaged. Engine mounts worn or damaged.

Burned Forward Clutch Plates

1. Check ball in clutch housing damaged, stuck or missing.
2. Clutch piston cracked, seals damaged or missing.
3. Low line pressure.
4. Manual valve mispositioned.
5. Restricted oil feed to forward clutch.
6. Pump cover oil seal rings missing, broken or undersize or ring groove oversize.
7. Case valve body face not flat or porosity between channels.
8. Manual valve bent and center land not ground properly.

Burned Intermediate Clutch Plates

1. Rear accumulator piston oil ring damaged or missing.
2. 1-2 accumulator valve stuck in control valve assembly.
3. Intermediate clutch piston seals damaged or missing.
4. Center support bolt loose.
5. Low line pressure.
6. Intermediate clutch plug in case missing.

7. Case valve body face not flat or porosity between channels.
8. Manual valve bent and center land not ground properly.

Burned Direct Clutch Plates

1. Restricted orifice in vacuum line to modulator.
2. Check ball in direct clutch piston damaged, stuck or missing.
3. Defective modulator bellows.
4. Center support bolt loose.
5. Center support oil rings or grooves damaged or missing.
6. Clutch piston seals damaged or missing.
7. Front and rear servo pistons and seals damaged.
8. Manual valve bent and center land not cleaned up.
9. Case valve body face not flat or porosity between channels.
10. Intermediate sprag clutch installed backwards.

BUICK SUPER TURBINE 300
1964-69 OLDS JETAWAY
1964-69 PONTIAC 2-SPEED, Fig. 11

Oil Forced Out of Filler Tube

1. Oil level too high. Foaming caused by planet carrier running in oil.
2. Water in oil.
3. Leak in pump suction circuits.

Oil Leaks

1. Check extension oil seal.
2. Check outer shift lever oil seal.
3. Check speedometer driven gear fitting.
4. Check oil cooler pipe connections.
5. Check vacuum modulator assembly and case.

No Drive in Any Position

1. Low oil level.

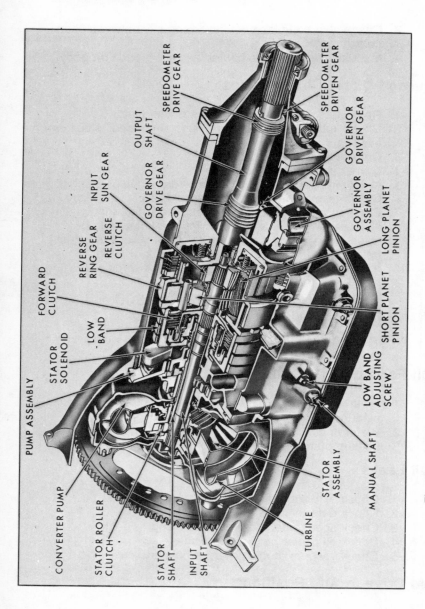

Fig. 11. Cutaway of Super Turbine 300. Some models use a fixed stator.

2. Clogged oil strainer screen or suction pipe loose.
3. Defective pressure regulator valve.
4. Front pump defective.
5. Input shaft broken.

Erratic Operation and Slippage Light to Medium Throttle

1. Low oil level.
2. Clogged oil strainer screen.
3. Servo piston seal leaking.
4. Band facing worn.
5. Low band apply struts disengaged or broken.
6. Vacuum modulator.

Engine Speed Flares on Upshifts

1. Low oil level.
2. Improper band adjustment.
3. Clogged oil strainer screen.
4. Forward clutch not fully engaging.
6. Forward clutch plates worn.
6. Forward clutch piston hanging up.
7. Forward clutch drum relief ball not sealing.
8. Vacuum modulator.

Upshifts Harsh

1. Vacuum modulator line broken or disconnected.
2. Vacuum modulator diaphragm leaks.
3. Vacuum modulator valve stuck.

Close Throttle (Coast) Downshift Harsh

1. High engine idle speed.
2. Improper low band adjustment.
3. Downshift timing valve malfunction.
4. High main line pressure. Check the following: a) vacuum modulator line broken or disconnected, b) modulator diaphragm ruptured, c) sticking pressure regulator coast valve, pressure regulator valve or vacuum modulator valve.

Car Creeps Excessively in Drive

1. Idle speed too high.
2. Closed throttle stator switch improperly adjusted (except Tempest and Oldsmobile 6-cylinder models).

Car Creeps in Neutral

1. Forward clutch not released.
2. Low band not released.

No Drive in Reverse

1. Reverse clutch piston stuck.
2. Reverse clutch plates worn out.
3. Reverse clutch seal leaking excessively.
4. Blocked reverse clutch apply orifice.

TURBO HYDRA-MATIC 250, 350 & 375B, Figs. 12 & 13

No Drive in Drive Range

1. Low oil level (check for leaks).
2. Manual control linkage improperly adjusted.
3. Low oil pressure. Check for blocked strainer, defective pressure regulator, pump assembly or pump drive gear. See that tangs have not been damaged by converter. Check case for porosity in intake bore.
4. Check control valve assembly to be sure manual valve has not been disconnected from inner lever.
5. Forward clutch may be stuck or damaged. Check pump feed circuits to forward clutch, including clutch drum ball check.
6. Roller clutch assembly broken or damaged.

Oil Pressure High or Low

High Pressure
1. Vacuum line or fittings leaking.
2. Vacuum modulator.

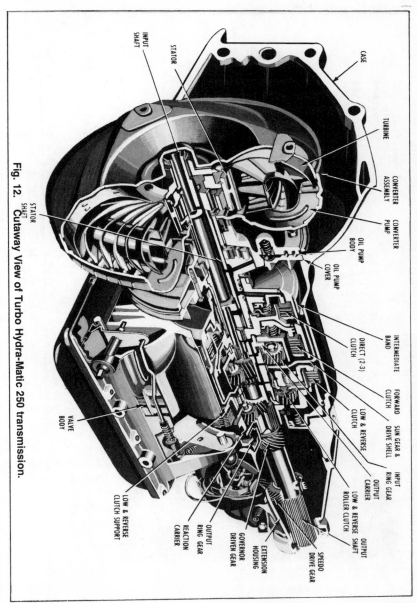

Fig. 12. Cutaway View of Turbo Hydra-Matic 250 transmission.

INPUT SHAFT

STATOR

CASE

TURBINE

CONVERTER ASSEMBLY

CONVERTER PUMP

OIL PUMP BODY

OIL PUMP COVER

STATOR SHAFT

INTERMEDIATE BAND

DIRECT (2-3) CLUTCH

FORWARD CLUTCH

SUN GEAR & DRIVE SHELL

INPUT RING GEAR

OUTPUT CARRIER

LOW & REVERSE CLUTCH

LOW & REVERSE ROLLER CLUTCH

OUTPUT SHAFT

VALVE BODY

LOW & REVERSE CLUTCH SUPPORT

OUTPUT RING GEAR

REACTION CARRIER

GOVERNOR DRIVEN GEAR

EXTENSION HOUSING

SPEEDO DRIVE GEAR

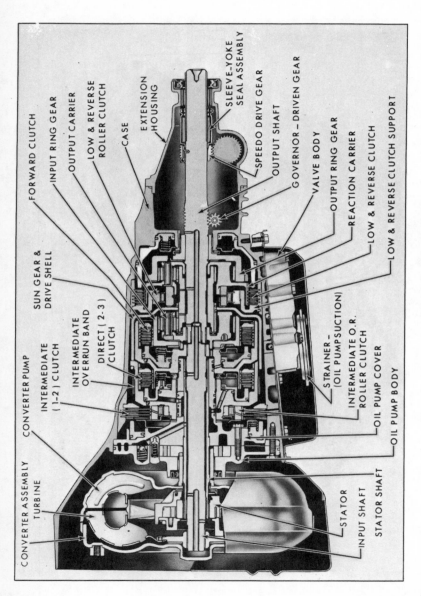

Fig. 13.   Cutaway of Turbo Hydra-Matic 350.

FORWARD CLUTCH

INPUT RING GEAR

OUTPUT CARRIER

LOW & REVERSE ROLLER CLUTCH

CASE

EXTENSION HOUSING

SLEEVE-YOKE SEAL ASSEMBLY

SPEEDO DRIVE GEAR

OUTPUT SHAFT

GOVERNOR – DRIVEN GEAR

VALVE BODY

OUTPUT RING GEAR

REACTION CARRIER

LOW & REVERSE CLUTCH

LOW & REVERSE CLUTCH SUPPORT

SUN GEAR & DRIVE SHELL

INTERMEDIATE (1-2) CLUTCH

INTERMEDIATE OVERRUN BAND

DIRECT (2-3) CLUTCH

CONVERTER PUMP

CONVERTER ASSEMBLY

TURBINE

INPUT SHAFT

STATOR SHAFT

STATOR

OIL PUMP BODY

OIL PUMP COVER

INTERMEDIATE O.R. ROLLER CLUTCH

STRAINER – (OIL PUMP SUCTION)

3. Modulator valve.
4. Pressure regulator.
5. Oil pump.

Low Pressure
1. Vacuum line or fittings obstructed.
2. Vacuum modulator.
3. Modulator valve.
4. Pressure regulator.
5. Governor.
6. Oil pump.

1-2 Shift at Full Throttle Only

1. Detent valve may be sticking or linkage may be misadjusted.
2. Vacuum line or fittings leaking.
3. Control valve body gaskets leaking, damaged or incorrectly installed. Detent valvetrain or 1-2 valve stuck.
4. Check case for porosity.

First Gear Only, No 1-2 Shift
Turbo Hydra-Matic 250, 350 & 375B

1. Governor valve may be sticking.
2. Driven gear in governor assembly loose, worn or damaged. If driven gear shows damage, check output shaft drive gear for nicks or rough finish.
3. Control valve governor feed channels blocked, or gaskets leaking. 1-2 shift valvetrain stuck closed.
4. Check case for blocked governor feed channels or for scored governor bore which will allow cross pressure leak. Check case for porosity.
5. Intermediate clutch or seals damaged.
6. Intermediate roller clutch damaged.

Turbo Hydra-Matic 250

1. Intermediate servo piston seals damaged, missing or installed improperly.
2. Intermediate band improperly adjusted.
3. Intermediate servo apply rod broken.

125

First and Second Only, No 2-3 Shift

1. Control valve 2-3 shift train stuck. Valve body gaskets leaking, damaged or incorrectly installed.
2. Pump hub-direct clutch oil seal rings broken or missing.
3. Direct clutch piston seals damaged. Piston ball check stuck or missing.

No First Gear
Turbo Hydra-Matic 250

1. Intermediate band adjusted too tightly.
2. 1-2 shift valve stuck in upshift position.

No First Gear
Turbo Hydra-Matic 350, 375B

1. Excessive number of clutch plates in intermediate clutch pack.
2. Incorrect intermediate clutch piston.

Moves Forward in Neutral

1. Manual linkage maladjusted.
2. Forward clutch not releasing.

No Drive in Reverse or Slips in Reverse

1. Low oil level.
2. Manual linkage maladjusted.
3. Modulator valve stuck.
4. Modulator and reverse boost valve stuck.
5. Pump hub-direct clutch oil seal rings broken or missing.
6. Direct clutch piston seal cut or missing.
7. Low and reverse clutch piston seal cut or missing.
8. Number 1 check ball missing.
9. Control valve body gaskets leaking or damaged.
10. 2-3 valvetrain stuck in upshifted position.
11. 1-2 valvetrain stuck in upshifted position.
12. Intermediate servo piston or pin stuck so intermediate overrun band is applied.
13. Low and reverse clutch piston out or seal damaged.
14. Direct clutch plates burned—may be caused by stuck ball check in piston. Outer seal damaged.
15. Forward clutch not releasing.

Slips in All Ranges

1. Low oil level.
2. Vacuum modulator valve defective or sticking.
3. Filter assembly plugged or leaking.
4. Pressure regulator valve stuck.
5. Pump to case gasket damaged.
6. Check case for cross leaks or porosity.
7. Forward clutch slipping.

Slips 1-2 Shift
Turbo Hydra-Matic 250, 350 and 375B

1. Low oil level.
2. Vacuum modulator assembly defective.
3. Modulator valve sticking.
4. Pump pressure regulator valve defective.
5. 2-3 accumulator oil ring damaged or missing. 1-2 accumulator oil ring damaged or missing. Case bore damaged.
6. Pump to case gasket mispositioned or damaged.
7. Check case for porosity.
8. Intermediate clutch piston seals damaged. Clutch plates burned.

Slips 1-2 Shift
Turbo Hydra-Matic 250 Only

1. Intermediate servo piston seals damaged or missing.
2. Burned intermediate band.

Rough 1-2 Shift
Turbo Hydra-Matic 250, 350 and 375B

1. Vacuum modulator—check for loose fittings, restrictions in line or defective modulator assembly.
2. Modulator valve stuck.
3. Valve body regulator or boost valve stuck.
4. Pump to case gasket mispositioned or damaged.
5. Check case for porosity.
6. Check 1-2 accumulator assembly for damaged oil rings,

127

stuck piston, broken or missing spring, or damaged case bore.

7. Improper number and location of check balls in case.

Rough 1-2 Shift
Turbo Hydra-Matic 250 Only

1. Intermediate band improperly adjusted.
2. Improper or broken servo spring.

Rough 1-2 Shift
Turbo Hydra-Matic 350, 375B Only

1. Burned intermediate clutch plates.
2. Improper number of intermediate clutch plates.

Slips 2-3 Shift

1. Low oil level.
2. Modulator valve or vacuum modulator assembly defective.
3. Pump pressure regulator valve or boost valve; pump to case gasket mispositioned.
4. Check case for porosity.
5. Direct clutch piston seals or ball check leaking.

Rough 2-3 Shift

1. High oil pressure. Vacuum leak, modulator valve sticking or pressure regulator or boost valve inoperative.
2. 2-3 accumulator piston stuck, spring broken or missing.

No Engine Braking in Second Gear

1. Intermediate servo or 2-3 accumulator oil rings or bores leaking or accumulator piston stuck.
2. Intermediate overrun band burned or broken.
3. Low oil pressure: Pressure regulator and/or boost valve stuck.

No Engine Braking in First Gear

1. Manual low control valve assembly stuck.

2. Low oil pressure: Pressure regulator and/or boost valve stuck.
3. Low and reverse clutch piston inner seal damaged.

No Part Throttle Downshift

1. Oil pressure: Vacuum modulator assembly, modulator valve or pressure regulator valvetrain malfunctioning.
2. Detent valve and linkage sticking, disconnected or broken.
3. 2-3 shift valve stuck.

No Detent Downshifts

1. 2-3 valve stuck.
2. Detent valve and linkage sticking, disconnected or broken.

Low or High Shift Points

1. Oil pressure: Check engine vacuum at transmission end of the modulator pipe.
2. Vacuum modulator assembly vacuum line connections at engine and transmission modulator valve, pressure regulator valvetrain.
3. Check governor for sticking valve, restricted or leaking feed holes, damaged pipes or plugged feed line.
4. Detent valve stuck open.
5. 1-2 or 2-3 valvetrain sticking.
6. Check case for porosity.

Won't Hold in Park

1. Manual linkage maladjusted.
2. Parking brake lever and actuator assembly defective.
3. Parking pawl broken or inoperative.

Burned Forward Clutch Plates

1. Check ball in clutch drum damaged, stuck or missing.
2. Clutch piston cracked, seals damaged or missing.
3. Low line pressure.
4. Pump cover oil seal rings missing, broken or undersize; ring groove oversize.
5. Transmission case valve body face not flat or porosity between channels.

Burned Intermediate Clutch Plates

1. Intermediate clutch piston seals damaged or missing.
2. Low line pressure.
3. Transmission case valve body face not flat or porosity between channels.

Burned Intermediate Band
Turbo Hydra-Matic 250

1. Intermediate servo piston seals damaged or missing.
2. Low line pressure.
3. Transmission case valve body face not flat or porosity between channels.

Burned Direct Clutch Plates

1. Restricted orifice in vacuum line to modulator.
2. Check ball in clutch drum damaged, stuck or missing.
3. Defective modulator.
4. Clutch piston cracked, seals damaged or missing.
5. Transmission case valve body face not flat or porosity between channels.

BUICK TWIN TURBINE PROBLEMS, Fig. 14

Engine Stalls While Decelerating Car with Brakes Applied

1. Improper adjustment of throttle dashpot.
2. Engine not properly tuned.

Transmission Oil Foams and Spews Out of Breather

1. Transmission overfilled. If transmission is overfilled, check for blackened condition of oil, indicating leakage of rear axle lubricant into transmission due to defective propeller shaft seals. Check for low oil level in rear axle housing. Correct cause of leakage and completely drain and refill transmission.
2. Water in transmission, indicated by overfilled condition and brown color of transmission oil. Water in transmission usually comes from a leaking oil cooler. In this case there

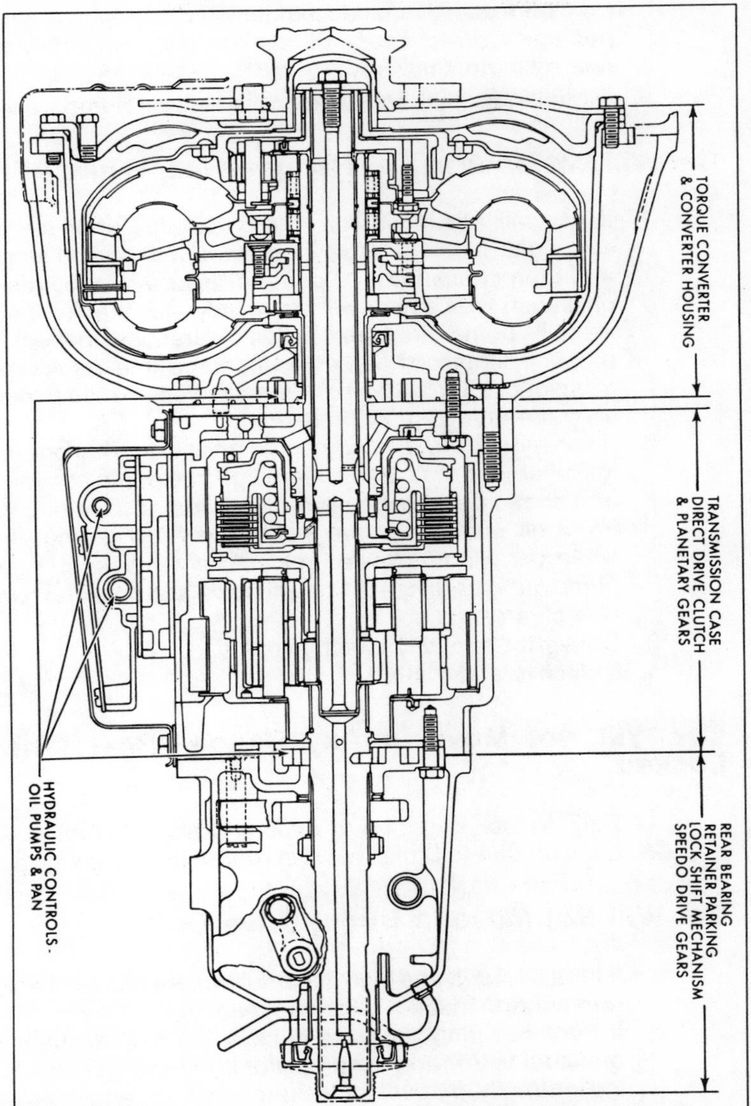

Fig. 14. Sectional view of Twin Turbine transmission.

TORQUE CONVERTER & CONVERTER HOUSING

TRANSMISSION CASE DIRECT DRIVE CLUTCH & PLANETARY GEARS

REAR BEARING RETAINER PARKING LOCK SHIFT MECHANISM SPEEDO DRIVE GEARS

HYDRAULIC CONTROLS - OIL PUMPS & PAN

131

may be excessive oil accumulation in top tank of engine radiator. Correct cause of leakage and completely drain and refill transmission.

3. Air leak into hydraulic system at rear oil pump gaskets.

Car Will Not Move in Any Range—Rear Wheels Free

1. If car will not move for 1 to 8 minutes after standing overnight, park car for several hours with engine stopped and then check front oil pump pressure. A zero reading until such time as car will move indicates that front pump loses its prime due to excessive clearances. Inspect front pump. If condition has existed for some time it is advisable to inspect clutch and bands for excessive wear due to slippage at low apply pressure.

2. If car will not move in any range after extended operation in Reverse, it indicates air leakage into pump suction line and suction and excessive clearance at front oil pump. Front oil pump pressure will be very low during period when car will not move. Inspect for air leaks at rear oil pump gaskets. Inspect front oil pump and cover for excessive clearances.

3. Converter one-way clutch slipping.

4. Defective stator shaft.

Car Will Not Move in Any Range—Rear Wheels Locked

1. Parking lock engaged or parking brake applied.

2. Lock up due to broken part in rear axle or transmission.

Car Will Not Move in Direct Drive Only

1. If front oil pump and high accumulator pressures are okay, remove and inspect clutch assembly.

2. If front oil pump pressure is okay but high accumulator pressure is low and accumulator body gasket is not leaking internally, inspect for leaks in reaction flange gasket. If gasket is satisfactory, inspect clutch piston outer seal and ball check, also oil sealing rings on hubs of reaction shaft flange and low drum.

Car Will Not Move in Reverse Only

1. Reverse servo inoperative.
2. Band improperly adjusted or band operating strut has dropped out of place.
3. Reverse ring gear.

Excessive Slip in All Ranges

1. If condition occurs only after operation in Reverse, see Condition 2 under *Car Will Not Move in Any Range—Rear Wheels Free*.
2. Low oil level.
3. Manual control linkage improperly adjusted.
4. If front oil pump pressure is low, remove and inspect pressure regulator valve and all valve and servo body gaskets. If cause is not found, remove and inspect front oil pump for wear or excessive clearances. Inspect pump cover and reaction shaft flange gaskets for leaks.
5. Defective sun gear and sprag assembly.

Excessive Slip in Direct Drive Only

1. Manual control linkage improperly adjusted.
2. Leak at high accumulator gasket, indicated by low oil pressure at high accumulator.
3. If above items are okay, remove and inspect clutch plates, sealing rings and clutch piston. Inspect for stuck check ball in pistion.

Excessive Slip in Low Only

1. Manual control linkage improperly adjusted.
2. Low band improperly adjusted.
3. If pressure at low accumulator is low, check for leak at accumulator body gasket. If gasket is okay remove valve and servo body and check for gasket leaks and condition of low servo piston seal.
4. Low band and drum scored or worn.

Excessive Slip in Reverse Only

1. Manual control linkage improperly adjusted.

2. Reverse band improperly adjusted. Check for strut out of place or broken anchor.
3. If front oil pump pressure is low, remove valve and servo body and check for gasket leaks and condition of reverse servo piston seal.
4. Reverse band and ring gear scored or worn.

Car Creeps in Neutral

1. Manual control linkage improperly adjusted.
2. Remove valve and servo body and check for low servo piston sticking up.
3. Remove clutch and inspect for sticking, warped or improperly assembled clutch plates. Note whether dish of steel plates is in same direction on all plates. If creep occurs only when engine is accelerated to about 2500 rpm, pay particular attention to condition of check balls at vents in clutch piston and reaction shaft flange.

Car Creeps Forward in Reverse or Backward in Low

Manual control linkage improperly adjusted.

Low-to-Direct Shift Abnormally Rough, or Slip Occurs

1. If high accumulator pressure is low, remove accumulator and check body gaskets. Check for accumulator piston sticking down. Top land of piston must be fully visible through top port in body.
2. If accumulator and gasket are okay, inspect for leaks in valve and servo body gaskets.
3. Low band improperly adjusted.
4. Binding or worn clutch plates.

Excessive Chatter or Clunk When Starting in Low or Reverse

NOTE: A very slight chatter just as car starts to move in reverse, which disappears as soon as car is in motion, may be considered normal. A slight clunk when shifting into Low or Reverse is also normal.

1. Check engine and transmission mountings for tightness. Inspect for broken rubber thrust pad at transmission mounting.
2. Low or Reverse band improperly adjusted.
3. If conditions 1 and 2 do not correct the trouble, direct drive clutch may be dragging. Remove clutch and inspect for sticking, warped, or improperly assembled clutch plates. Note whether dish of steel plates is in same direction on all plates.
4. Inspect for excessive wear of reverse ring gear bushing. Check for foreign matter in planet pinion needle bearings.

Hard Shifting Out of Parking

This condition is caused by binding of transmission shift rod in shift idler lever. If a burr exists on shift rod where it enters idler lever, remove burr with a file. If idler lever is distorted, replace the lever.

TRANSMISSION NOISES

When diagnosing abnormal noises in the transmission, consideration should be given to the parts that are in motion when the noise occurs. The presence or absence of noise in each range should be noted so that the parts which cause the noise can be determined by a process of elimination.

Hum or Low Whine in Neutral or Parking

A hum or low whine in Neutral or Park is normal since all planetary gears are free to rotate without the steadying effect of a load. Some hum may also be expected in Low and Reverse.

Low Growl in Transmission

A low growl in the transmission which disappears in several minutes after the engine is started, following extended parking in extremely cold weather, is caused by cavitation of the cold oil. This is a normal condition which requires no correction.

Buzzing Noise

A buzzing noise can be caused by a low oil level, or by the front pump delivery check valve seating on the edge of the gasket between valves and servo bodies.

A buzzing noise, noticeable in Park and Neutral, may be caused by excessive clearance of the pressure regulator valve in the valve body or an oversize orifice in the valve land. Correction requires replacement of the valve.

Clicking Noise in All Ranges

This sound may be caused by a foreign object going through the converter. A clicking noise which occurs only when the car is in motion may be caused by the parking lock pawl contacting the ratchet wheel due to improper manual control linkage adjustment.

Abnormal Hum or Whine in All Ranges

This condition may be attributed to worn parts or excessive clearances in the front oil pump. A noise caused by the front pump will increase in Low and will diminish at car speeds above 45 mph in Direct Drive. It increases and decreases with engine speed in all ranges. When excessive clearances exist in the front oil pump, a pressure test will usually indicate low front pump pressure.

Abnormal Hum or Whine in All Ranges but Direct Drive

This may be attributed to conditions in the planetary gear train since these gears are locked in Direct Drive but are either idling or transmitting power in all other ranges.

Squealing or Screeching

Squealing or screeching immediately following installation of front oil pump parts indicates that the driving gear has been installed backwards. This condition should be corrected without further operation of the transmission as severe damage will result.

Whistling Noise

A whistling noise which occurs during low speed acceleration in Drive, Low and Reverse, accompanied by unsatisfactory transmission performance indicates cavitation of oil due to incomplete filling of torque convertor. Remove the valve and servo body assembly and check for restrictions in the passages leading to the torque converter. If these passages are clear, check the passages in the reaction shaft flange.

A whistling noise during low speed acceleration in Drive, Low and Reverse, but with otherwise satisfactory transmission performance, may be caused by thin, weak, or cracked turbine vanes, or vanes which are bent over at the exit edges. Such vanes will vibrate under load, causing a whistle. Replacement of the turbine is required for correction.

CHEVROLET POWERGLIDE AND TORQUE DRIVE PROBLEMS—TYPE WITH ALUMINUM CASE

Oil Forced Out Filler Tube

1. Oil level too high. Aeration and foaming caused by planet carrier running in oil.
2. Water in oil.
3. Leak in pump suction circuits.

Oil Leaks

1. Transmission case and extension: extension oil seal, shifter shaft oil seal, speedometer driven gear fitting, pressure taps, oil cooler pipe connections, vacuum modulator and case, transmission oil pan gasket.
2. A very smoky exhaust indicates a ruptured vacuum modulator diaphragm.
3. Converter cover pan; front pump attaching bolts, pump seal ring, pump oil seal, plugged oil drain in front pump, porosity in transmission case.

No Drive in Any Position

1. Low oil level.

2. Clogged oil suction screen.
3. Defective pressure regulator valve.
4. Front pump defective.
5. Input shaft broken.
6. Front pump priming valve stuck.

Erratic Operation and Slippage—Light to Medium Throttle

1. Low oil level.
2. Clogged oil suction screen.
3. Improper band adjustment.
4. Band facing worn.
5. Low band apply linkage disengaged or broken.
6. Servo apply passage blocked.
7. Servo piston ring broken or leaking.
8. Converter stator not holding (rare).

Engine Flares on Standstill Starts but Acceleration Lags

1. Low oil level.
2. Clogged oil suction screen.
3. Improper band adjustment.
4. Band facing worn.
5. Low band apply linkage disengaged or broken.
6. Servo apply passage blocked.
7. Servo piston ring broken or leaking.
8. Converter stator not holding (rare).

Engine Speed Flares on Upshift

1. Low oil level.
2. Improper band adjustment.
3. Clogged oil suction screen.
4. High clutch partially applied—blocked feed orifice.
5. High clutch plates worn.
6. High clutch seals leak.
7. High clutch piston hung up.
8. High clutch drum relief ball not sealing.
9. Vacuum modulator line plugged.
10. Vacuum modulator defective.

Will Not Upshift

1. Maladjusted manual valve lever.
2. Throttle valve stuck or maladjusted.
3. No rear oil pump output caused by stuck priming valve, sheared drive pin or defective pump, 1962-66.
4. Defective governor.
5. Stuck low-drive valve.

No Downshift

1. Low TV pressure.
2. High governor pressure.
3. Sticking low and drive shift plug.
4. Sticking low and drive shift valve.

Harsh Upshifts

1. Throttle valve linkage improperly adjusted.
2. Vacuum modulator line broken or disconnected.
3. Vacuum modulator diaphragm leaks.
4. Vacuum modulator valve stuck.
5. Hydraulic modulator valve stuck.
6. Improper low band adjustment.

Harsh Closed Throttle (Coast) Downshifts

1. High engine idle speed.
2. Improper band adjustment.
3. Vacuum modulator line broken or disconnected.
4. Modulator diaphragm ruptured.
5. Sticking hydraulic modulator valve, pressure regulator valve or vacuum modulator valve.
6. Downshift timing valve malfunction.

No Downshift (Direct-to-Low) Accelerator Floored

1. Throttle control linkage improperly adjusted.
2. Sticking shifter valve or throttle and detent valve.

Car Creeps in Neutral

1. Manual control linkage improperly adjusted.
2. High clutch or low band not released.

No Drive in Reverse

1. Manual control linkage improperly adjusted.
2. Reverse clutch piston stuck.
3. Reverse clutch plates worn out.
4. Reverse clutch leaking excessively.
5. Blocked reverse clutch apply orifice.

Improper Shift Points

1. Throttle valve linkage improperly adjusted.
2. Incorrectly adjusted throttle valve.
3. Defective governor.
4. Rear pump priming valve stuck, 1962-66.

Unable to Push Start, 1962-66

1. Rear pump drive gear not engaged with drive pin on output shaft.
2. Drive pin sheared off or missing.
3. Rear pump priming valve not sealing.
4. Rear pump defective.

Burned Clutch Plates

1. Band adjusting screw backed off more than specified.
2. Improper order of clutch plate assembly.
3. Extended operation with low oil level.
4. Stuck relief ball in clutch drum.
5. Abnormally high speed upshift, probably due to improper governor action; transmission operated at high speed in manual Low.

DUAL COUPLING HYDRA-MATIC, Fig. 15

Slips in First and Third

1. Front sprag clutch slipping.
2. Front sprag clutch broken.

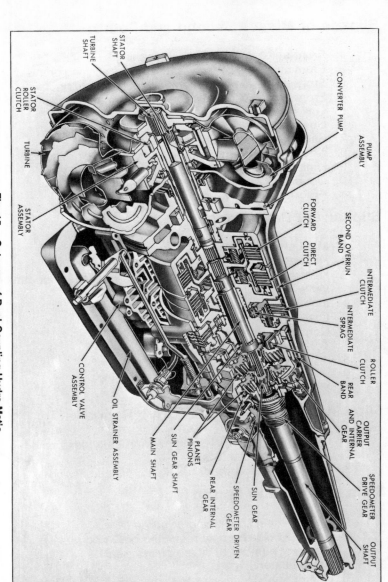

Fig. 15. Cutaway of Dual Coupling Hydra-Matic.

TURBINE SHAFT

STATOR SHAFT

STATOR ROLLER CLUTCH

TURBINE

STATOR ASSEMBLY

CONVERTER PUMP

PUMP ASSEMBLY

FORWARD CLUTCH

DIRECT CLUTCH

SECOND OVERRUN BAND

INTERMEDIATE CLUTCH

INTERMEDIATE SPRAG

ROLLER CLUTCH

REAR BAND

OUTPUT CARRIER AND INTERNAL GEAR

SPEEDOMETER DRIVE GEAR

OUTPUT SHAFT

SPEEDOMETER DRIVEN GEAR

SUN GEAR

REAR INTERNAL GEAR

PLANET PINIONS

SUN GEAR SHAFT

MAIN SHAFT

OIL STRAINER ASSEMBLY

CONTROL VALVE ASSEMBLY

Slips in or Misses Second and Fourth

1. Front unit torus cover seals leaking.
2. Front unit torus cover exhaust valves sticking or missing.
3. Front unit torus cover feed restriction or leak.
4. Front unit torus cover signal restriction or leak.
5. Low oil pressure.
6. Coupling valve sticking.
7. Sticking valves or dirt in valve body.
8. Coupling snap ring improperly installed or missing.
9. Limit valve.
10. Coupling passage restricted or leaking.
11. Front unit torus vanes damaged.

Slips in All Drive Ranges

1. Manual linkage.
2. Neutral clutch slipping or burned.
3. Neutral clutch apply restricted or leaking (case support or valve body).
4. Incorrect number of neutral clutch plates.
5. Low oil pressure.
6. Control valve.
7. Torus members (check valve).
8. Intake pipe O-ring damaged or missing.
9. Pressure regulator valve stuck in pump.
10. Pump slide stuck.

Slips in First and Second (Drive Range)

1. Rear sprag clutch slipping or improperly assembled.
2. Rear sprag clutch broken.
3. Neutral clutch burned, restricted, piston sticking.

Slips in Third and Fourth

1. Rear unit clutch slipping or burned.
2. Rear unit clutch apply restricted or O-ring leaking.
3. Incorrect number of clutch plates (rear).
4. Accumulator.
5. Center support, leak at 2-3 passage.
6. Low oil pressure.
7. Accumulator valve stuck (3rd only).

Slips in Third in Drive Right on Coast

1. Overrun clutch slipping or burned.
2. Overrun clutch apply restricted or leaking.
3. Sticking valves or dirt in valve body.
4. Overrun clutch passages restricted or leaking.

Slips in First and Second in Low Range on Coast

1. Low servo apply restricted or leaking.
2. Low band not anchored to case or broken.
3. Low servo piston and rod binding in case or servo and accumulator body.
4. Band facing worn or loose.
5. Anchor dowel pin missing or loose in case.

No Drive in Drive Range

1. Manual linkage incorrectly adjusted.
2. Manual valve not engaged with drive pin.
3. Low oil pressure.
4. Pressure regulator stuck.
5. Pump intake pipe improperly installed.
6. Front sprag broken, pump bushing, front unit drive torus shaft.
7. Front and/or rear sprag incorrectly installed.
8. Rear sprag broken.
9. Front sprag inner race broken.
10. Rear sprag outer race broken.
11. Neutral clutch plates burned.
12. Neutral clutch piston.
13. Control valve.
14. Pump.

Erratic or No Upshifts

1. Governor valves stuck.
2. Broken governor rings.
3. Sticking valves or dirt in valve body.
4. G-2 bushing turned.

Misses in Second

1. Governor boost valve stuck closed.

2. Transition valve stuck away from plate.
3. Sticking valves or dirt in valve body.
4. Governor sticking.

Misses in Third

1. Transition valve sticking.
2. Sticking valves or dirt in valve body.
3. TV adjustment—too long.
4. Rear clutch.
5. Transition valve spring.

Locks Up in Second and Fourth

1. Front sprag clutch broken or reversed.
2. Overrun clutch applied or sticking.

Locks Up in Third and Fourth

1. Rear sprag clutch broken.
2. Low band not releasing.

Rough 2-3 Shift

1. Accumulator valve stuck.
2. Accumulator piston stuck.
3. Accumulator gasket broken or missing.
4. Restricted or leaking oil passages.
5. Broken accumulator spring.
6. Broken or leaking piston oil seal rings.
7. Control valve.
8. TV adjusted incorrectly.
9. Rear clutch pack.
10. Case passages; TV oil, 2-3 oil, leaks or restrictions.

Upshifts High

1. Throttle linkage adjusted short.
2. Governor valves sticking.
3. Broken governor rings.
4. Sticking valves or dirt in valve body.
5. Leaking or restricted main line feed to governor.

Upshifts Low

1. Throttle linkage adjusted long.
2. Governor valves sticking.
3. Broken governor rings.
4. Sticking valves or dirt in valve body.
5. Leaking TV oil.

No Reverse, Slips or Locks Up

1. Manual linkage incorrectly adjusted.
2. Manual valve not engaged with drive pin.
3. Reverse piston apply restricted or leaking.
4. Low oil pressure.
5. Pressure regulator.
6. Neutral clutch not released.
7. Flash restricting neutral clutch exhaust port on manual body.

Selector Lever Won't Go in Reverse

1. Governor valves sticking.
2. Broken governor rings.
3. Reverse blocker piston stuck.
4. Manual linkage interference.

Reverse Drive in Neutral

1. Reverse stationary cone sticking.

Delayed 1-2 Shift

1. Coupling valve sticking.
2. Governor boost valve sticking.
3. G-1 valve sticking.
4. Wrong spring on coupling valve.

Drive in Low Range Only

1. Rear sprag broken.
2. Neutral clutch not applying.

No Forced Downshifts 4-3 or 3-2

1. Control valve.
2. Linkage.

2-3 Runaway

1. 2-3 passage in center bearing support.
2. Plug out of accumulator.
3. Rear clutch burned.
4. Valve body, transition valve, case passages (2-3 circuit).

Won't Go Into Park

1. Parking links broken.
2. Mechanical interference.
3. Manual linkage.
4. Parking pawl.

Starts in Second Gear

1. Valves sticking.
2. Governor sticking.
3. Governor boost valve stuck.

Drives Forward in Reverse and Neutral

1. Neutral clutch piston stuck in applied position.

Lunges Forward Before Backup When Placing Selector in Reverse

1. G-2 plunger stuck in outward position.
2. Restricted neutral clutch release oil.

Noise Diagnosis

P, R, N, D First and Third

1. Front unit planetary gears.

P, R, N, D First and Second

1. Rear unit planetary gears.

All Ranges, Especially During Warmup

1. Pump noisy; cut O-ring on intake pipe, cut O-ring on cooler sleeves.

1-2 and 3-4 with Hot Oil

1. Front unit coupling leaks.

All Ranges—Loaded Only in Reverse

1. Reverse planetary gears.

Clicking—Low Speed Forward

1. Pressure regulator.
2. Low oil pressure or level.
3. Coupling valve.
4. Governor.

Buzzing

1. Pressure regulator.
2. Oil pressure.
3. Throttle valve.
4. Rear bearing (at about 35 mph).

Rattle or Buzz Under Light Load in Third and Fourth

1. Torus cover; damper spring.

Squeak When Engaging Reverse

1. Low oil pressure or leak in front clutch overrun piston.
2. Rear pump (prior to 1959).

Vibration

1. Flywheel balance.
2. Torus cover balance.
3. Front unit assembly balance.
4. Rear brake drum balance.

OLDS F-85 HYDRA-MATIC, Fig. 16

Low Oil Pressure

1. Boost plug stuck.

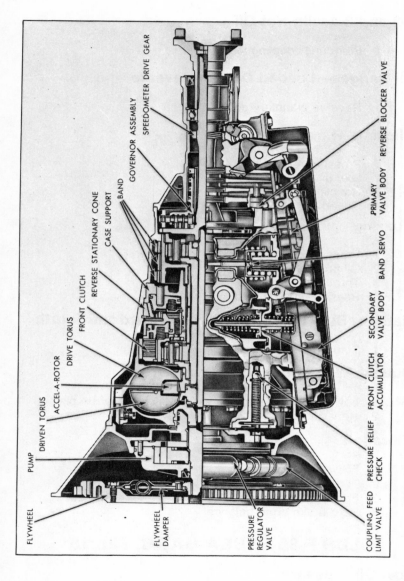

Fig. 16. Cross section of 1963 Oldsmobile F-85 Hydra-Matic transmission.

2. Pressure regulator valve stuck or spring damaged.
3. Strainer O-ring damaged.
4. Manual valve misaligned with pin.
5. Internal leaks.
6. Control valve assembly may have sticking valves.
7. Leak in pump suction circuit.
8. Front pump defective.
9. Ball check valve in control valve assembly defective.

High Oil Pressure

1. Pressure regulator valve may be stuck or damaged.
2. Boost plug sticking.
3. Manual valve misaligned with pin.
4. Sticking valve in control valve assembly.
5. Pump slide sticking. Cover-to-slide clearance too great.

No Drive in Drive Range

1. Low oil level.
2. Low oil pressure.
3. Manual control linkage improperly adjusted.
4. Adjust or replace servo band.
5. Sticking valve in valve body.
6. Leaking or restricted circuit in servo, coupling, case cover, governor.
7. Reverse clutch.

Missing All Shifts

1. Sticking governor valve.
2. Sticking valve in control valve assembly.
3. Clutch not applying.

Drive in Second and Third Only

1. Sticking valve in control valve assembly.
2. Clutch locked—too many plates.

Drive in First and Third Only, 1961

1. Sticking valve in control valve assembly.
2. Coupling not emptying.

Drive in First Only, 1962-63

1. Sticking valve in control valve assembly.
2. Inspect front clutch and accumulator for leaks.
3. Governor rings broken, worn ring lands, sticking valves.

Drive in First and Second Only

1. G-2 governor valve sticking.
2. Sticking valve in control valve assembly.

Drive in Third Only

1. Sticking valve in control valve assembly.
2. Band not applying, 1961.
3. Governor valves sticking.

Drive in Neutral (Reverse or Forward)

1. Internal linkage (manual) engaging.
2. Mispositioned front clutch.
3. Reverse cone clutch not applying.

No Reverse

1. Manual linkage (internal) mispositioned.
2. Low oil pressure.
3. Reverse cone clutch not engaging.
4. Restricted passage.
5. Band not releasing.

Rough 1-2 Shift

1. TV linkage maladjusted.
2. Stuck valves in control valve assembly.
3. Defective accumulator (sticking parts).
4. Coupling not emptying fast enough.
5. Front clutch slipping.
6. 1-2 oil passages restricted.

Rough 2-3 Shift

1. Band not releasing quickly.
2. Sticking servo parts.

Slipping in All Ranges

1. Low oil pressure.

Slipping 1-2 Shift

1. TV linkage adjusted too long.
2. Low oil pressure.
3. Check for restrictions or sticking accumulator parts.
4. Stuck valves in control valve assembly.
5. Slipping band.
6. Front clutch (check number of plates).
7. Restricted 1-2 oil passages.

Slipping 2-3 Shift

1. Stuck valves in control valve assembly.
2. Coupling not filling fast enough, 1961.
3. Front clutch slipping.

Slipping 3-4 Shift, 1962-63

1. Stuck valves in control valve assembly.
2. Front clutch slipping.

No Engine Braking

1. Stuck valves in control valve assembly.
2. Slipping band.
3. Servo not applying.

No Part Throttle or Detent Downshifts

1. TV linkage adjusted too long.
2. Stuck valves in control valve assembly.
3. Accelerator travel short.
4. Governor valves sticking.

Selector Valve Won't Go into Reverse

1. Manual linkage (internal) mispositioned.
2. Reverse blocker valve stuck open.
3. Governor G-2 valve sticking.

Selector Lever Won't Go into Park

1. Parking linkage broken, improperly assembled, distorted.
2. Manual linkage maladjusted.

Drives Forward in Reverse

1. Manual linkage (internal) improperly assembled or distorted.

Upshifts High

1. TV linkage adjusted short.
2. Stuck valve in control valve assembly.
3. Sticking governor valve.
4. TV lever bent.
5. TV pressure high.
6. Line pressure high.
7. Governor oil passage restricted.

Upshifts Low

1. TV linkage adjusted long.
2. Stuck valve in control valve assembly.
3. Governor valve sticking.
4. TV lever bent.
5. TV pressure low.
6. Line pressure low.
7. Governor oil passage restricted.

Hanging in Second—Engine Stall upon Stop

1. Sticking governor valve.
2. Sticking valve in control valve assembly.
3. TV linkage adjusted short.
4. Clutch not releasing.

ROTO HYDRA-MATIC 375, Fig. 17

High Oil Pressure

1. Pressure regulator valve stuck or damaged.
2. Boost plug sticking.

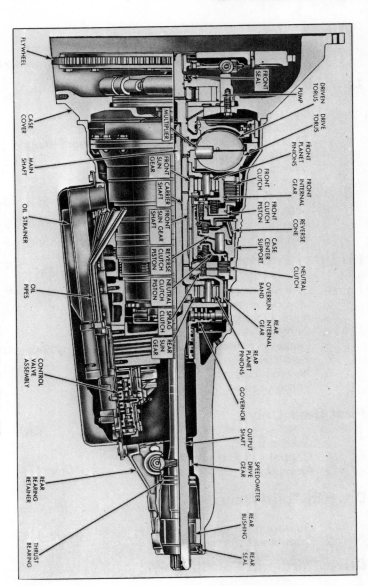

Fig. 17. Cross section of Roto Hydra-Matic 375.

FLYWHEEL

CASE COVER

MAIN SHAFT

OIL STRAINER

OIL PIPES

CONTROL VALVE ASSEMBLY

REAR BEARING RETAINER

THRUST BEARING

MULTIPLIER

FRONT SUN GEAR

CARRIER SHAFT

FRONT SUN GEAR SHAFT

REVERSE CLUTCH PISTON

NEUTRAL CLUTCH PISTON

SPRAG CLUTCH

REAR SUN GEAR

DRIVEN TORUS

PUMP

FRONT SEAL

DRIVE TORUS

FRONT PLANET PINIONS

FRONT CLUTCH

FRONT INTERNAL GEAR

FRONT CLUTCH PISTON

REVERSE CONE

CASE CENTER SUPPORT

NEUTRAL CLUTCH

OVERRUN BAND

REAR INTERNAL GEAR

REAR PLANET PINIONS

GOVERNOR

OUTPUT SHAFT

SPEEDOMETER DRIVE GEAR

REAR BUSHING

REAR SEAL

153

3. Manual valve misaligned with pin.
4. Sticking valve in control valve body.
5. Pump slide sticking; cover-to-slide clearance too great.

Low Oil Pressure

1. Oil level low.
2. Boost plug stuck.
3. Pressure regulator valve stuck or spring damaged.
4. Strainer O-ring seal damaged.
5. Manual valve misaligned with pin.
6. Internal leaks.
7. Sticking valves in control valve body.
8. Leak in pump suction circuit.
9. Front pump defective.
10. Ball check valve in control valve assembly defective.

No Drive in Drive Range

1. Low oil level.
2. Low oil pressure.
3. Manual control linkage.
4. Control valve assembly.
5. Leaking or restricted circuit in coupling, neutral clutch, case cover, governor.
6. Reverse clutch.
7. Sprag or race.

First Gear Only

1. Governor.
2. Control valve assembly.
3. Front clutch.

Drive in Third Only

1. Governor.
2. Control valve assembly.

Drive Third and Fourth Only

1. Control valve assembly.
2. Governor.

No Fourth

1. Governor.
2. Control valve assembly.
3. Oil passages in clutch, accumulator, compensator, drive passages or TV passages.

Drive in Neutral—Forward or Reverse

1. Manual linkage improperly adjusted.
2. Neutral clutch.
3. Reverse clutch.

No Reverse

1. Manual linkage improperly adjusted.
2. Low oil pressure.
3. Reserve clutch.
4. Governor.

Slipping All Ranges

1. Low oil level.
2. Low oil pressure.
3. Coupling.

Slipping 2-3 Shift

1. Throttle linkage improperly adjusted.
2. Low oil level.
3. Low oil pressure.
4. Leaking or restricted circuit in front clutch, accumulator, compensator, TV passage, drive passage.
5. Control valve assembly.

Rough 1-2 Shift

1. Neutral clutch bypass valve broken.

Rough 2-3 Shift

1. Throttle linkage improperly adjusted.

2. Control valve assembly.
3. Leaking or restricted circuit in front clutch, accumulator, compensator, TV passage, drive passage.

Slipping 3-4 Shift

1. Control valve assembly.
2. Leaking or restricted circuit in coupling, front clutch, accumulator, compensator, TV passage, drive passage.

No Engine Braking—Third or Low

1. Control valve assembly.
2. Overrun band servo.

No Part Throttle or Detent Downshifts

1. Throttle linkage improperly adjusted; accelerator pedal height.
2. Control valve assembly.
3. Governor.

Selector Lever Won't Go into Reverse

1. Manual linkage improperly adjusted.
2. Reverse blocker piston.
3. Governor.

Selector Lever Won't Go into Park

1. Manual linkage improperly adjusted.
2. Parking linkage (internal).

Forward Drive in Reverse

1. Manual linkage improperly adjusted.
2. Manual valve.
3. Neutral clutch.

Low or High Upshifts

1. Throttle linkage improperly adjusted.
2. TV pressure high.
3. Governor.

CHEVROLET POWERGLIDE
TYPE WITH CAST IRON CASE

Oil Forced Out Filler Tube

1. Oil level too high.
2. Damaged suction pipe seal.
3. Ears on suction pipe retainer bent.
4. Bore for suction pipe in housing too deep.
5. Sand hole in suction bore in transmission case or housing.
6. Sand hole in suction cavity of valve body.
7. Water in oil.

Oil Leaks

1. At transmission case side cover.
2. At low-drive valve body and transmission case.
3. At servo cover and transmission case.
4. At transmission housing and case.
5. At front of flywheel housing.
6. At oil cooler pipes and connections.
7. At transmission case oil seals.
8. Ruptured diaphragm in vacuum modulator.
9. At O-ring seal between converter cover and pump.
10. At front O-ring seal and front pump oil seal.
11. Plugged oil drain in front pump.
12. Leaks between front pump and converter cavity due to sand hole in housing.

Car Won't Move in Any Range—Rear Wheels Free

1. If car will not move in any range after extended operation in reverse, it indicates air leakage into suction lines and excessive clearances at front oil pump. Front pump pressure will be very low during the period when car will not move. Inspect for air leaks at rear pump gasket.

2. If car will not move for several minutes after standing overnight, park car for several hours with engine stopped and then check front pump pressure. A zero pressure will indicate that the front pump loses its prime due to excessive clearances. If condition has existed for some time it is advisable to inspect clutch and bands for excessive wear due to slippage.
3. Broken internal parts.
4. Converter one-way clutch slipping.
5. Defective stator shaft.

Won't Move in Any Range—Rear Wheels Locked

1. Parking lock pawl engaged.
2. Parking brake applied.
3. Lock up due to broken part in transmission or rear axle.

Won't Move in Reverse

1. Low band needs adjusting.
2. Clutch relief valve stuck.
3. Clutch plates binding in hub or flange.
4. Clutch plates not properly installed.
5. Clutch piston stuck.
6. Reverse band strut broken.
7. Broken reverse band. This problem, which occurs on 1958 V8's, is generally caused by harsh application of reverse pressure. To prevent its reoccurrence, a pressure regulator and damper valve kit (Part No. 3759998) is available for installation. An alternate remedy is to remove the reverse servo and pipe tap at $1/8$-inch plug in the reverse oil passage. Then drill a $1/16$-inch hole in the plug to restrict the oil pressure and soften the application of the reverse band.

Slips When Transmission is Hot

1. No clutch pressure. Clutch drum bushing needs replacing.

Excessive Slip in All Ranges

1. Low oil level.
2. Throttle linkage needs adjusting.
3. Oil suction pipe not seating properly.
4. Oil suction screen clogged.
5. Front pump worn or damaged.
6. Faulty pressure regulator valve or gasket.

Excessive Slip in Manual Low and First Gear or Drive Range

1. Improper linkage adjustment.
2. Improper low band adjustment.
3. Broken low band.
4. Accumulator band stuck.
5. Broken low servo piston ring.
6. Worn clutch drum.
7. Defective servo-to-case gaskets.
8. Defective valve body gaskets.

Excessive Slip in Reverse Only

1. Improper linkage adjustment.
2. Improper reverse band adjustment or broken band.
3. No oil pressure due to stuck accumulator valve.
4. Broken reverse servo piston ring.
5. Defective valve body gaskets.

Car Creeps in Neutral

1. Improper manual linkage adjustment.
2. Low band adjusted too tight.

3. Clutch may be inoperative due to:
   a. Plates not properly assembled.
   b. Plates sticking.
   c. Clutch relief valve stuck closed.
   d. Defective valve body gasket.
   e. Control lever not attached to manual control valve inside transmission.

Car Creeps Forward in Reverse or Backward in Low

1. Manual linkage improperly adjusted.

Low-to-Direct Shift Very Rough

1. Improper low band adjustment.
2. Modulator vacuum line leaking.
3. Worn clutch plates.
4. Clutch plates binding in drum or flange.
5. Inoperative accumulator dump valve.

Engine Races on Low-to-Direct Shift

1. Modulator spring weak.
2. Clutch plates worn or burned.
3. Oil passage to clutch restricted.

Rough Shift Direct-to-Low

1. Vacuum modulator valve stuck.
2. Improper low band adjustment.
3. High speed downshift timing valve inoperative.

No Upshift in Drive Range

1. Broken rear pump drive pin.
2. Defective governor.
3. Stuck shift valve.
4. Clutch plates worn or burned.

No Shift Direct-to-Low With Accelerator Floored

1. Throttle linkage improperly adjusted.
2. Sticking shifter valve or shuttle and detent valve.

Rough Shift Neutral-to-Reverse

1. Engine idling speed too high.
2. Improper reverse band adjustment.
3. Accumulator piston stuck closed.
4. Excessive end play in transmission main shaft.

Chatter in Manual Low and First Gear Drive Range

1. Improper low band adjustment.
2. Worn low band or drum.
3. Defective clutch plates.
4. Clutch piston stuck.
5. Clutch relief valve stuck.

Chatter in Reverse

1. Improper reverse band adjustment.
2. Worn reverse band or drum.
3. Worn or damaged reverse ring gear bushing.
4. Worn or damaged transmission case rear bushing.

Buzzing in All Ranges

1. Low oil level.
2. Front or rear pumps not functioning properly.

Ringing Noise in Converter

1. Low oil level.
2. Oil suction pipe damaged or not seating properly.
3. Defective pressure regulator valve.
4. Front oil pump worn.

CHEVROLET TURBOGLIDE PROBLEMS

No Drive in Any Range

1. Low oil level.
2. Front pump defective or assembled backwards.
3. Front pump priming ball not seating.
4. Defective converter pump.
5. Converter one-way clutch slipping.
6. Defective stator shaft.

No Drive Except in Grade Retard

1. Both overrun clutches assembled backwards.

No Drive Except in Grade Retard and Reverse. Cannot Load Engine in Drive

1. Outer overrun clutch assembled backwards.
2. Forward and neutral clutch not applied due to severe leakage in forward clutch hydraulic circuit.

Drive is Poor at Low Speed, No Reverse, Grade Retard Normal

1. Inner overrun clutch assembled backwards.
2. Stator overrun clutch not holding.

Car Drives Very Slightly in Neutral, Reverse Normal

1. Neutral clutch not released.

Car Drives Normal in Neutral and Drive at Low Speeds, No Reverse

1. Forward clutch not released.

Transmission Will Not Shift to Performance Stator Angle

1. Stator control linkage out of adjustment.
2. Converter charging pressure is low for one of the following reasons:
    a. Leakage which will reduce line pressure enough to cause pressure regulator valve to shut off converter in line.
    b. Leakage in converter circuit.
    c. Discharge orifice in transfer plate plugged.
    d. Damaged or leaking seal rings on second turbine shaft. Damage to front ring allows converter out pressure to leak to stator passage. Damage to middle ring allows neutral pressure to leak to converter out passage.

Unable to Push Start

1. Rear oil pump drive pin broken.

Clutch Slippage on Wide Open Throttle Starts

1. Low oil pressure due to leakage. Especially check forward pressure tube O-ring.
2. Mechanical interference which will prevent forward piston from fully applying.
3. Forward clutch facing failure.

Grade Retard Slow to Apply

1. Control linkage out of adjustment preventing manual valve getting into grade retard position.
2. Low pressure resulting from leakage. Check pressure tube O-ring seals and other O-ring seals.
3. Mechanical interference of grade retard piston.
4. Glazed grade retard plates.

No Drive, Reverse Normal, No Grade Retard

1. Reverse clutch not disengaged.

Grade Retard Brakes Violently

1. Vacuum hose disconnected.
2. Vacuum modulator diaphragm ruptured or hose disconnected.

Shifts From Standstill Very Slowly

1. Check linkage to ascertain that shift lever is positioned by transmission detents.
2. Accumulator control valve stuck closed.
3. Leakage in hydraulic system. Check pressure tube O-ring seals and other seals and gaskets.
4. Front pump priming ball seating poorly, 1959-60.
5. Front pump side clearance excessive.

Shifts From Standstill Very Harsh and Fast

1. Accumulator control valve spring too strong or valve stuck open.
2. Vacuum modulator diaphragm ruptured.
3. Vacuum hose disconnected.
4. Excessively high idle speed.
5. Defective neutral accumulator spring, 1959-60.
6. Kinked vacuum to modulator supply hose.

Excess Vibration in Neutral

1. Converter and flywheel not in proper alignment.

Transmission Operates OK When Cold but Not When Hot

1. If transmission operates properly when cold but has excessive slip when hot, along with no reverse, it indicates that the sun gear free wheeling sprags are worn.

TORQUEFLITE WITH ALUMINUM CASE, Fig. 18

Harsh Engagement in D-1-2-R

1. Engine idle speed too high.
2. Hydraulic pressures too high or too low.
3. Low-reverse band out of adjustment.
4. Accumulator sticking, broken rings or spring.
5. Low-reverse servo, band or linkage malfunction.
6. Worn or faulty front and/or rear clutch.
7. Valve body malfunction or leakage.

Delayed Engagement in D-1-2-R

1. Low fluid level.
2. Incorrect manual linkage adjustment, 1966-69, or incorrect control cable adjustment, 1960-65.
3. Oil filter clogged.
4. Hydraulic pressures too high or low.
5. Valve body malfunction or leakage.
6. Accumulator sticking, broken rings or spring.
7. Clutches or servos sticking or not operating.
8. Faulty front oil pump.
9. Worn or faulty front and/or rear clutch.
10. Worn or broken input shaft and/or reaction shaft support seal rings.
11. Aerated fluid.

Runaway or Harsh Upshift and 3-2 Kickdown

1. Low fluid level.
2. Incorrect throttle linkage adjustment.
3. Hydraulic pressures too high or low.
4. Kickdown band out of adjustment.
5. Valve body malfunction or leakage.
6. Governor malfunction.
7. Accumulator sticking, broken rings or spring.
8. Clutches or servos sticking or not operating.
9. Kickdown servo, band or linkage malfunction.

165

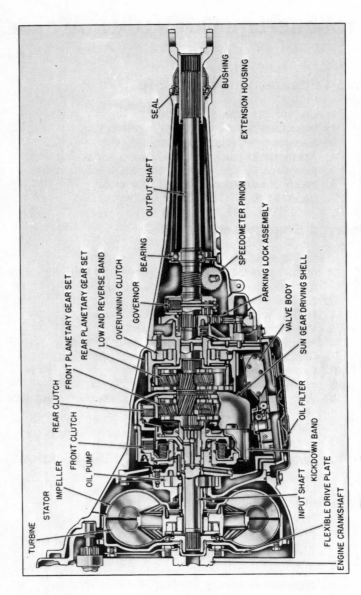

TURBINE
STATOR
IMPELLER
FRONT CLUTCH
OIL PUMP
REAR CLUTCH
FRONT PLANETARY GEAR SET
REAR PLANETARY GEAR SET
LOW AND REVERSE BAND
OVERRUNNING CLUTCH
GOVERNOR
BEARING
OUTPUT SHAFT
SEAL
BUSHING
EXTENSION HOUSING
SPEEDOMETER PINION
PARKING LOCK ASSEMBLY
VALVE BODY
SUN GEAR DRIVING SHELL
OIL FILTER
KICKDOWN BAND
INPUT SHAFT
FLEXIBLE DRIVE PLATE
ENGINE CRANKSHAFT

Fig. 18.   Cutaway of Torqueflite transmission. Earlier models used a rear pump.

166

10. Worn or faulty front clutch.
11. Worn or broken input shaft and/or reaction shaft support seal rings.
12. Aerated oil.
13. Clogged oil filter.

No Upshift

1. Low fluid level.
2. Incorrect throttle linkage adjustment.
3. Kickdown band out of adjustment.
4. Hydraulic pressures too high or low.
5. Governor sticking or leaking.
6. Valve body malfunction or leakage.
7. Accumulator sticking, broken rings or spring.
8. Clutches or servos sticking or not operating.
9. Faulty oil pump, 1966-69.
10. Faulty rear oil pump, 1960-65.
11. Kickdown servo, band or linkage malfunction.
12. Worn or faulty front clutch.
13. Worn or broken input shaft and/or reaction shaft support seal rings.
14. Gearshift linkage misadjusted.
15. Governor support seal rings broken or worn.

Delayed Upshift

1. Incorrect throttle linkage adjustment.
2. Kickdown band out of adjustment.
3. Governor support seal rings broken or worn.
4. Worn or broken reaction shaft support seal rings.
5. Governor malfunction.
6. Kickdown servo band or linkage malfunction.
7. Worn or faulty front clutch.

No Kickdown or Normal Downshift

1. Incorrect throttle linkage adjustment.
2. Incorrect gearshift linkage adjustment, 1966-69.
3. Incorrect control cable adjustment, 1960-65.
4. Kickdown band out of adjustment.
5. Hydraulic pressure too high or low.
6. Governor sticking or leaking.

7. Valve body malfunction or leakage.
8. Accumulator sticking, broken rings or spring.
9. Clutches or servos sticking or not operating.
10. Kickdown servo, band or linkage malfunction.
11. Overrunning clutch not holding.

Erratic Shifts

1. Low fluid level.
2. Aerated fluid.
3. Incorrect throttle linkage adjustment.
4. Incorrect gearshift control linkage adjustment, 1966-69.
5. Incorrect control cable adjustment, 1960-65.
6. Hydraulic pressures too high or low.
7. Governor sticking or leaking.
8. Oil filter clogged.
9. Valve body malfunction or leakage.
10. Clutches or servos sticking or not operating.
11. Faulty oil pump, 1966-69.
12. Faulty front and/or rear oil pump, 1960-65.
13. Worn or broken input shaft and/or reaction shaft support seal rings.
14. Governor support seal rings broken or worn.
15. Kickdown servo band or linkage malfunction.
16. Worn or faulty front clutch.

Slips in Forward Drive Positions

1. Low oil level.
2. Aerated fluid.
3. Incorrect throttle linkage adjustment.
4. Incorrect gearshift control linkage adjustment, 1966-69.
5. Incorrect control cable adjustment, 1960-65.
6. Hydraulic pressures too low.
7. Valve body malfunction or leakage.
8. Accumulator sticking, broken rings or spring.
9. Clutches or servos sticking or not operating.
10. Worn or faulty front and/or rear clutch.
11. Overrunning clutch not holding.
12. Worn or broken input shaft and/or reaction shaft support seal rings.
13. Accumulator sticking, broken rings or springs.

14. Overrunning clutch not holding.
15. Clogged oil filter.
16. Faulty oil pump.
17. Overrunning clutch worn, broken or seized.

Slips in Reverse Only

1. Low fluid level.
2. Aerated fluid.
3. Incorrect gearshift control linkage adjustment, 1966-69.
4. Incorrect control cable adjustment, 1960-65.
5. Hydraulic pressures too high or low.
6. Low-reverse band out of adjustment.
7. Valve body malfunction or leakage.
8. Front clutch or rear servo sticking or not operating.
9. Low-reverse servo, band or linkage malfunction.
10. Faulty oil pump (front on 1960-65).

Slips in All Positions

1. Low fluid level.
2. Hydraulic pressures too low.
3. Valve body malfunction or leakage.
4. Faulty oil pump (front on 1960-65).
5. Clutches or servos sticking or not operating.
6. Worn or broken input shaft and/or reaction shaft support seal rings.
7. Aerated oil.
8. Oil filter clogged.

No Drive in Any Position

1. Low fluid level.
2. Hydraulic pressures too low.
3. Oil filter clogged.
4. Valve body malfunction or leakage.
5. Faulty oil pump (front on 1960-65).
6. Clutches or servos sticking or not operating.
7. Torque converter failure.
8. Planetary gearsets broken or seized.

No Drive in Forward Drive Positions

1. Hydraulic pressures too low.
2. Valve body malfunction or leakage.
3. Accumulator sticking, broken rings or spring.
4. Clutches or servos, sticking or not operating.
5. Worn or faulty rear clutch.
6. Overrunning clutch not holding.
7. Worn or broken input shaft and/or reaction shaft support seal rings.
8. Low fluid level.
9. Planetary gearsets broken or seized.
10. Overrunning clutch broken, worn or seized.

No Drive in Reverse

1. Incorrect gearshift control linkage adjustment, 1966-69.
2. Incorrect control cable adjustment, 1960-65.
3. Hydraulic pressures too low.
4. Low-reverse band out of adjustment.
5. Valve body malfunction or leakage.
6. Front clutch or rear servo sticking or not operating.
7. Low-reverse servo, band or linkage malfunction.
8. Worn or faulty front clutch.
9. Planetary gearsets broken or seized.

Drives in Neutral

1. Incorrect gearshift control linkage adjustment, 1966-69.
2. Incorrect control cable adjustment, 1960-65.
3. Valve body malfunction or leakage.
4. Rear clutch inoperative.
5. Insufficient clutch plate clearance.

Drags or Locks

1. Kickdown band out of adjustment.
2. Low-reverse band out of adjustment.
3. Kickdown and/or Low-Reverse servo, band or linkage malfunction.

4. Front and/or rear clutch faulty.
5. Planetary gear sets broken or seized.
6. Overrunning clutch worn, broken or seized.

Grating, Scraping or Growling Noise

1. Kickdown band out of adjustment.
2. Low-reverse band out of adjustment.
3. Output shaft bearing and/or bushing damaged.
4. Governor support binding or broken seal rings.
5. Oil pump scored or binding (either pump on 1960-65).
6. Front and/or rear clutch faulty.
7. Planetary gear sets broken or seized.
8. Overrunning clutch worn, broken or seized.

Buzzing Noise

1. Low fluid level.
2. Pump sucking air (both pumps on 1960-65).
3. Valve body malfunction.
4. Overrunning clutch inner race damaged.

Hard to Fill, Oil Flows Out Filler Tube

1. High fluid level.
2. Breather clogged.
3. Oil filter clogged.
4. Aerated fluid.

Transmission Overheats

1. Low fluid level.
2. Kickdown band adjustment too tight.
3. Low-reverse band adjustment too tight.
4. Faulty cooling system.
5. Cracked or restricted oil cooler line or fitting.
6. Faulty oil pump (either pump on 1960-65).
7. Insufficient clutch plate clearance in front and/or rear clutches.
8. Engine idle too low.
9. Hydraulic pressures too low.

171

10. Incorrect gearshift linkage adjustment.
11. Kickdown band adjustment too tight.

Starter Will Not Energize in Neutral or Park

1. Incorrect gearshift control linkage adjustment, 1966-69.
2. Incorrect control cable adjustment, 1960-65.
3. Faulty or incorrectly adjusted neutral starting switch.
4. Broken lead to neutral switch.

Impossible to Push Start, 1960-65 Only

1. Low fluid level.
2. Low-Reverse band slipping.
3. Valve body malfunction or leakage.
4. Rear oil pump faulty.
5. Low-Reverse servo, band or linkage malfunction.
6. Worn or faulty rear clutch.
7. Worn or broken input shaft and/or reaction shaft support seal rings.

TORQUEFLITE WITH CAST IRON CASE, Fig. 19

SHIFT DIFFICULTIES

Harsh N to D or N to R

1. Pressure checks, line lube, etc.
2. Low-Reverse band adjustment.
3. Engine idle.
4. L-R servo band or linkage.
5. Accumulator.
6. Front clutch.
7. Rear clutch.

Delayed N to D

1. Oil level.
2. Pressure checks, line lube, etc.
3. Valve body—bolts, mating surfaces.

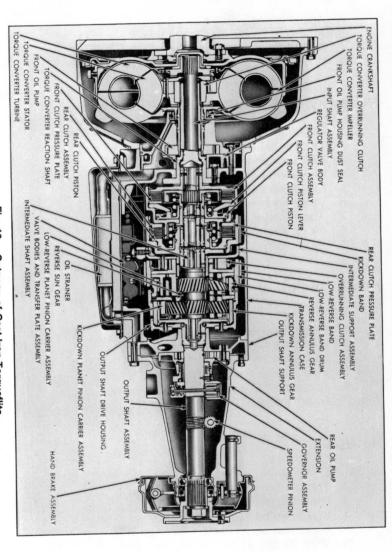

ENGINE CRANKSHAFT
TORQUE CONVERTER OVERRUNNING CLUTCH
TORQUE CONVERTER IMPELLER
FRONT OIL PUMP HOUSING DUST SEAL
INPUT SHAFT ASSEMBLY
REGULATOR VALVE BODY
FRONT CLUTCH ASSEMBLY
FRONT CLUTCH PISTON LEVER
FRONT CLUTCH PISTON

TORQUE CONVERTER TURBINE
TORQUE CONVERTER STATOR
FRONT OIL PUMP
TORQUE CONVERTER REACTION SHAFT
FRONT CLUTCH PRESSURE PLATE
REAR CLUTCH ASSEMBLY
REAR CLUTCH PISTON

REAR CLUTCH PRESSURE PLATE
KICKDOWN BAND
INTERMEDIATE SUPPORT ASSEMBLY
OVERRUNNING CLUTCH ASSEMBLY
LOW-REVERSE BAND
LOW-REVERSE BAND DRUM
REVERSE ANNULUS GEAR
TRANSMISSION CASE
KICKDOWN ANNULUS GEAR
OUTPUT SHAFT SUPPORT

INTERMEDIATE SHAFT ASSEMBLY
VALVE BODIES AND TRANSFER PLATE ASSEMBLY
LOW-REVERSE PLANET PINION CARRIER ASSEMBLY
REVERSE SUN GEAR
OIL STRAINER
KICKDOWN PLANET PINION CARRIER ASSEMBLY
OUTPUT SHAFT DRIVE HOUSING
OUTPUT SHAFT ASSEMBLY

REAR OIL PUMP
EXTENSION
GOVERNOR ASSEMBLY
SPEEDOMETER PINION

HAND BRAKE ASSEMBLY

Fig. 19. Cutaway of Cast Iron Torqueflite.

173

4. Accumulator.
5. Air pressure check.
6. Front pump.
7. Front clutch.

Runaway on Upshift and 3-2 Kickdown

1. Oil level.
2. Throttle linkage adjustment.
3. Pressure checks, line lube, etc.
4. Kickdown band adjustment.
5. Kickdown servo band or linkage.
6. Valve body—bolts, mating surfaces.
7. Accumulator.
8. Air pressure check.
9. Rear clutch.

Harsh Upshift and 3-2 Kickdown

1. Throttle linkage adjustment.
2. Pressure checks, line lube, etc.
3. Kickdown band adjustment.
4. Kickdown servo band or linkage.
5. Valve body—bolts, mating surfaces.
6. Accumulator.
7. Rear clutch.

No Upshift

1. Oil level.
2. Throttle linkage adjustment.
3. Pressure checks, line lube, etc.
4. Kickdown band adjustment.
5. Kickdown servo band or linkage.
6. Valve body—bolts, mating surfaces.
7. Accumulator.
8. Air pressure check.
9. Governor.
10. Rear clutch.

No Kickdown or Normal Downshift

1. Oil level.
2. Throttle linkage adjustment.
3. Gearshift control cable adjustment.
4. Pressure checks, line lube, etc.
5. Kickdown band adjustment.
6. Kickdown servo band or linkage.
7. Valve body—bolts, mating surfaces.
8. Accumulator.
9. Air pressure check.
10. Governor.
11. Overrunning clutch.

Shifts Erratically

1. Oil level.
2. Throttle linkage adjustment.
3. Gearshift control cable adjustment.
4. Pressure checks, line lube, etc.
5. Engine idle.
6. Regulator valve or spring.
7. Output shaft rear bearing.
8. Oil strainer.
9. Valve body—bolts, mating surfaces.
10. Air pressure check.
11. Governor.
12. Front pump—drive sleeve.

OPERATING DIFFICULTIES

Slips in Forward Drive Position

1. Oil level.
2. Pressure checks, line lube, etc.
3. Valve body—bolts, mating surfaces.
4. Accumulator.
5. Air pressure check.
6. Regulator valve body, gasket, mating surfaces.
7. Front clutch.
8. Rear clutch.
9. Overrunning clutch.

Slips in L-R Only

1. Pressure checks, line lube, etc.
2. Low-Reverse band adjustment.
3. Low-Reverse servo band or linkage.
4. Valve body—bolts, mating surfaces.
5. Air pressure check.
6. Regulator valve body, gasket, mating surfaces.

Slips in All Positions

1. Oil level.
2. Pressure checks, line lube, etc.
3. Regulator valve or spring.
4. Valve body—bolts, mating surfaces.
5. Air pressure check.
6. Front pump.
7. Regulator valve body, gasket, mating surfaces.

No Drive in Any Position

1. Oil level.
2. Pressure checks, line lube, etc.
3. Regulator valve or spring.
4. Oil strainer.
5. Valve body—bolts, mating surfaces.
6. Air pressure check.
7. Front pump.
8. Regulator valve body, gasket, mating surfaces.
9. Converter one-way clutch slipping.
10. Defective stator shaft.

No Drive in Forward Ranges

1. Pressure checks, line lube, etc.
2. Kickdown band adjustment.
3. Kickdown servo band or linkage.
4. Valve body—bolts, mating surfaces.
5. Accumulator.
6. Air pressure check.
7. Front clutch.
8. Rear clutch.
9. Overrunning clutch.

No Drive in Reverse

1. Pressure checks, line lube, etc.
2. Low-Reverse band adjustment.
3. Low-Reverse servo band or linkage.
4. Air pressure check.
5. Rear clutch.
6. Stuck reverse blocker valve (one piece valve body).
7. Broken reverse servo piston ring.

Drives in Neutral

1. Gearshift control cable adjustment.
2. Valve body—bolts, mating surfaces.
3. Front clutch.

MISCELLANEOUS

Drags or Locks

1. Kickdown hand adjustment.
2. Low-Reverse band adjustment.
3. Hand brake adjustment.
4. Kickdown servo band on linkage.
5. Low-Reverse servo band or linkage.
6. Front clutch.
7. Rear clutch.
8. Planetary gear set.
9. Overrunning clutch.

Grating, Scraping Noise

1. Hand brake adjustment.
2. Output shaft rear bearing.
3. Governor.
4. Rear pump.
5. Front pump.
6. Front clutch.
7. Rear clutch.
8. Planetary gear set.

Buzzing Noises

1. Oil level.

2. Regulator valve or spring.
3. Converter control valve.
4. Regulator valve body, gasket, mating surfaces.

Transmission Hard to Fill—Oil Blows Out Fill Tube

1. Oil level.
2. Regulator valve or spring.
3. Converter control valve.
4. Breather.
5. Oil strainer.
6. Front pump.
7. Regulator valve body, gasket, mating surfaces.

Transmission Overheats

1. Oil level.
2. Kickdown band adjustment.
3. Low-Reverse band adjustment.
4. Hand brake adjustment.
5. Regulator valve or spring.
6. Converter control valve.
7. Torque converter cooling.
8. Rear pump.
9. Front pump.
10. Regulator valve body, gasket, mating surfaces.
11. Front clutch.
12. Rear clutch.

Impossible to Push

1. Oil level.
2. Pressure checks, line lube, etc.
3. Low-Reverse band adjustment.
4. Low-Reverse servo band or linkage.
5. Valve body—bolts, mating surfaces.
6. Rear pump.

Starter Won't Energize

1. Gearshift control cable adjustment.
2. Starting switches.

FORD
C3 AND C4
TRANSMISSION, Figs. 20 & 21

Rough Initial Engagement in D, D2, 2, D1

1. Engine idle speed.
2. Vacuum diaphragm unit or tubes restricted, leaking or maladjusted.
3. Check control pressure.
4. Pressure regulator.
5. Valve body.
6. Forward clutch.

1-2 or 2-3 Shift Points Erratic

1. Check fluid level.
2. Vacuum diaphragm unit or tubes restricted, leaking or maladjusted.
3. Intermediate servo.
4. Manual linkage adjustment.
5. Governor.
6. Check control pressure.
7. Valve body.
8. Make air pressure check.

Rough 1-2 Upshifts

1. Vacuum diaphragm unit or tubes restricted, leaking or maladjusted.
2. Intermediate servo.
3. Intermediate band.
4. Check control pressure.
5. Valve body.
6. Pressure regulator.

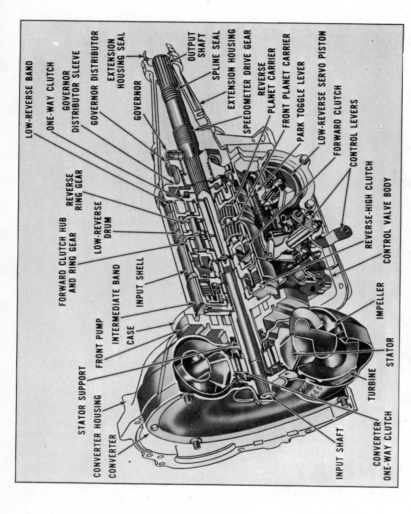

Fig. 20. Cutaway of C3 & C4 transmission.

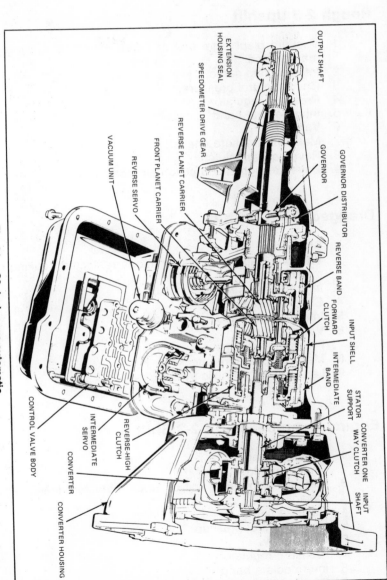

Fig. 21. C3 dual range automatic.

OUTPUT SHAFT

EXTENSION HOUSING SEAL

SPEEDOMETER DRIVE GEAR

REVERSE PLANET CARRIER

FRONT PLANET CARRIER

VACUUM UNIT

REVERSE SERVO

GOVERNOR

GOVERNOR DISTRIBUTOR

REVERSE BAND

FORWARD CLUTCH

INPUT SHELL

INTERMEDIATE BAND

STATOR SUPPORT

CONVERTER ONE WAY CLUTCH

INPUT SHAFT

CONTROL VALVE BODY

INTERMEDIATE SERVO

REVERSE-HIGH CLUTCH

CONVERTER

CONVERTER HOUSING

181

Rough 2-3 Upshift

1. Vacuum diaphragm unit or tubes restricted, leaking or maladjusted.
2. Intermediate servo.
3. Check control pressure.
4. Pressure regulator.
5. Intermediate band.
6. Valve body.
7. Make air pressure check.
8. Reverse-High clutch.
9. Reverse-High clutch piston air bleed valve.

Dragged Out 1-2 Shift

1. Check fluid level.
2. Vacuum diaphragm unit or tubes restricted, leaking or maladjusted.
3. Intermediate servo.
4. Check control pressure.
5. Intermediate band.
6. Valve body.
7. Pressure regulator.
8. Make air pressure check.
9. Leakage in hydraulic system.

Engine Overspeeds on 2-3 Shift

1. Manual linkage.
2. Check fluid level.
3. Vacuum diaphragm unit or tubes restricted, leakage or maladjusted.
4. Reverse servo.
5. Check control pressure.
6. Valve body.
7. Pressure regulator.
8. Intermediate band.
9. Reverse-High clutch.
10. Reverse-High clutch piston air bleed valve.

No 1-2 or 2-3 Shift

1. Manual linkage.
2. Downshift linkage, including inner lever position.
3. Vacuum diaphragm unit or tubes restricted, leaking or maladjusted.
4. Governor.
5. Check control pressure.
6. Valve body.
7. Intermediate band.
8. Intermediate servo.
9. Reverse-High clutch.
10. Reverse-High clutch piston air bleed valve.

No 3-1 Shift in D1 or 2 or 3-2 Shift in D or D2

1. Governor.
2. Valve body.

No Forced Downshift

1. Downshift linkage, including inner lever position.
2. Valve body.
3. Vacuum diaphragm unit or tubes restricted, leaking or maladjusted.

Runaway Engine on Forced 3-2 Downshift

1. Check control pressure.
2. Intermediate servo.
3. Intermediate band.
4. Pressure regulator.
5. Valve body.
6. Vacuum diaphragm unit or tubes restricted, leaking or maladjusted.
7. Leakage in hydraulic system.

Rough 3-2 or 3-1 Shift at Closed Throttle

1. Engine idle speed.
2. Vacuum diaphragm unit or tubes restricted, leaking or maladjusted.

3. Intermediate servo.
4. Valve body.
5. Pressure regulator.

Shifts 1-3 in Either D Position

1. Intermediate band.
2. Intermediate servo.
3. Vacuum diaphragm unit or tubes restricted, leaking or maladjusted.
4. Valve body.
5. Governor.
6. Make air pressure check.

No Engine Braking in First Gear—Manual Low

1. Manual linkage.
2. Reverse band.
3. Reverse servo.
4. Valve body.
5. Governor.
6. Make air pressure check.

Slips or Chatters in First Gear—Drive 1

1. Check fluid level.
2. Vacuum diaphragm unit or tubes restricted, leaking or maladjusted.
3. Check control pressure.
4. Pressure regulator.
5. Valve body.
6. Forward clutch.
7. Leakage in hydraulic system.
8. Planetary one-way clutch.

Slips or Chatters in Second Gear

1. Check fluid level.
2. Vacuum diaphragm unit or tubes restricted, leaking or maladjusted.
3. Intermediate servo.
4. Intermediate band.

5. Check control pressure.
6. Pressure regulator.
7. Valve body.
8. Make air pressure check.
9. Forward clutch.
10. Leakage in hydraulic system.

Slips or Chatters in R

1. Check fluid level.
2. Vacuum diaphragm unit or tubes restricted, leaking or maladjusted.
3. Reverse band.
4. Check control pressure.
5. Reverse servo.
6. Pressure regulator.
7. Valve body.
8. Make air pressure check.
9. Reverse-High clutch.
10. Leakage in hydraulic system.
11. Reverse-High piston air bleed valve.

No Drive in Drive 1 Only

1. Check fluid level.
2. Manual linkage.
3. Check control pressure.
4. Valve body.
5. Make air pressure check.
6. Planetary one-way clutch.

No Drive in L Only

1. Check fluid level.
2. Manual linkage.
3. Check control pressure.
4. Intermediate servo.
5. Valve body.
6. Make air pressure check.
7. Leakage in hydraulic system.
8. Planetary one-way clutch.

185

No Drive in L or 1 Only

1. Check fluid level.
2. Manual linkage.
3. Check control pressure.
4. Valve body.
5. Reverse servo.
6. Make air pressure check.
7. Leakage in hydraulic system.
8. Planetary one-way clutch.

No Drive in R Only

1. Check fluid level.
2. Manual linkage.
3. Reverse band.
4. Check control pressure.
5. Reverse servo.
6. Valve body.
7. Make air pressure check.
8. Reverse-high clutch.
9. Leakage in hydraulic system.
10. Reverse-High clutch piston air bleed valve.

No Drive in Any Selector Position

1. Check fluid level.
2. Manual linkage.
3. Check control pressure.
4. Pressure regulator.
5. Valve body.
6. Make air pressure check.
7. Leakage in hydraulic system.
8. Front pump.

Lockup in Drive 1 Only

1. Reverse-High clutch.
2. Parking linkage.
3. Leakage in hydraulic system.

Lockup in Drive 2 Only

1. Reverse band.
2. Reverse servo.
3. Reverse-high clutch.
4. Parking linkage.
5. Leakage in hydraulic system.
6. Planetary one-way clutch.

Lockup in L Only

1. Intermediate band.
2. Intermediate servo.
3. Reverse-High clutch.
4. Parking linkage.
5. Leakage in hydraulic system.

Lockup in R Only

1. Intermediate band.
2. Intermediate servo
3. Forward clutch.
4. Parking linkage.
5. Leakage in hydraulic system.

Parking Lock Binds or Does Not Hold

1. Manual linkage.
2. Parking linkage.

Maximum Speed Too Low, Poor Acceleration

1. Engine performance.
2. Brakes bind.
3. Converter one-way clutch.

Noisy in N or P

1. Check fluid level.
2. Pressure regulator.
3. Front pump.
4. Planetary assembly.

Noisy in All Gears

1. Check fluid level.
2. Pressure regulator.
3. Planetary assembly.
4. Forward clutch.
5. Front pump.
6. Planetary one-way clutch.

Car Moves Forward in N

1. Manual linkage.
2. Forward clutch.

FORD C6 TRANSMISSION, Fig. 22

No Drive in Forward Ranges

1. Manual linkage adjustment.
2. Check control pressure.
3. Valve body.
4. Make air pressure check.
5. Forward clutch.
6. Leakage in hydraulic system.

Rough Initial Engagement in D, D1, D2 or 2

1. Engine idle speed too high.
2. Vacuum diaphragm unit or tubes restricted, leaking or maladjusted.
3. Check control pressure.
4. Valve body.
5. Forward clutch.

1-2 or 2-3 Shift Points Incorrect or Erratic

1. Check fluid level.
2. Vacuum diaphragm unit or tubes restricted, leaking or maladjusted.
3. Downshift linkage, including inner lever position.

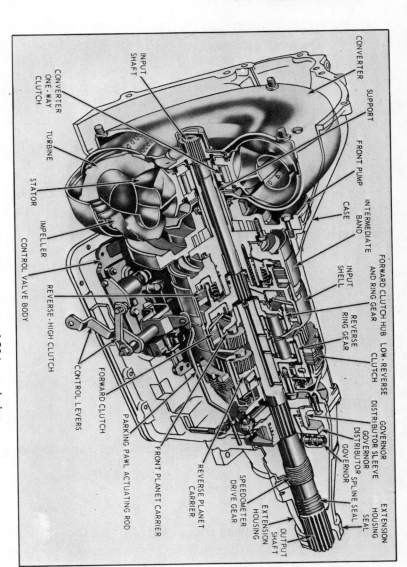

Fig. 22.   Cutaway of C6 transmission.

189

4. Manual linkage adjustment.
5. Governor defective.
6. Check control pressure.
7. Valve body.
8. Make air pressure check.

Rough 1-2 Upshift

1. Vacuum diaphragm unit or tubes restricted, leaking or maladjusted.
2. Intermediate servo.
3. Intermediate band.
4. Check control pressure.
5. Valve body.

Rough 2-3 Shift

1. Vacuum diaphragm or tubes restricted, leaking or maladjusted.
2. Intermediate servo.
3. Check control pressure.
4. Intermediate band.
5. Valve body.
6. Make air pressure check.
7. Reverse-high clutch.
8. Reverse-high clutch piston air bleed valve.

Dragged Out 1-2 Shift

1. Check fluid level.
2. Vacuum diaphragm unit or tubes restricted, leaking or maladjusted.
3. Intermediate servo.
4. Check control pressure.
5. Intermediate band.
6. Valve body.
7. Make air pressure check.
8. Leakage in hydraulic system.

Engine Overspeeds on 2-3 Shift

1. Manual linkage adjustment.
2. Check fluid level.

3. Vacuum diaphragm unit or tubes restricted, leaking or maladjusted.
4. Intermediate servo.
5. Check control pressure.
6. Valve body.
7. Intermediate band.
8. Reverse-high clutch.
9. Reverse-high clutch piston air bleed valve.

No 1-2 or 2-3 Shift

1. Manual linkage adjustment.
2. Downshift linkage including inner lever position.
3. Vacuum diaphragm unit or tubes restricted, leaking or maladjusted.
4. Governor.
5. Check control pressure.
6. Valve body.
7. Intermediate band.
8. Intermediate servo.
9. Reverse-High clutch.
10. Leakage in hydraulic system.

No 3-1 Shift in D1, 2 or 3-2 Shift in D2, D

1. Governor.
2. Valve body.

No Forced Downshift

1. Downshift linkage, including inner lever position.
2. Check control pressure.
3. Valve body.

Runaway Engine on Forced 3-2 Shift

1. Check control pressure.
2. Intermediate servo.
3. Intermediate band.
4. Valve body.
5. Vacuum diaphragm unit or tubes restricted, leaking or maladjusted.
6. Leakage in hydraulic system.

Rough 3-2 Shift or 3-1 Shift at Closed Throttle

1. Engine idle speed.
2. Vacuum diaphragm unit or tubes restricted, leaking or maladjusted.
3. Intermediate servo.
4. Check control pressure.
5. Valve body.

Shifts 1-3 in D1, D2, D, 2

1. Intermediate band.
2. Intermediate servo.
3. Valve body.
4. Governor.
5. Make air pressure check.

No Engine Braking in First Gear—Manual Low Range

1. Manual linkage adjustment.
2. Low-Reverse clutch.
3. Valve body.
4. Governor.
5. Make air pressure check.
6. Leakage in hydraulic system.

Creeps Excessively

1. Engine idle speed too high.

Slips or Chatters in First, D1 or 2

1. Check fluid level.
2. Vacuum diaphragm unit or tubes restricted, leaking or maladjusted.
3. Check control pressure.
4. Valve body.
5. Forward clutch.
6. Leakage in hydraulic system.
7. Planetary one-way clutch.

Slips or Chatters in Second Gear

1. Check fluid level.
2. Vacuum diaphragm unit or tubes restricted, leaking or maladjusted.
3. Intermediate servo.
4. Intermediate band.
5. Check control pressure.
6. Valve body.
7. Make air pressure check.
8. Forward clutch.
9. Leakage in hydraulic system.

Slips or Chatters in Reverse

1. Check fluid level.
2. Vacuum diaphragm unit or tubes restricted, leaking or maladjusted.
3. Manual linkage adjustment.
4. Low-Reverse clutch.
5. Check control pressure.
6. Valve body.
7. Make air pressure check.
8. Reverse-High clutch.
9. Leakage in hydraulic system.
10. Reverse-High clutch piston air bleed valve.

No Drive in D1 or 2

1. Manual linkage adjustment.
2. Check control pressure.
3. Valve body.
4. Planetary one-way clutch.

No Drive in D2 or D

1. Check fluid level.
2. Manual linkage adjustment.
3. Check control pressure.
4. Intermediate servo.
5. Valve body.
6. Make air pressure check.
7. Leakage in hydraulic system.

193

No Drive in L or 1

1. Check fluid level.
2. Check control pressure.
3. Valve body.
4. Make air pressure check.
5. Leakage in hydraulic system.

No Drive in R Only

1. Check fluid level.
2. Manual linkage adjustment.
3. Low-Reverse clutch.
4. Check control pressure.
5. Valve body..
6. Make air pressure check.
7. Reverse-High clutch.
8. Leakage in hydraulic system.
9. Reverse-High clutch piston air bleed valve.

No Drive in Any Selector Position

1. Check fluid level.
2. Manual linkage adjustment.
3. Check control pressure.
4. Valve body.
5. Make air pressure check.
6. Leakage in hydraulic system.
7. Front pump.

Lockup in D1 or 2

1. Valve body.
2. Parking linkage.
3. Leakage in hydraulic system.

Lockup in D2 or D

1. Low-Reverse clutch.
2. Valve body.
3. Reverse-High clutch.
4. Parking linkage.
5. Leakage in hydraulic system.
6. Planetary one-way clutch.

Lockup in L or 1

1. Valve body.
2. Parking linkage.
3. Leakage in hydraulic system.

Lockup in R Only

1. Valve body.
2. Forward clutch.
3. Parking linkage.
4. Leakage in hydraulic system.

Parking Lock Binds or Does Not Hold

1. Manual linkage adjustment.
2. Parking linkage.

Transmission Overheats

1. Oil cooler and connections.
2. Valve body.
3. Vacuum diaphragm unit or tubes restricted, leaking or maladjusted.
4. Check control pressure.
5. Converter one-way clutch.
6. Converter pressure check valves.

Maximum Speed Too Low, Poor Acceleration

1. Engine performance.
2. Car brakes.
3. Forward clutch.

Transmission Noisy in N and P

1. Check fluid level.
2. Valve body.
3. Front pump.

Noisy in First, Second, Third or Reverse

1. Check fluid level.
2. Valve body.
3. Planetary assembly.
4. Forward clutch.
5. Reverse-high clutch.
6. Planetary one-way clutch.

Fluid Leak

1. Check fluid level.
2. Converter drain plugs.
3. Oil pan gasket, filler tube or seal.
4. Oil cooler and connections.
5. Manual or downshift lever shaft seal.
6. 1/8-inch pipe plugs in case.
7. Extension housing-to-case gasket.
8. Extension housing rear oil seal.
9. Speedometer driven gear adapter seal.
10. Vacuum diaphragm unit or tubes.
11. Intermediate servo.
12. Engine rear oil seal.
13. Front pump oil seal.
14. Front pump-to-case gasket or seal.

Car Moves Forward in N

1. Manual linkage adjustment.
2. Forward clutch.

FoMoCo CW AND THREE-SPEED UNITS WITH CAST IRON CASE, Figs. 23 & 24

Rough Initial Engagement

1. Idle speed.
2. Vacuum unit or tubes, 1961-76
3. Throttle linkage, 1959-60.
4. Rear band, 1959-60.

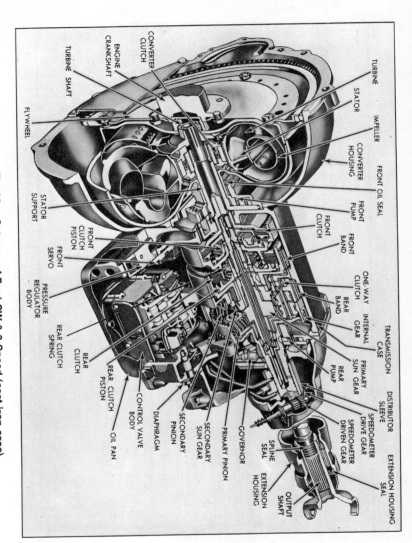

Fig. 23.   Cutaway of Ford CW & 3 Speed (cast iron case).

CONVERTER CLUTCH

ENGINE CRANKSHAFT

TURBINE SHAFT

FLYWHEEL

TURBINE

STATOR

IMPELLER

CONVERTER HOUSING

FRONT OIL SEAL

STATOR SUPPORT

FRONT PUMP

FRONT CLUTCH

FRONT CLUTCH PISTON

FRONT SERVO

FRONT BAND

FRONT CLUTCH

ONE-WAY CLUTCH

INTERNAL GEAR

REAR BAND

PRIMARY SUN GEAR

REAR PUMP

TRANSMISSION CASE

PRESSURE REGULATOR BODY

REAR CLUTCH SPRING

REAR CLUTCH

REAR CLUTCH PISTON

CONTROL VALVE BODY

DIAPHRAGM

OIL PAN

SECONDARY PINION

SECONDARY SUN GEAR

PRIMARY PINION

GOVERNOR

DISTRIBUTOR SLEEVE

SPEEDOMETER DRIVE GEAR

SPEEDOMETER DRIVEN GEAR

SPLINE SEAL

EXTENSION HOUSING

OUTPUT SHAFT

EXTENSION HOUSING SEAL

197

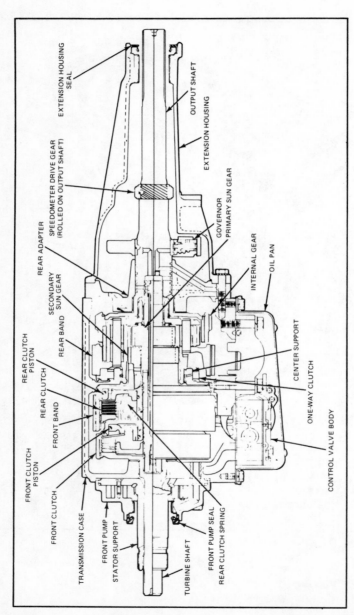

Fig. 24. CW transmission cutaway.

EXTENSION HOUSING SEAL

OUTPUT SHAFT

EXTENSION HOUSING

REAR ADAPTER

SPEEDOMETER DRIVE GEAR (ROLLED ON OUTPUT SHAFT)

GOVERNOR

PRIMARY SUN GEAR

INTERNAL GEAR

OIL PAN

SECONDARY SUN GEAR

REAR BAND

CENTER SUPPORT

REAR CLUTCH PISTON

REAR CLUTCH

FRONT BAND

ONE-WAY CLUTCH

FRONT CLUTCH PISTON

FRONT CLUTCH

CONTROL VALVE BODY

TRANSMISSION CASE

FRONT PUMP

STATOR SUPPORT

TURBINE SHAFT

FRONT PUMP SEAL

REAR CLUTCH SPRING

5. Front band, 1961-76.
6. Check control pressure.
7. Pressure regulator.
8. Valve body.

Shift Points High, Low or Erratic

1. Fluid level.
2. Vacuum unit or tubes, 1961-76.
3. Throttle linkage, 1959-60.
4. Manual linkage.
5. Governor.
6. Check control pressure.
7. Valve body.
8. Inner and outer throttle levers, 1959-60.
9. Downshift linkage, 1961-76.

Rough 2-3 Shift

1. Throttle linkage, 1959-60.
2. Manual linkage, 1961-76.
3. Front band.
4. Vacuum unit or tubes, 1961-75.
5. Pressure regulator.
6. Valve body.
7. Front servo.

Engine Overspeeds, 2-3 Shift

1. Vacuum unit or tubes, 1961-76.
2. Throttle linkage, 1959-60.
3. Front band.
4. Valve body.
5. Pressure regulator, 1961-76.

No 1-2 or 2-3 Shifts

1. Governor.
2. Valve body.
3. Manual linkage, 1961-76.

4. Rear clutch.
5. Front band, 1961-76.
6. Front servo, 1961-76.
7. Leakage in hydraulic system.
8. Fluid distributor sleeve in output shaft, 1959-60.
9. Pressure regulator, 1961-76.

No Forced Downshift

1. Throttle linkage, 1959-60.
2. Downshift linkage, 1961-76.
3. Check control pressure.
4. Valve body.
5. Inner and outer throttle levers, 1959-60.

Rough 3-2 or 3-1 Shifts

1. Engine idle speed.
2. Vacuum unit or tubes, 1961-76.
3. Throttle linkage, 1959-60.
4. Valve body.

Slips or Chatters in Second

1. Fluid level.
2. Vacuum unit or tubes, 1961-76.
3. Throttle linkage, 1959-60.
4. Front band.
5. Check control pressure.
6. Pressure regulator.
7. Valve body.
8. Front servo.
9. Front clutch.
10. Leakage in hydraulic system.

Slips or Chatters in First

1. Fluid level.
2. Vacuum unit or tubes, 1961-76.
3. Throttle linkage, 1959-60.
4. Rear band, 1959-60.
5. Check control pressure.

6. Pressure regulator.
7. Valve body.
8. Inner and outer throttle levers, 1959-60.
9. Front clutch.
10. Leakage in hydraulic system.
11. Fluid distributor sleeve in output shaft.
12. Planetary one-way clutch.

Slips or Chatters in Reverse

1. Fluid level.
2. Throttle linkage, 1959-60.
3. Rear band.
4. Check control pressure.
5. Pressure regulator.
6. Valve body.
7. Rear servo, 1961-76.
8. Rear clutch.
9. Vacuum unit or tubes, 1961-76.
10. Leakage in hydraulic system.
11. Fluid distributor sleeve in output shaft.

No Drive in D Range

1. Front band, 1959-60.
2. Valve body.
3. Make air pressure check.
4. Manual linkage, 1961-76.
5. Front clutch.
6. Leak in hydraulic system.
7. Fluid distributor sleeve in output shaft.

No Drive in D1 or D

1. Manual linkage.
2. Valve body.
3. Planetary one-way clutch.

No Drive in L or 1

1. Manual linkage.
2. Rear band, 1959-60.

3. Front clutch, 1961-76.
4. Rear servo, 1959-60.
5. Valve body.
6. Make air pressure check.
7. Leak in hydraulic system.
8. Fluid distributor sleeve in output shaft.

No Drive in R

1. Rear band.
2. Rear servo.
3. Valve body.
4. Make air pressure check.
5. Rear clutch.
6. Leak in hydraulic system.
7. Fluid distributor sleeve in output shaft.

No Drive in Any Range

1. Fluid level.
2. Manual linkage.
3. Check control pressure.
4. Pressure regulator.
5. Valve body.
6. Make air pressure check.
7. Leak in hydraulic system.

Lockup in D, D1, D2 or 2

1. Manual linkage.
2. Rear band, 1959-60.
3. Rear servo.
4. Front servo.
5. Rear clutch.
6. Parking linkage.
7. Leak in hydraulic system.

Lockup in D2 or D

1. Manual linkage.
2. Rear band.
3. Rear servo.
4. Rear clutch.

   5. Parking linkage.
   6. Leak in hydraulic system.
   7. Planetary one-way clutch.

Lockup in R

   1. Front band.
   2. Front servo.
   3. Front clutch.
   4. Parking linkage.
   5. Leak in hydraulic system.

Lockup in L or 1

   1. Front band.
   2. Pressure regulator, 1961-76.
   3. Front servo, 1959-60.
   4. Valve body.
   5. Rear clutch.
   6. Parking linkage.
   7. Leak in hydraulic system.

Parking Lock Binds or Won't Hold

   1. Manual linkage.
   2. Parking linkage.

Unable to Push Start

   1. Fluid level.
   2. Manual linkage.
   3. Pressure regulator.
   4. Valve body.
   5. Rear pump.
   6. Leak in hydraulic system.

Transmission Overheats

   1. Converter cooling air passages, 1959-60.
   2. Oil cooler and connections.
   3. Pressure regulator.
   4. Converter one-way clutch.

Engine Runaway on Forced Downshift

1. Front band.
2. Pressure regulator.
3. Valve body.
4. Front servo.
5. Vacuum unit or tubes, 1961-76.
6. Leak in hydraulic system.

Maximum Speed Below Normal, Acceleration Poor

1. Converter one-way clutch.

No 2-1 Downshift, 1959-60

1. Throttle linkage.
2. Valve body.
3. Rear servo.

No 3-1 Downshift

1. Engine idle speed.
2. Vacuum unit or tubes, 1961-76.
3. Throttle linkage, 1959-60.
4. Valve body.

Noise in Neutral

1. Pressure regulator.
2. Engine rear oil seal, 1959-60.
3. Front clutch.
4. Front pump.

Noise in 1-2-3 or R

1. Pressure regulator.
2. Planetary assembly.
3. Front clutch.
4. Rear clutch.
5. Front pump.

Noise in Reverse

1. Pressure regulator.
2. Front pump.

Noise on Coast in Neutral

1. Rear pump.

FoMoCo TWO-SPEED AUTOMATIC TRANSMISSIONS, Fig. 25

Harsh Initial Engagement in D, L and R

1. Engine idle speed.
2. Vacuum unit or tube leaking.
3. Throttle linkage.
4. Check control pressure.

Slips or Chatters in D or L

1. Fluid level.
2. Check control pressure.
3. Control valve body.
4. Low band adjustment.
5. Make air pressure check.
6. Leakage in low servo apply circuit.
7. Engine-transmission mounts.
8. Low servo and band.
9. Planetary gears.

Car Won't Move in D but Will in L

1. Low servo piston check valve.

Slips or Chatters in R

1. Fluid level.
2. Check control pressure.
3. Manual linkage.

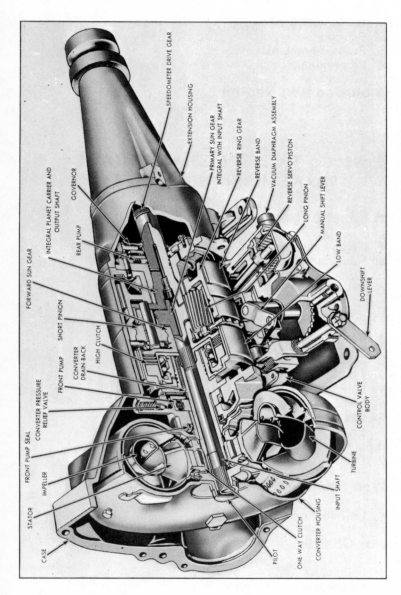

Fig. 25. Cutaway of Ford 2 Speed with vacuum controlled throttle valve.

SPEEDOMETER DRIVE GEAR

EXTENSION HOUSING

PRIMARY SUN GEAR
INTEGRAL WITH INPUT SHAFT

REVERSE RING GEAR

REVERSE BAND

VACUUM DIAPHRAGM ASSEMBLY

REVERSE SERVO PISTON

LONG PINION

MANUAL SHIFT LEVER

LOW BAND

DOWNSHIFT LEVER

CONTROL VALVE BODY

TURBINE

INPUT SHAFT

CONVERTER HOUSING

ONE-WAY CLUTCH

PILOT

INTEGRAL PLANET CARRIER AND OUTPUT SHAFT

GOVERNOR

REAR PUMP

FORWARD SUN GEAR

SHORT PINION

HIGH CLUTCH

CONVERTER DRAIN-BACK

FRONT PUMP

CONVERTER PRESSURE RELIEF VALVE

FRONT PUMP SEAL

IMPELLER

STATOR

CASE

4. Control valve body.
5. Reverse band adjustment.
6. Air pressure check.
7. Leakage in reverse servo apply circuit.
8. Engine-transmission mounts.
9. Reverse servo and band.
10. Cracked or broken rear band anchor.

Engine Overspeeds During 1-2 Shift

1. Fluid level.
2. Check for burned clutch plates if there is fluid odor.
3. Check control pressure.
4. Low band adjustment.
5. Air pressure check.
6. Control valve body.
7. Leakage in clutch apply or low servo release circuit.
8. High clutch.

Momentary Lockup During 1-2 Shift

1. Fluid level.
2. Control pressure check.
3. Control valve body.
4. Low band adjustment.
5. Low servo and band.
6. High clutch.
7. Low servo piston return spring.

Severe 2-1 Shift During Coast-Down

1. Engine idle speed.
2. Throttle linkage.
3. Control valve body.
4. Control pressure check.
5. Low band adjustment.

No 1-2 Shift in D

1. Fluid level.
2. Check for burned clutch plates if there is fluid odor.

3. Manual linkage.
4. Governor.
5. High clutch piston.
6. Low servo and band.
7. Leakage in control pressure main circuit.
8. High clutch.
9. High clutch piston.
10. Rear pump.

Delayed or Severe 1-2 Shift

1. Vacuum diaphragm or tube leakage.
2. Throttle linkage.
3. Governor.
4. Control valve body.
5. Leakage in control pressure main circuit.
6. Low servo piston check valve.

Slips Continuously After 1-2 Shift

1. Check for burned clutch plates if there is fluid odor.
2. Fluid level.
3. Check control pressure.
4. Air pressure check.
5. Control valve body.
6. High clutch.
7. Leakage in clutch apply or low servo release circuit.

No 2-1 Forced Downshift

1. Downshift linkage.
2. Control valve body.
3. Leakage in control pressure main circuit.

No 2-1 Shift During Coast-Down

1. Control valve body.
2. Governor.

Fluid Forced Out Vent

1. Fluid level.

2. Transmission external vent.
3. Fluid aeration.
4. Fluid contaminated with engine coolant.
5. Cooler flow check.

Transmission Overheats

1. Fluid level.
2. Control pressure check.
3. Converter cooler air passages.
4. Cooler flow check.
5. Converter one-way clutch.
6. Fluid check for engine coolant contamination.
7. Transmission external vent.

Acceleration Normal—Maximum Speed About 50 mph

1. Converter one-way clutch.

Acceleration Poor—Operation Above 30 mph Normal with Steady Throttle

1. Converter one-way clutch.

Engine Won't Push Start

1. Fluid level.
2. Manual linkage.
3. Control valve body.
4. Low band adjustment.
5. Low servo piston check valve.
6. Rear pump.
7. Leakage in control pressure main circuit.
8. Low servo and band.
9. Leakage in low servo apply circuit.

Parking Lock Doesn't Hold or Binds

1. Manual linkage.
2. Parking linkage.
3. Front band installed backwards—strut out of position.

Other Automatic Transmissions

BORG-WARNER AUTOMATIC TRANS RAMBLER AND J-SERIES JEEP AND SCOUT, Fig. 26

Harsh Engagement

1. Front clutch seized or plates distorted.
2. Rear clutch seized or plates distorted.

Delayed Forward Engagement

1. Sealing rings missing or broken.
2. Front clutch piston check valve leaks.

Delayed Reverse Engagement

1. Sealing rings missing or broken.

No Engagement

1. Sealing rings missing or broken.
2. Broken input shaft.
3. Front pump drive tangs or converter hub broken.
4. Front pump worn.
5. Defective converter.

No Forward D-1

1. Sealing rings missing or broken.
2. Front clutch slipping, worn plates or faulty parts.
3. One-way (sprag) clutch slipping or incorrectly installed.
4. Front clutch piston check valve leaks.

No Forward D-2

1. Sealing rings missing or broken.
2. Front clutch slipping, worn plates or faulty parts.
3. Front clutch piston check valve leaks.

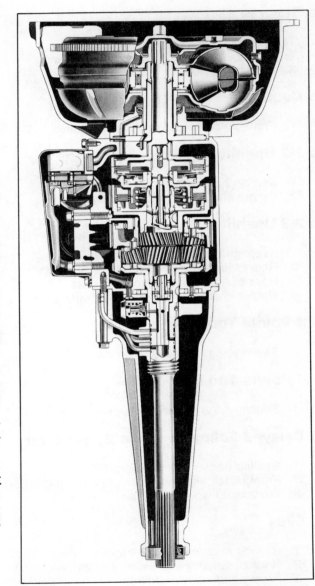

Fig. 26. Sectional view of typical Warner Automatic Transmission, cast iron case. Rear pump is not used on 1967-73 units.

No Reverse

1. Sealing rings missing or broken.
2. Rear clutch slipping, worn or faulty parts.
3. Rear band worn or broken.

No Neutral

1. Front clutch seized or distorted plates.

No 1-2 Upshift

1. Sealing rings missing or broken.
2. Output shaft plug missing (6 cylinder).

No 2-3 Upshift

1. Sealing rings missing or broken.
2. Rear clutch slipping, worn or faulty parts.
3. Rear clutch piston ball check leaks.
4. Output shaft plug missing (6 cylinder).

Shift Points Too High

1. Sealing rings missing or broken.

Shift Points Too Low

1. Sealing rings missing or broken.

1-2 Delayed Followed Close By 2-3 Shift

1. Sealing rings missing or broken.
2. Front clutch slipping, worn plates or faulty parts.
3. Front band worn or broken.

2-3 Slips

1. Sealing rings missing or broken.
2. Rear clutch slipping, worn or faulty parts.
3. Front band worn or broken.
4. Rear clutch pistol ball check leaks.

Harsh 1-2 Shift

1. Front clutch slipping, worn plates or faulty parts.

Harsh 2-3 Shift

1. Rear clutch seized or plates distorted.

1-2 Ties Up

1. Rear clutch seized or plates distorted.
2. One-way (sprag) clutch seized.

No 2-1 in D-1

1. One-way (sprag) clutch slipping or incorrectly installed.
2. Output shaft plug missing (6 cylinder).

No 2-1 in L Range

1. Rear band worn or broken.
2. Output shaft plug missing (6 cylinder).

No 3-2 Shift

1. Front band worn or broken.
2. Output shaft plug missing (6 cylinder).

Shift Points Too High or Too Low

1. Sealing rings missing or broken.

2-1 Slips

1. Front clutch slipping, worn plates or faulty parts.
2. Front pump drive tangs or converter hub broken.
3. Front clutch piston check valve leaks.

3-2 Slips

1. Sealing rings missing or broken.
2. Rear clutch slipping, worn or faulty parts.
3. Front band worn or broken.
4. Rear clutch piston ball check leaks.

Harsh 2-1 Shift

1. Sealing rings missing or broken.
2. Front clutch slipping, worn plates or faulty parts.
3. One-way (sprag) clutch slipping or incorrectly installed.

Harsh 3-2 Shift

1. Rear clutch slipping, worn or faulty parts.
2. Rear clutch seized or plates distorted.

3-1 Shift Above 30 mph

1. Sealing rings missing or broken.
2. Front band worn or broken.

Clips or Chatters in Reverse

1. Sealing rings missing or broken.
2. Front clutch seized or plates distorted.
3. Rear clutch slipping, worn or faulty parts.
4. Rear band worn or broken.
5. Rear clutch piston ball check leaks.

Reverse Tie Up

1. Sealing rings missing or broken.
2. Front clutch seized or plates distorted.

Low Idle Pressure

1. Sealing rings missing or broken.
2. Front pump worn.

Low Stall Pressure

1. Sealing rings missing or broken.
2. Front pump worn.
3. Output shaft plug missing (6 cylinder).

Stall Speed Too Low

1. Converter.

Stall Speed Too High D-1

1. Broken output shaft.
2. Broken gears.
3. Sealing rings missing or broken.
4. Front clutch slipping, worn plates or faulty parts.
5. One-way (sprag) clutch slipping or incorrectly installed.
6. Broken input shaft.
7. Converter.
8. Front clutch piston check valve leaks.

Reverse Stall Speed Too High

1. Broken output shaft.
2. Broken gears.
3. Rear band worn or broken.
4. Rear clutch slipping, worn or faulty parts.
5. Broken input shaft.
6. Converter.

Poor Acceleration

1. Output shaft plug missing (6 cylinder).
2. Converter.

Noisy in Neutral

1. Rear clutch seized or plates distorted.
2. Front pump.
3. Front clutch hub thrust washer missing (detectable in N, P, R only).
4. Converter.

Noisy in Park

1. Front pump.
2. Front clutch hub thrust washer missing (detectable in N, P, R only).
3. Converter.

Noisy in All Gears

1. Front pump.
2. Planetary assembly.
3. Converter.

Noisy in First and Second Gears Only

1. Front pump.
2. Planetary assembly.
3. Forward sun gear thrust washer missing.

Park Brake Does Not Hold

1. Parking linkage.

Oil Out Breather

1. Sealing rings missing or broken.
2. Breather baffle missing.

Oil Out Fill Tube

1. Sealing rings missing or broken.
2. Breather baffle missing.

Ties Up in L or D-1, First Gear

1. Rear clutch seized or plates distorted.
2. Sealing rings missing or broken.

Ties Up in D-1 or D-2, Second and Third Gears

1. Rear clutch seized or plates distorted.
2. Sealing rings missing or broken.
3. One-way (sprag) clutch seized.

Chatters D-1, D-2 or Low

1. Sealing rings missing or broken.
2. Front clutch slipping, worn plates or faulty parts.
3. Front clutch piston check valve leaks.

VOLKSWAGEN AUTOMATIC, Fig. 27

No Drive in Any Range

1. Low oil level.
2. Oil pump or drive defective.
3. Shafts or planet gear set broken.
4. Drive plate broken.
5. Fluid filter clogged.

No Drive in Any Forward Range

1. Forward clutch defective.

No Drive with Lever in First or Reverse

1. First and Reverse band or servo faulty.

No Drive in First Gear with Lever in 3 Position

1. First gear one-way clutch in annulus gear defective.

No Drive in Second Gear with Lever in 2 or 3 Position

1. Second gear band or servo faulty.

No Drive in Third or Reverse

1. Direct and Reverse clutch faulty.

No Upshift Out of First Gear

1. Governor drive defective.
2. Governor valve sticking.
3. Valve body defective.

Power Transmission Erratic

1. Low oil level.
2. Selector lever incorrectly adjusted.

217

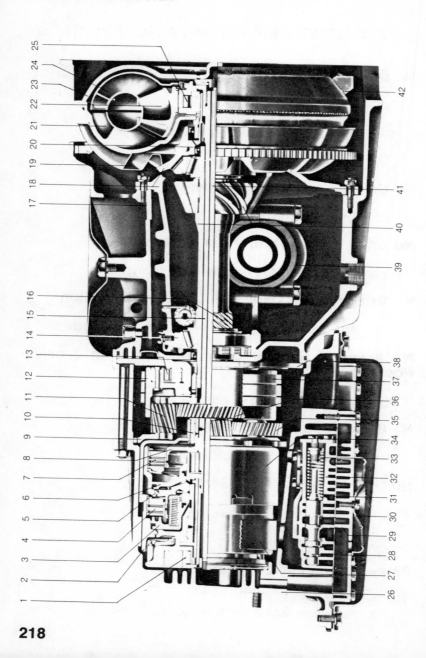

1 - Oil pump
2 - Clutch drum
3 - Piston for direct and reverse clutch
4 - Direct and reverse clutch
5 - Forward clutch drum with ball valve
6 - Piston for forward clutch
7 - Forward clutch
8 - Forward clutch hub
9 - Planetary gear carrier
10 - Small sun gear
11 - Small planet pinion
12 - Annulus or ring gear
13 - 1st gear one-way clutch
14 - Adjusting ring for pinion bearing
15 - Turbine shaft
16 - Governor drive
17 - Final drive housing
18 - Differential carrier
19 - Cooling fins
20 - Torque converter support tube
21 - Impeller
22 - Stator
23 - Converter housing
24 - Turbine
25 - One-way clutch
26 - Transmission case
27 - 2nd gear brake band
28 - Control valve
29 - Transfer plate
30 - Oil strainer
31 - Separator plate
32 - Valve body
33 - Spring for valve
34 - Driving shell
35 - Large planet pinion
36 - Large sun gear
37 - 1st and reverse brake band
38 - Bearing flange
39 - Bearing cap for differential
40 - Pinion with shaft
41 - Impeller shaft
42 - Connecting lug

Fig. 27. Volkswagen automatic transmission.

219

    3. Fluid filter clogged.
    4. Primary throttle pressure valve sticking.

Delayed Engagement, Engine Races

    1. Oil level incorrect.
    2. Friction linings burned or worn.
    3. Oil pressure wrong due to incorrect adjustment of vacuum unit.
    4. Incorrect oil pressure due to internal leakage.

Shifts Occur When Speed is Too Low

    1. Defective governor.
    2. Defective valve body.
    3. Maladjusted vacuum unit.
    4. Leakage in transmission.

Shifts Occur When Speed is Too High

    1. Vacuum unit or hose leaking.
    2. Defective valve body.
    3. Defective governor.
    4. Misadjusted vacuum unit.
    5. Leakage in transmission.
    6. Primary throttle pressure incorrect.
    7. Kickdown switch lever bent.
    8. Kickdown solenoid defective.

No Upshift to Third

    1. Incorrect governor pressure.
    2. Defective valve body.
    3. Direct and reverse clutch defective.

Harsh Engagement when Lever is Shifted into Gear

    1. Idle speed too high.
    2. Vacuum hose leaking.
    3. Primary throttle pressure incorrect.

Vehicle Creeps

1. Idle speed too high.

No Kickdown

1. Incorrect throttle linkage and switch adjustment.
2. Electrical fault in kickdown circuit.
3. Valve body defective or dirty.

Poor Acceleration; Low Maximum Speed

1. Faulty converter.
2. Bands or clutches slipping.
3. Low oil level.

Poor Acceleration; Screeching Noise When Moving Off

1. Converter or one-way clutch faulty. Make stall test to check.

Scraping Noise From Converter

1. Thrust washer in converter worn.

Oil Consumption Without External Leakage

1. Vacuum unit leaking.
2. Oil seals on pinion or governor shaft faulty (oil getting into final drive housing).

Parking Lock Not Working

1. Incorrect selector lever adjustment.
2. Operating linkage broken.

Rear Axle Problems

Noise When Pulling Straight Ahead

1. Not enough oil.
2. Wrong grade of oil.
3. Poor quality oil.
4. Ring gear and pinion have excessive backlash.
5. Ring gear and pinion worn.
6. Pinion shaft bearings worn or loose.
7. Pinion shaft end play excessive.
8. Ring gear and pinion misaligned because of bent axle housing or distorted differential case.
9. Ring gear warped.
10. Differential bearings worn or loose.
11. Ring gear rivets or screws loose.
12. Ring gear and pinion not matched set.

Noise When Coasting in Gear

Any axle noise which is heard when the engine is pulling the car is likely to be heard when the car is coasting. However, it will not be as loud as when pulling.

If the ring gear and pinion are meshed too tight, the noise will be greater when decelerating. The noise will disappear when the engine is pulling unless the gears are very tight.

Excessive end play of the pinion shaft is due to a loose pinion nut or incorrect adjustment.

Intermittent Noise

1. Warped ring gear.
2. Loose ring gear rivets or screws.
3. Ring gear improperly installed on differential case due to dirt or burrs between the two.

Knocks or Clicks

1. Flat spot on ring gear or pinion tooth, or tooth chipped, or particle of metal lodged on tooth.

2. Flat spot on bearing.
3. Loose axle shaft key.
4. Loose splined shafts.
5. Mismatched differential case halves.

Noise on Turns

1. Differential pinions or side gears chipped, scuffed or teeth broken.
2. Differential pinions binding on pinion shaft.
3. Differential pinions or side gears loose due to worn bushings or shaft.
4. Excessive backlash between pinions and side gears.
5. Excessive axle shaft end play.
6. Contacting surfaces between side gear and differential case burred, scored or otherwise damaged.

Noise Is the Same in Drive or Coast

1. Road noise.
2. Tire noise.
3. Front wheel bearing noise.
4. Incorrect driveline angle.

Noise Changes on Different Types of Road

1. Road noise.
2. Tire noise.

Noise Tone Lowers As Car Speed Is Lowered

1. Tire noise.

Vibration

1. Rough rear wheel bearing.
2. Unbalanced or damaged propeller shaft.
3. Tire unbalance.
4. Worn universal joint in propeller shaft.
5. Incorrect driveline angle.
6. Improperly indexed propeller shaft at companion flange.
7. Companion flange runout too great.

A Knock or Click Approximately Every Two Revolutions of Rear Wheel

    1. Rear wheel bearing.

A Continuous Low Pitch Whirring or Scraping Noise Starting at Relatively Low Speed

    1. Pinion bearing noise.

Drive Noise, Coast Noise or Float Noise

    1. Ring and pinion gear noise.

Clunk on Acceleration or Deceleration

    1. Worn differential pinion shaft in case or side gear hub counterbore in case worn oversize.
    2. Insufficient lubrication on propeller shaft slip yoke.

Chatter on Turns

    1. Wrong lubricant in differential.
    2. Clutch plates worn.

Clunk or Knock on Rough Road Operation

    1. Excessive end play of axle shafts.

Oil Leaks at Axle Ends

    1. Oil level too high.
    2. Oil too light or poor quality.
    3. Axle shaft oil seals worn.
    4. Axle shaft bearing retainer loose.
    5. Cracked rear axle housing.
    6. Vent (if any) clogged.

Oil Leak at Pinion Shaft

1. Oil level too high.
2. Oil too light or poor quality.
3. Pinion oil seal worn.
4. Pinion oil seal retainer distorted, loose in housing or improperly installed.
5. Oil return passage in carrier housing restricted.
6. Universal joint companion flange hub rough, scored or out of round.
7. Universal joint companion flange loose on pinion shaft.

Drum Brake Problems

One Brake Drags

1. Brake line restricted.
2. Improperly adjusted or worn wheel bearing.
3. Distorted or improperly adjusted brake shoe.
4. Faulty retracting spring.
5. Drum out of round.
6. Loose backing plate.
7. Faulty wheel cylinder.
8. Dirty brake fluid.
9. Air in hydraulic system.
10. Insufficient shoe-to-backing plate lubrication.

All Brakes Drag

1. Mechanical resistance at pedal or shoes. Damaged linkage.
2. Brake line restricted.
3. Distorted or improperly adjusted brake shoes.
4. Dirty brake fluid.
5. Faulty master cylinder.
6. Sticking booster control valve.

Hard Pedal

1. Mechanical resistance at pedal or shoes. Damaged linkage.

225

2. Brake line restricted.
3. Distorted or improperly adjusted brake shoes.
4. Linings glazed or worn.
5. Oil or grease in lining.

Spongy Pedal

1. Leaks or insufficient fluid.
2. Air in hydraulic system.

Car Pulls to One Side

1. Brake line restricted.
2. Improper tire pressure.
3. Improperly adjusted or worn wheel bearing.
4. Distorted or improperly adjusted brake shoes.
5. Faulty retracting spring.
6. Drum out of round.
7. Linings glazed or worn.
8. Oil or grease in lining.
9. Loose lining.
10. Faulty wheel cylinder.
11. Self-adjusters not operating.

One Wheel Locks

1. Distorted or improperly adjusted brake shoes.
2. Linings glazed or worn.
3. Oil or grease in lining.
4. Loose backing plate.
5. Faulty wheel cylinder.
6. Tire tread worn.

Brakes Chatter

1. Drum out of round.
2. Linings glazed or worn.
3. Oil or grease in lining.
4. Loose backing plate.
5. Loose lining.
6. Poor lining-to-drum contact.
7. Loose front suspension.

Excessive Pedal Travel

1. Leaks or insufficient fluid.
2. Distorted or improperly adjusted brake shoes.
3. Linings glazed or worn.
4. Faulty master cylinder.
5. Air in hydraulic system.
6. Self-adjusters not operating.
7. Cracked drum.

Pedal Gradually Goes to Floor

1. Leaks or insufficient fluid.
2. Faulty master cylinder.

Brakes Uneven

1. Improper tire pressure.
2. Oil or grease in lining.
3. Scored drum.
4. Dirty brake fluid.

Shoe Click Release

1. Self-adjusters not operating.
2. Insufficient shoe-to-backing plate lubrication.
3. Threads left by drum turning tool pull shoes sideways.

Noisy or Grabbing Brakes

1. Distorted or improperly adjusted brake shoes.
2. Linings glazed or worn.
3. Oil or grease in lining.
4. Scored drum.
5. Dirt on drum lining surface.
6. Faulty wheel cylinder.
7. Sticking booster control valve.

Brakes Do Not Apply

1. Leaks or insufficient fluid.
2. Linings glazed or worn.
3. Oil or grease in lining.
4. Dirty brake fluid.
5. Faulty master cylinder.
6. Air in hydraulic system.

Disc Brake Problems

Excessive Pedal Travel

1. Shoe and lining knock back after violent cornering or rough road travel.
2. Piston and shoe and lining assembly not properly seated or positioned.
3. Air leak or insufficient fluid in system or caliper.
4. Loose wheel bearing adjustment.
5. Damaged or worn caliper piston seal.
6. Improper booster push rod adjustment.
7. Shoe out of flat more than .005-inch.
8. Rear brake automatic adjusters inoperative.
9. Improperly ground rear brake shoe and lining assemblies.
10. Partial system failure.

Brake Roughness or Chatter; Pedal Pumping

1. Excessive lateral run-out of rotor.
2. Rotor excessively out of parallel.
3. Wheel bearings not adjusted.
4. Rear drums out of round.
5. Shoe reversed, steel against iron.

Excessive Pedal Effort

1. Frozen or seized pistons.
2. Brake fluid, or grease on linings.

3. Shoe and lining worn below specifications.
4. Proportioning valve malfunction.
5. Booster inoperative.
6. Leaking booster vacuum check valve.
7. Partial system failure.
8. Fading brakes due to incorrect lining.

Pull, Uneven or Grabbing Brakes

1. Frozen or seized pistons.
2. Brake fluid, oil or grease on linings.
3. Caliper out of alignment with rotor.
4. Loose caliper attachment.
5. Unequalized front tire pressure.
6. Incorrect front end alignment.
7. Lining protruding beyond end of shoe.
8. Unmatched tires on same axle.
9. Restriction in brake hoses or tubing.
10. Grease or brake fluid on lining or bent shoe.
11. Malfunctioning rear brakes.

Brake Rattle

1. Excessive clearance between shoe and caliper or between shoe and splash shield.
2. Shoe hold-down clips missing or improperly positioned.

Heavy Brake Drag

1. Frozen or seized pistons.
2. Operator riding brake pedal.
3. Incomplete brake pedal return due to linkage interference.
4. Faulty booster check valve holding pressure in hydraulic system.
5. Residual pressure in front brake hydraulic system.

Caliper Brake Fluid Leak.

1. Damaged or worn caliper piston seal.
2. Scores in cylinder bore.
3. Corrosion build-up in cylinder bore or on piston surface.
4. Metal clip in seal groove.

No Braking Effect When Pedal is Depressed

1. Piston and shoe and lining assembly not properly seated or positioned.
2. Air leak or insufficient fluid in system or caliper.
3. Damaged or worn caliper piston seal.
4. Bleeder screw open.
5. Air in hydraulic system or improper bleeding.

Power Brake Problems

Trouble Diagnosis

To tell whether the power sytem is operating at all, stop the engine and apply the brakes several times to exhaust vacuum reserve. Now depress the brake pedal, and while maintaining light pressure on the pedal, start the engine. If the power system is operating, the pedal will tend to move forward and less effort will be required to keep brakes applied.

If the power system is not operating, first check the vacuum supply as a possible cause. Start the engine and bring it up to medium speed. Turn off ignition and immediately close throttle to increase manifold vacuum. Wait at least 90 seconds, then try the brakes. If there is insufficient reserve for three or more power applications, the vacuum check valve is faulty or there is a leak or obstruction in the power cylinder, reserve tank or lines.

When the vacuum supply is adequate, failure of the system to supply the proper assist is to be found in the power unit itself.

Don't forget that some of the troubles listed may be in the brakes themselves, rather than in the power unit. A hard pedal may be due to a swollen wheel or master cylinder cups, or to a defective or kinked flexible hydraulic line. Grabbing can be caused by grease or hydraulic fluid on the lining. Drag can be caused by misadjustment. A spongy pedal may arise from air in the lines.

To pinpoint the source of vacuum leakage, connect a vacuum gauge to a T fitting inserted between the power unit and the reserve tank. Start the engine and read the vacuum at slow idle. Shut off the engine. With the system in good condition, the reading will be maintained on the gauge for at least 15 seconds. If it drops, there is leakage.

To find the point of leakage, disconnect the line to the reserve tank and plug that end of the T fitting. Then repeat the test. If the reading is now maintained for at least 15 seconds, the reserve tank is leaking. If the reading still drops, the leak is in the power cylinder or the check valve.

To determine which, insert the T into a vacuum line running directly from the check valve to the reserve tank. This disconnects the power cylinder. Repeat the test. If the gauge drops, there is leakage past the check valve. If it now holds the reading, the leakage is in the power cylinder. Not all cars are equipped with reserve tanks but the same method of eliminating one unit at a time can be used in making the test on any car.

Hard Pedal

1. Broken or damaged hydraulic brake lines.
2. Vacuum failure.
3. Defective diaphragm.
4. Restricted air filter element.
5. Worn or badly distorted reaction disc (tandem diaphragm).
6. Worn or distorted reaction plate or levers (single diaphragm).
7. Cracked or broken power pistons or retainer.
8. Incorrect selective reaction piston (tandem diaphragm).

Grabby Brakes (Apparent Off-and-On Condition)

1. Broken or damaged hydraulic brake lines.
2. Insufficient fluid in master cylinder.
3. Defective master cylinder seals.
4. Cracked master cylinder casting.
5. Leaks at front disc brake calipers or rear wheel cylinders in pipes or connections.
6. Air in hydraulic system.

Brakes Fail to Release

1. Blocked passage in power piston.
2. Air valve sticking shut.
3. Broken piston return spring.
4. Broken air valve spring.
5. Tight pedal linkage.

The cause of power brake problems in general as they apply to the different makes and types of power units are as follows:

BENDIX DIAPHRAGM TYPE

Hard Pedal or No Assist—Air cleaner element clogged, control valve faulty, defective diaphragm, worn or distorted reaction plate or levers, cracked or broken power piston or levers, internal or external leaks.

Brakes Grab—Control valve defective or sticking, bind in linkage, reaction diaphragm leaking, worn or distorted levers or plate.

No or Slow Release—Push rod adjustment incorrect, linkage binding, return spring defective.

BENDIX HYDROVAC

Hard Pedal—Internal or external vacuum or hydraulic leak. low fluid level, control valve defective.

Brakes Grab—Sticky control valve, power piston sticking, sticking ball check in hydraulic piston in slave cylinder chamber.

No or Slow Release—Internal friction, sluggish control valve.

Brake Pedal Chatter—Residual check valve defective.

Brakes Apply When Engine Is Started—Control valve piston sticking, atmospheric poppet return spring defective.

BENDIX TREADLE-VAC, REACTION TYPE

Hard Pedal—Internal vacuum hose loose or restricted, jammed vacuum cylinder plate screws, faulty piston seal.

Brake Grab—Counter reaction spring broken, poppet valve sticking.

Slow or No Release—Air passages restricted, hydraulic seal friction excessive, compensating valve or valve plunger sticking, poppet valve stuck in closed position.

BENDIX POWER-VAC

Hard Pedal—Blocked air cleaner element.
Slow Release—Pedal trigger arm improperly adjusted.

BENDIX MASTER-VAC

Hard Pedal—Internal vacuum hose loose or restricted, jammed vacuum cylinder piston, vacuum leaks from loose piston screws, faulty piston seal, leak between power and master cylinders, control valve jammed.
Brakes Grab—Counter reaction spring broken, sticking poppet valve.
Slow or No Release—Piston return spring broken, valve plunger sticking, air passage restricted, piston stroke interference.

BENDIX PISTON TYPE

Hard Pedal—Internal vacuum hose loose or restricted, jammed vacuum cylinder piston, vacuum leaks from loose piston plate screws, faulty piston seal, leak between power and master cylinders, control valve jammed.
Brakes Grab—Counter reaction spring broken, sticking poppet valves.
Slow or No Release—Piston return spring broken, valve plunger sticking, air passage restricted, piston stroke interference.

DELCO-MORAINE AIR SUSPENDED DIAPHRAGM TYPE

Hard Pedal—Vacuum hose in unit loose or restricted, air cleaner, internal vacuum leak, jammed sliding valve.

233

Brakes Grab—Floating valve diaphragm leakage due to faulty rubber bumper pad in valve, improper number of shims on air valve. *Slow or No Release*—Broken vacuum piston return spring, restricted air cleaner, bent or dented vacuum cylinder.

DELCO-MORAINE, PISTON TYPE

Hard Pedal—Vacuum hose in unit loose or restricted, restricted air cleaner, internal vacuum leak, jammed sliding valve.
Brakes Grab—Floating valve diaphragm leakage due to faulty rubber bumper pad in valve, improper number of shims on air valve.
Slow or No Release—Broken vacuum piston return spring, restricted air cleaner, bent or dented vacuum cylinder.

DELCO-MORAINE VACUUM SUSPENDED DIAPHRAGM TYPE, 1959-61

Hard Pedal—Internal vacuum hose loose or restricted, jammed air valve, vacuum leak in unit, defective diaphragm, restricted air cleaner, badly distorted reaction plate or levers.
Brakes Grab—Reaction diaphragm leaks or passage restricted, valve sticking, dislodged reaction levers, broken reaction spring, faulty control valve.
Slow or No Release—Blocked air passage, air cleaner blocked, broken piston return spring, broken air valve spring.

DELCO-MORAINE VACUUM SUSPENDED DIAPHRAGM TYPE, 1962-70

Hard Pedal—Internal vacuum leak, faulty control valve.
Brakes Grab—Faulty control valve.
Slow or No Release—Faulty push rod adjustment, bind in linkage.

KELSEY-HAYES DIAPHRAGM TYPE

Hard Pedal—Faulty vacuum check valve, vacuum hose or pipe collapsed, plugged, kinked or disconnected, internal leaks, vacuum leaks in unit caused by improper assembly, missing parts, damaged parts or foreign matter, cups swollen by improper fluid, improper push rod adjustment, badly dented vacuum cylinder, bound up pedal linkage, improperly adjusted stop light switch, scored valve plunger, broken or missing springs.

Brakes Grab—Faulty pedal linkage, dented vacuum cylinder, sticking control piston, defective vacuum check valve, loose vacuum connections.

KELSEY-HAYES OVAL BELLOWS TYPE

Hard Pedal—Blocked air passage in piston guide sleeve assembly or in air cleaner element, inspection screw or gasket loose or missing, vacuum passage blocked in valve housing, vacuum valve binding in guide due to defective spring or dry seal, valve operating rod binding.

Brakes Grab—Seals binding.

Slow or No Release—Push rod incorrectly adjusted, guide sleeve bearing seal binding on sleeve.

Brake Pedal Chatter—Power brake trigger bent or out of adjustment, trigger pivot rubber collar defective, guide sleeve bearing seal binding on sleeve, pedal push rod incorrectly adjusted.

KELSEY-HAYES ROUND BELLOWS TYPE

Hard Pedal—Valve eccentric or push rod incorrectly adjusted, bent pedal trigger.

Brake Pedal Chatter—Valve eccentric or push rod incorrectly adjusted.

No or Slow Release—Clogged air filter, incorrectly adjusted push rod.

235

MIDLAND-ROSS DIAPHRAGM TYPE

Hard Pedal—Leak in bellows, diaphragm assembly out of place in housing.
Brakes Grab—Sticking actuating valve assembly.
Brakes Drag—Sticking valve plunger.
Brakes Self-Apply When Engine Is Started—Leak in rear housing, diaphragm out of position in housing allowing air into rear chamber, sticking or unseated air valve.

FORD SURE-TRACK ANTI-SKID BRAKING SYSTEM, Fig. 28

Brake Warning Light Comes on and Stays on Immediately (not 5 seconds later) After Key Is Turned to ON or ACCESSORY Position and: Actuator Cycles and 4 Amp Fuse OK

1. Differential valve shuttled.
2. Short in brake warning light ground circuit.
3. Inoperative computer module.

Actuator Does Not Cycle and 4 Amp Fuse OK

1. Open B+ lead to module.
2. Inoperative computer module.

Actuator Does Not Cycle and 4 Amp Fuse Is Blown

1. Shorted B+ lead to module.
2. Shorted actuator solenoid circuit.
3. Defective computer module.

236

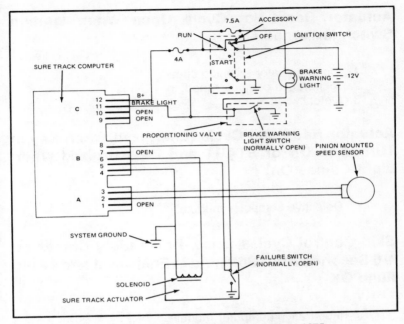

Fig. 28.   Sure-Track brake system wiring. 1975.

Brake Warning Light Comes on 4 to 6 Seconds After Key Is Turned To ON or START Position, 4 Amp Fuse OK and:
Actuator Cycles Once When Ignition Switch Is Turned On.

1. Open sensor circuit.
2. Open failure switch connector.
3. Closed differential failure switch in actuator.
4. Defective computer module.

237

Actuator Does Not Cycle Once When Ignition Switch Is Turned On

1. Open actuator solenoid circuit.
2. Inoperative computer module.
3. Defective actuator.

Actuator Has Long Cycle (Energized When Key Is Turned to ON or START and De-energized When Light Comes On)

1. Defective computer module.

Skid Control Cycles Once, Brake Light Comes on 4-6 Seconds After Solenoid Is Energized and 4 Amp Fuse OK

1. Inoperative computer module.

Brake Warning Light Off and Actuator Cycles While Driving Over Rough Roads Or During Normal Braking Conditions (False Cycling)

1. Loose ground connection.
2. Loose sensor connection.
3. Loose B+ and failure light connector at computer module.
4. Defective computer module.

Actuator Cycles After Key Is Turned to ON or ACCESSORY Position But Does Not Cycle During a Maximum Braking Condition

1. Shorted sensor circuit.
2. Defective computer module.

Actuator Cycles Slowly or Not At All During An Impending Skid Braking Condition

    1. Plugged actuator filter.

GENERAL MOTORS MAX-TRAC SYSTEM
Figs. 29, 30 & 31

The purpose of the Max-Trac System is to aid the operator in maintaining vehicle directional stability and maneuverability during acceleration and/or cornering. The system accomplishes this purpose by automatically limiting engine power to a value required for maximum acceleration without excessive rear wheel slippage.

Basic system components include the transmission speed sensor, front wheel speed sensor and speed disc, electronic controller, on-off switch, and electrical harness. In addition, the system uses the existing ignition switch, brake switch, brake light, and ignition components.

Transmission Speed Sensor

This sensor is a mechanically driven electro-magnetic device which produces an AC voltage with frequency proportional to the transmission output shaft speed. The sensor is mounted in the transmission at the speedometer cable connection. Its function is to convert the rear wheel speed into an electrical signal at a frequency of 25 Hz/mph. This rear wheel speed signal is transmitted via the electrical harness to the electronic controller.

Front Wheel Speed Sensor and Speed Disc

This sensor is an electro-magnetic device which, in conjunction with the rotating speed disc, produces an AC voltage with frequency proportional to the speed of the disc. The speed disc is mounted on the hub of the left front wheel. The sensor is mounted at a predetermined distance from the disc and the gap is adjustable at the sensor mounting. The function of the sensor is to convert the front wheel speed into an electrical signal at a frequency of 6.25 Hz/mph.

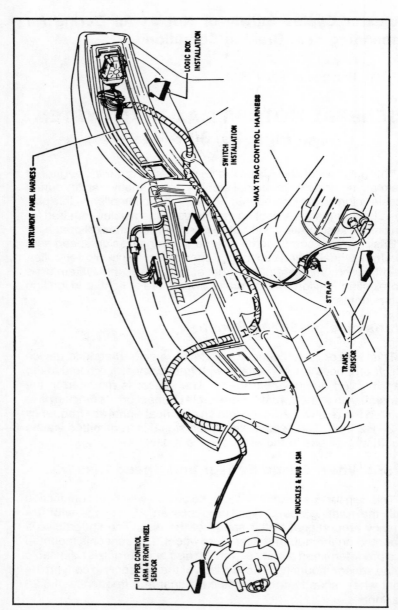

Fig. 29. Max-Trac system component location. Less Air Cushion Restraint system.

LOGIC BOX INSTALLATION

SWITCH INSTALLATION

MAX TRAC CONTROL HARNESS

INSTRUMENT PANEL HARNESS

STRAP

TRANS. SENSOR

KNUCKLES & HUB ASM

UPPER CONTROL ARM & FRONT WHEEL SENSOR

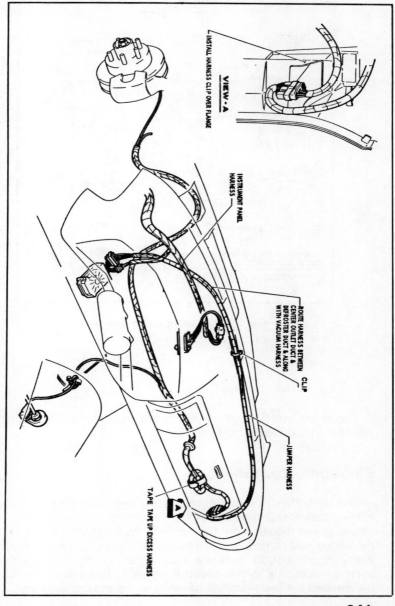

Fig. 30. Max-Trac system component location. With Air Cushion Restraint system.

INSTALL HARNESS CLIP OVER FLANGE

VIEW - A

INSTRUMENT PANEL HARNESS

ROUTE HARNESS BETWEEN CENTER OUTLET DUCT & DEFROSTER DUCT & ALONG WITH VACUUM HARNESS

CLIP

JUMPER HARNESS

TAPE TAPE UP EXCESS HARNESS

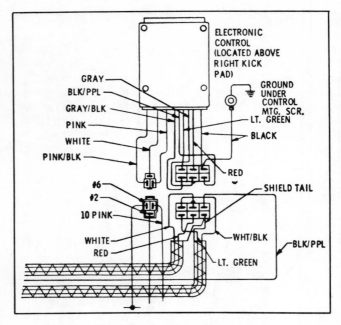

Fig. 31.   Controller wiring (typical).

This front wheel speed signal is transmitted via the electrical harness to the electronic controller.

Electronic Controller

The controller is a solid state electronic computer that is mounted in the passenger compartment. It receives the driven and undriven wheel speed signals from the sensors. Its function is to compare the two-speed signals and, when the difference exceeds a predetermined amount, to generate a 30 Hz output signal with a duty cycle proportional to the speed difference. This output signal is transmitted via the electrical harness to the ignition system.

On-Off Switch

The on-off switch is located on the vehicle's instrument panel. It allows the operator to make the Max-Trac operation optional. It is recommended that the switch normally be in the On position. However, it is desirable to have the system inoperative under certain driving conditions, i.e., rocking the car in snow. Also, should a malfunction in the system occur the vehicle may be driven with the switch off until repairs are made. In the off position, this switch shorts the controller output signal and prevents it from being transmitted to the ignition system.

Electrical Harness

The harness provides the electrical connection between the sensors, controller, power source, ignition switch, brake switch, and ignition coil.

Diverter Valve Solenoid

On cars equipped with Max-Trac and A. I. R., a solenoid is mounted on the A. I. R. pump to prevent engine backfire when the Max-Trac is operating.

The components of the Max-Trac System are interconnected. The system is not operable whenever the ignition switch is off and/or the on-off switch is off and/or the brakes are applied. When the ignition switch is on, the vehicle can be driven in the normal manner without Max-Trac operation, regardless of the amount of rear wheel slippage.

The system is operable whenever the ignition switch is on, and the on-off switch is on and the brakes are not applied. The vehicle can then be driven in the normal manner and no ignition interrupts will occur if the slippage does not exceed a predetermined value. However, under particular driving conditions, i.e., excessive acceleration or hard cornering, which reduces the normal load on the rear wheels, the amount of slippage can exceed the predetermined amount. The controller, continuously comparing the speed signals from the two sensors, determines that the excessive slippage has occurred and generates an output signal which interrupts the ignition in the prescribed manner, resulting in a power reduction and a corresponding reduction in slippage.

System Inoperative at Speeds

1. On-off switch set at Off.
2. No ground connection to the controller.
3. Brake lights dead.
4. No signal from transmission speed sensor (faulty harness or an open circuit in the sender).
5. No signal from front wheel speed sensor (a faulty harness or open circuit in sensor).
6. Controller faulty.

Engine Will Start But Will Not Run Until On-Off Switch Is Set At Off

1. No battery (positive) electrical supply to controller.
2. No connection between controller output and ignition ballast resistor.
3. Faulty controller.

System Functions Or Engine Stops During Braking

1. No B (positive) from brake circuit.
2. Brake lights dead.
3. No connection from controller to brake.
4. Malfunctioned controller.

System Functions Properly At High Speeds But Is Inoperative At Lower Vehicle Speeds

1. Low signal from the front wheel speed sensor (excessive gap between sensor and speed disc).
2. Malfunctioned controller.

System Operates When Not Necessary

1. Incorrect speedo gear.

Engine Backfires

1. A.I.R. bypass system not connected.
2. A.I.R. bypass solenoid not grounded.
3. Front wheel sensor improperly positioned.

System Functions at Low Speeds Causing Engine Hesitation

1. Low signal from the front wheel speed sensor (excessive gap between sensor and speed disc).

GENERAL MOTORS TRACK MASTER
AND
TRUE TRACK ANTI-SKID BRAKING
SYSTEM, Figs. 32 & 33

This system incorporates a speed sensor mounted on each rear wheel on 1971-75 Eldorado and Toronado models and a transmission mounted speed sensor on 1972-75 Cadillac models. It combines a controller under the instrument panel and a modulator on the cowl in the engine compartment to prevent rear wheel lockup.

The sensors produce an electrical signal that is proportional to wheel speed. This signal is monitored by the controller. A wheel that is not locking during brake application will gradually decelerate. When a wheel has started to lock, it will decelerate abruptly at a rate much greater than the car's deceleration. When the controller determines that the signal from the sensors changes too rapidly, and the car is approaching a skid, the controller energizes the modulator solenoid.

The modulator contains a diaphragm, both sides of which are exposed to intake manifold vacuum as long as the solenoid is not energized. When the solenoid is energized, atmospheric pressure is allowed to reach the top side of the diaphragm, forcing it down against the support spring. The displacement piston is lowered along with the diaphragm. This seals off hydraulic pressure from the master cylinder to the rear wheel cylinders by closing the

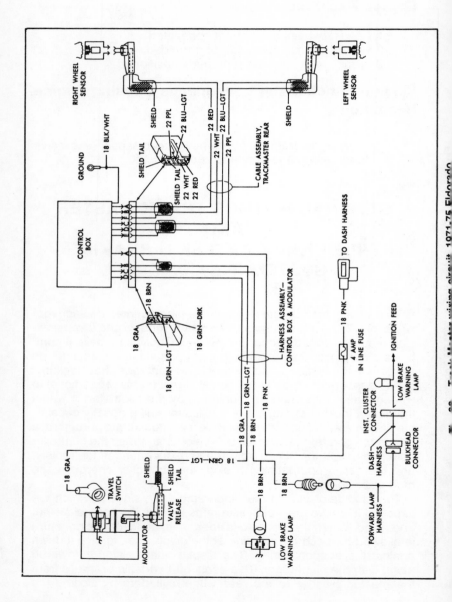

Track Master wiring circuit, 1971-75 Eldorado

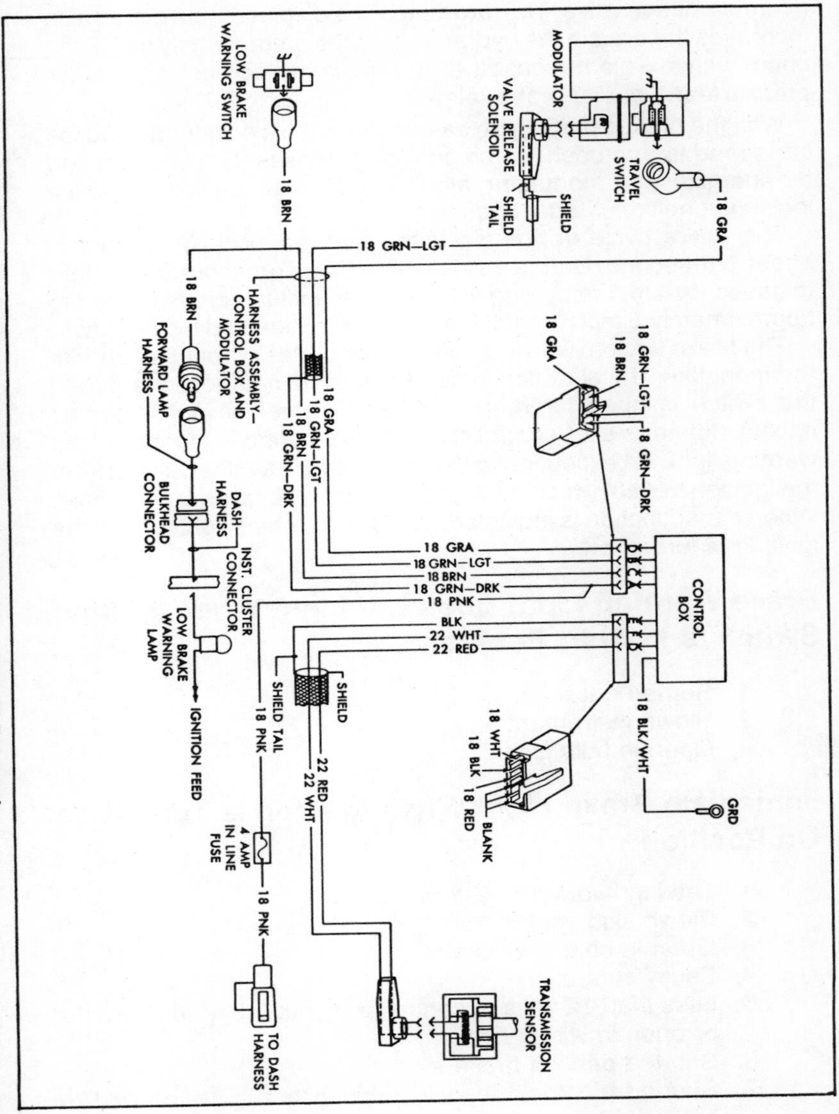

Fig. 33. True Track wiring circuit. 1971-75 Toronado.

hydraulic check valve. The lowering of the displacement piston also increases the area in the hydraulic chamber immediately below the check valve. This increased area results in decreased hydraulic pressure and partial brake release.

With the brakes partially released, the wheels accelerate and, as car speed is approached, the controller senses the condition and de-energizes the modulator, allowing full brake application until a locking condition is again sensed.

The entire cycle of brake release and reapplication occurs in about 1/3-second. During a stop where brake pressure is sufficient to cause lockup, the cycling will continue until the car is slowed to approximately 5 mph or until the brakes are released by the driver.

The brake system warning light also operates in conjunction with the modulator travel switch in case of system malfunctions. When the switch is open for more than approximately four seconds, except during a skid controlled stop, the controller turns on the warning light. An exception to this is an open in the feed circuit from the ignition switch, which is indicated without the four second delay. When a malfunction is indicated, the lamp remains lighted until the ignition is turned off.

Brake Warning Light Does Not Light When Ignition Switch Is in Start Position

1. Burned out bulb.
2. Blown instrument fuse.
3. Open in bulb circuit.

Immediate Brake Light When Ignition Is Turned To On Position

1. Leak in hydraulic system.
2. Blown skid control fuse.
3. Open in controller circuit.
4. Faulty controller.
5. Less than 12 volts at controller due to faulty connections or open in wiring circuit.
6. Shorted parking brake switch.
7. Shorted electrical lead to parking brake switch and/or brake lamp.
8. Shorted solenoid or lead to ground blows skid control fuse.

9. Shorted pressure differential switch (System OK).

NOTE: For the following conditions, it is assumed that the brake lamp circuit operates normally and there are no hydraulic leaks or air trapped in the brake system. All the following conditions are with ignition switch ON or engine running.

No Brake Light, System Inoperative, Exercise Cycle OK With Engine Running Or Ignition Switch On

1. Wheel sensor not being driven due to missing dust cap or sensor quill (Eldorado and Toronado).
2. Transmission sensor seized or not being driven (Cadillac).
3. Incorrect sensor adjustment (Eldorado and Toronado).
4. Both sensor leads shorted to each other (not shorted to ground).
5. Faulty controller.

No Brake Light, System Inoperative, No Exercise Cycle

1. Loss of ground to controller.
2. Bad connection at controller or modulator.
3. Modulator seized in de-energized position.
4. Solenoid valve seized in de-energized position.
5. Faulty controller.

Brake Light Lights After 2-5 Second Delay, System Inoperative, Exercise Cycle OK

1. Speed sensor leads open.
2. Speed sensor leads shorted to ground.
3. Modulator travel switch open.
4. Faulty connection at travel switch.
5. Faulty controller.

Brake Light Lights After 2-5 Second Delay, System Inoperative, No Exercise Cycle

1. Solenoid leads open.
2. Faulty controller.

False Releases While Car Is In Motion

1. Frayed shield leads causing intermittent short.
2. Sensor drive shaft rubbing in wheel spindle due to improper adjustment (Eldorado and Toronado).
3. Faulty controller.

Brake Light On 2-5 Seconds After High Brake Pressure Is Applied

1. Defective differential and proportioning valve.

Brake Light Comes On During a Stop, Or When Brake Is Depressed Firmly, And Goes Off When Brake Pedal Is Released

1. Hydraulic fluid leak.
2. Air in brake system.
3. Missing or damaged insulators.
4. Sensor damper deteriorated.
5. Bad electrical connections.
6. Faulty controller.

False Releases While Vehicle Is Parked

1. Bad electrical connections.
2. Faulty controller.

Does Not Cycle Down To 5 mph During Maximum Braking

1. Insufficient operating vacuum.

Front End And Steering Problems

Hard Steering

1. Low or uneven tire pressure.
2. Steering gear or connections adjusted too tight.
3. Insufficient or incorrect lubricant used.
4. Excessive caster.
5. Suspension arms bent or twisted.
6. Front spring sagged.
7. Frame bent or broken.
8. Steering knuckle bent.
9. Kingpin galled or frozen in bushing.
10. Excessive steering shaft coupling misalignment.
11. Steering column to steering gear misaligned.
12. Shock absorber bound up (Eldorado and Toronado).

Excessive Play or Looseness in Steering

1. Steering gear connections adjusted too loose or worn.
2. Steering knuckle bushings worn.
3. Front wheel bearings incorrectly adjusted or worn.
4. Worn ball joints.
5. Worn or loose worm steering shaft bearings.
6. Worn control arm bushings.
7. Worn couplings or steering shaft U-joints.
8. Steering wheel loose on shaft.
9. Loose pitman arm, tie rods, steering arms or steering linkage studs.
10. Excessive pitman shaft or ball nut lash in steering gear.
11. Worn intermediate rod or tie rod sockets.
12. Shock absorber soft (Eldorado and Toronado).

Poor Returnability

1. Front end needs lubrication.
2. Steering gear adjusted too tightly.
3. Front end alignment incorrect.
4. Steering gear to steering column misalignment.

Rattle or Chuckle in Steering Gear

1. Insufficient or improper lubricant in steering gear.
2. Excessive backlash in steering gear.
3. Worn or loose worm steering shaft bearings.
4. Pitman arm loose on shaft.

Erratic Steering on Application of Brakes

1. Oil or brake fluid on lining.
2. Brakes improperly adjusted.
3. Front spring weak.
4. Low or uneven tire pressure.
5. Insufficient or uneven caster.
6. Steering knuckle bent.

Car Pulls to One Side

1. Low or uneven tire pressure.
2. Incorrect or uneven caster or camber.
3. Wheel bearings adjusted too tight.
4. Uneven front car height.
5. Toe-in incorrect.
6. Oil or brake fluid on brake lining.
7. Brakes incorrectly or unevenly adjusted.
8. Steering knuckle or knuckle support bent.
9. Frame bent or broken.
10. Shock absorbers inoperative.
11. Rear wheels not tracking with front wheels.
12. Rear axle shifted (spring U bolts loose or center bolt sheared).
13. Broken or weak rear springs.

Scuffed Tires

1. Tire improperly inflated.
2. Toe-in incorrect.
3. Excessive wheel or tire run-out.
4. Steering knuckle bushings worn.
5. Uneven camber.
6. Incorrect toe-out on turns.
7. Suspension arms bent or twisted.
8. Steering knuckle bent.
9. Excessive speed on turns.

Cupped Tires

1. Improper toe-in.
2. Tires improperly inflated.
3. Wheels, tires or brake drums out of balance.
4. Dragging brakes.
5. Worn steering knuckle bushings.
6. Wheel bearings incorrectly adjusted or worn.
7. Uneven camber.
8. Steering knuckle bent.
9. Excessive mileage without rotating tires.

Front Wheel Shimmy

1. Low or uneven tire pressure.
2. Wheels, tires or brake drums out of balance.
3. Excessive wheel or tire runout.
4. Shock absorbers inoperative.
5. Steering connections incorrectly adjusted or worn.
6. Steering gear incorrectly adjusted.
7. Front wheel bearings incorrectly adjusted or worn.
8. Incorrect or uneven caster.
9. Steering knuckle bushings worn.
10. Toe-in incorrect.
11. Steering knuckle bent.
12. Eccentric or bulged tires.
13. Stabilizer inoperative.
14. Worn ball joints.
15. Worn control arm bushings.

Front Wheel Tramp

1. Wheels, tires or brake drums out of balance.
2. Wheel or tire not concentric.
3. Shock absorbers inoperative.
4. Stabilizer inoperative.

Car Wanders

1. Low or uneven tire pressure.
2. Steering gear or connections adjusted too loose or worn.
3. Steering gear or connections adjusted too tight.
4. Steering knuckle bushings worn.
5. Improper toe-in.
6. Incorrect or uneven caster or camber.
8. Kingpin bent.
9. Rear axle shifted (spring U bolts loose or center bolt sheared).
10. Stabilizer inoperative.
11. Kingpins or bushings tight.
12. Bind in lower or upper control arm shaft.
13. Bind in rear spring shackles or dry rear springs.
14. Excessive backlash in steering gear.

Road Shocks

1. High air pressure in tires.
2. Steering gear or connections incorrectly adjusted.
3. Excessive caster.
4. Shock absorbers inoperative.
5. Front springs weak or sagged.
6. Wrong type or size of tires used.
7. Steering knuckle bent.

GENERAL MOTORS FRONT WHEEL DRIVE

Clicking Noise In Turns

1. Excessive wear or broken outboard joint.

Coast To Drive Clunk

1. Loose inboard joint flange bolts.
2. Inoperative rubber damper (RH side).
3. Loose spline (RH damper to shaft).

Shudder Or Vibration On Acceleration

1. Excessive wear on inboard joint housing.
2. Worn spider assembly.

Shimmy Vibration At Highway Speeds

1. Tires out of balance or out of round.

Power Steering Problems

CHRYSLER CONSTANT CONTROL TYPE

Hard Steering

1. Tires not properly inflated.
2. Low oil level in reservoir.
3. Loose pump belt.
4. Oil on pump belts.
5. Steering linkage needs lubrication.
6. Power steering pump output low.
7. Cross shaft adjustment too tight.
8. Pressure control valve stuck in closed position.
9. External oil leaks.
10. Defective or damaged valve lever.
11. Dirt or chips in steering gear.
12. Damaged column support worm shaft bearings.
13. Damaged thrust bearings or excessive preload adjustment.
14. Rough or hard to turn worm and piston assembly.
15. Excessive internal leakage.

Poor Recovery from Turns

1. Tires not properly inflated.
2. Steering linkage binding.
3. Improper wheel alignment.
4. Damaged or defective steering tube bearings.
5. Steering column jacket and steering gear not properly aligned.
6. Improper cross shaft mesh adjustment.
7. Pressure control valve piston stuck open.
8. Column support spanner nut loose.
9. Defective or damaged valve lever.
10. Improper worm thrust bearing adjustment.
11. Burrs or nicks in reaction ring grooves in cylinder head or column support.
12. Defective or damaged cylinder head worm shaft seal ring.
13. Dirt or chips in steering gear unit.
14. Rough or catchy worm and piston assembly.

Self-Steering or Leads to Either Side

1. Tires not properly inflated.
2. Improper wheel alignment.
3. Steering wheel off center when car is traveling straight ahead.
4. Valve body out of adjustment.
5. Valve lever damaged.
6. Column support spanner nut loose.

Temporary Increase in Effort When Turning Steering Wheel

1. Low oil level.
2. Loose pump belt.
3. Oil on pump belts.
4. Binding steerage linkage.
5. Engine idle too slow.
6. Defective power steering pump.
7. Air in system.
8. External adjustment.
9. Improper cross shaft adjustment.
10. Excessive internal leakage.

Excessive Steering Wheel Free Play

1. Improper cross shaft adjustment.
2. Column support spanner nut loose.
3. Improper worm thrust bearing adjustment.

Lack of Assistance in One Direction

1. Oil leaking past worm shaft cast iron seal ring or ferrule O-ring.

Lack of Assistance in Both Directions

1. Broken O-ring on worm piston.
2. Piston end plug loose.
3. Pump belt slipping.
4. Pump output low.

Noises

1. Buzzing noise in neutral only is caused by sticking pressure control valve.
2. Noisy power pump.
3. Damaged hydraulic lines.
4. Pressure control valve sticking.
5. Improper sector shaft adjustment.
6. Air in system.

FORD TORSION BAR TYPE

Hard Steering

1. Low or uneven tire pressure.
2. Improper gear adjustment.
3. Improper wheel alignment.
4. Low fluid level.
5. Twisted or bent suspension parts, frame and linkage components.
6. Tight wheel bearings.
7. Steering spindle bent.
8. Pump belt out of adjustment.

9. Pump output low.
10. Air in system.
11. Valve spool out of adjustment.
12. Valve spool sticking.
13. Steering linkage binding.

Hard Steering Straight Ahead

1. Steering adjustment too tight.
2. Steering gear shaft binding.

Hard Steering While Turning or Parking

1. Oil level low.
2. Pump pressure low.
3. Pressure loss in steering gear due to leakage past O-rings.
4. Pressure loss between valve spool and sleeve.
5. Pressure loss past piston ring or scored housing bore.

Loose Steering

1. Loose wheel bearings.
2. Loose tie rod ends or linkage.
3. Worn ball joints.
4. Worn suspension parts.
5. Insufficient mesh loads.
6. Insufficient worm bearing preload.
7. Valve spool out of adjustment.

Erratic Steering

1. Oil or brake fluid on brake lining.
2. Out of round brake drums.
3. Improperly adjusted brakes.
4. Under-inflated tires.
5. Broken spring or other details in suspension system.
6. Improper caster adjustment.
7. Fluid level low.

Binding or Poor Recovery

1. Steering gear shaft binding.
2. Steering gear out of adjustment.
3. Steering linkage binding.
4. Valve spool binding due to dirt or burred edges.
5. Valve spool out of adjustment.
6. Interference at sector shaft and ball stud.

Loss of Power Assist

1. Pump inoperative.
2. Hydraulic lines damaged.
3. Power cylinder damaged.
4. Valve spool out of adjustment.

Loss of Power Assist in One Direction

1. Valve spool out of adjustment.

Noisy Pump

1. Air being drawn into pump.
2. Lines touching other parts of car.
3. Oil level low.
4. Excessive back pressure caused by obstructions in lines.
5. Excessive wear of internal parts.

Poor Return of Steering Gear to Center

1. Valve spool sticking.
2. Valve spool out of adjustment.
3. All items given under *Binding or Poor Recovery*.

Steering Wheel Surge While Turning

1. Valve spool sticking.
2. Excessive internal leakage.
3. Belt slippage.

SAGINAW ROTARY VALVE TYPE

Hard Steering

1. Frozen steering shaft bearings.
2. Lower coupling flange rubbing against adjuster.
3. Steering adjustment tight.

Poor Return of Steering

1. Frozen steering shaft bearings.
2. Lower coupling flange rubbing against adjuster.
3. Tires not inflated properly.
4. Incorrect caster and toe-in.
5. Tight steering linkage.
6. Steering gear misalignment.
7. Tight suspension ball joints.
8. Steering adjustment tight.
9. Thrust bearing adjustment tight.
10. Tight sector-to-rack piston adjustment.
11. Rack piston nut and worm preload too tight.
12. Sticky valve spool.

Car Leads to One Side

1. Front end misalignment.
2. Unbalanced or badly worn valve.

Momentary Increase in Effort When Turning Wheel Fast

1. Low oil level in pump.
2. Pump belt slipping.
3. High internal leakage.

External Oil Leaks

1. Loose hose connections.
2. Damaged hose.
3. Side cover O-ring seal.

4. Pitman shaft seals.
5. Housing end plug seal.
6. Adjuster plug seals.
7. Torsion bar seal.

Steering Gear Noise

NOTE: There is some noise in all power steering systems. One of the most common is a hissing sound most evident at standstill parking. There is no relationship between this noise and performance of the steering. Hiss may be expected when steering wheel is at end of travel when slowly turning at standstill.

1. A rattle or chuckling noise caused by loose over-center adjustment, gear loose on frame, steering linkage looseness, or pressure hose touching other parts of car.
2. Chirp or squealing noise caused by a loose belt.
3. Growl noise caused by excessive back pressure in hoses due to restriction. If noise is most evident at standstill, it may be caused by scored pressure plates, thrust plate or rotor or extreme wear of cam ring.
4. Groan noise caused by low oil level, aerated oil, or loose pump mounting bolts.
5. Rattle or knock caused by loose pump pulley nut.
6. Rattle or noise caused by improperly installed vanes, or vanes sticking in rotor slots.
7. Swishing noise caused by malfunctioning flow control valve.
8. Whine noise caused by pump shaft bearing.

Excessive Wheel Kickback or Loose Steering

1. Lash in steering linkage.
2. Air in system.
3. Excessive lash between pitman shaft sector and rack piston.
4. Loose thrust bearing adjustment.
5. Ball nut and worm preload.

Wheel Surges or Jerks

1. Loose pump belt.
2. Low oil level.
3. Steering linkage striking oil pan at full turn.
4. Insufficient pump pressure.
5. Sticking flow control valve.

Hard Steering When Parking

1. Loose pump belt.
2. Low oil level in reservoir.
3. Lack of lubrication in linkage or front suspension.
4. Tires not properly inflated.
5. Insufficient oil pressure.
6. Low oil pressure due to restriction in hoses.
7. Low oil pressure due to worn piston ring or scored housing bore.
8. Pressure loss due to leakage at valve rings, valve body-to-worm seal or rack piston end plug seal.
9. Pressure loss due to loose fit of spool in valve body or leaky valve body.
10. Steering gear to steering column misalignment.
11. Lower coupling flange rubbing against steering gear adjuster plug.
12. Sticking flow control valve.
13. Excessive internal pump leakage.

Valve Squawk

1. Cut or worn damper ring on valve spool.
2. Loose or worn rotary valve parts.

No Effort Required to Turn

1. Broken torsion bar.

SAGINAW STANDARD
STEERING COLUMNS

Will Not Unlock

1. Sector collapsed.
2. Lock bolt damaged.
3. Defective lock cylinder.
4. Damaged housing.

Will Not Lock

1. Lock bolt spring broken or defective.
2. Damaged sector tooth.
3. Defective lock cylinder.
4. Burr on lock bolt or housing.
5. Damaged housing.
6. Transmission linkage adjustment incorrect.
7. Sector installed incorrectly.

High Effort

1. Lock cylinder defective.
2. Ignition switch defective.
3. Rack preload spring broken or deformed.
4. Burrs on sector, rack or housing.
5. Bent sector shaft.
6. Actuator rod restricted.

High Effort On Lock Cylinder Between Off and Off-Lock

1. Burr on tang of shift gate.
2. Distorted rack.

Will Stick in Start

1. Actuator rod deformed.
2. Any high effort condition.
3. Ignition switch defective.

Lock Bolt Hits Shaft Lock in Off Position and Park

1. Ignition switch is not set correctly.

Key Cannot Be Removed in Off-Lock

1. Ignition switch is not set correctly.
2. Defective lock cylinder.

Lock Cylinder Can be Removed Without Depressing Retainer

1. Lock cylinder with defective retainer.
2. Lock cylinder without retainer.
3. Burr over retainer slot in housing.

Electrical System Will Not Function

1. Defective fuse in accessory circuit.
2. Connector body loose or defective.
3. Defective wiring.
4. Defective ignition switch.

Switch Will Not Actuate Mechanically

1. Defective ignition switch.

Switch Cannot be Set Correctly

1. Switch actuator rod deformed.

Noise in Column

1. Coupling bolts not tightened.
2. Coupling pulled apart.
3. Horn contact ring not lubricated.
4. Lack of grease on bearings or bearing surface.
5. Lower shaft bearing tight or frozen.
6. Upper shaft bearing tight or frozen.
7. Shaft lock plate cover loose.
8. Lock plate retaining ring not seated.
9. Shaft lock plate cover loose.

High Steering Shaft Turning Effort

1. Column assembly misaligned in vehicle.
2. Improperly installed or deformed dust seal.
3. Tight or frozen upper or lower bearings.
4. U-joint binding.

High Shift Effort

1. Column not aligned correctly in car.
2. Lower bowl bearing not assembled correctly.
3. Improperly installed dust seal.
4. Lack of grease on seal or bearing areas.

Improper Transmission Shifting

1. Sheared shift tube joint.
2. Improper transmission linkage adjustment.
3. Improper gate plate.

Lash in Mounted Column Assembly

1. Instrument panel to dash mounting bolts loose.
2. Broken weld nuts on jacket.
3. Instrument panel bracket capsule sheared.
4. Instrument panel to jacket mounting bolts loose.

Shroud Loose on Shift
1. Housing loose on jacket—will be noticed with ignition in off-lock and a torque applied to the steering wheel.

SAGINAW TILT AND TELESCOPE STEERING COLUMNS

Will Not Unlock

1. Shear flange on sector shaft collapsed.
2. Lock bolt damaged.
3. Defective lock cylinder.

4. Damaged housing.
5. Damaged sector.
6. Damaged rack.

Will Not Lock

1. Lock bolt spring broken or defective.
2. Damaged sector tooth.
3. Defective lock cylinder.
4. Burr on lock bolt or housing.
5. Damaged housing.
6. Transmission linkage adjustment incorrect.
7. Damaged rack.
8. Interference between bowl and rack coupling.
9. Ignition switch stuck.
10. Actuator rod restricted.

High Effort

1. Lock cylinder defective.
2. Ignition switch defective.
3. Rack preload spring broken or deformed.
4. Burrs on sector, rack, housing, support or actuator rod coupling.
5. Bent sector shaft.
6. Defective rack.
7. Extreme misalignment of housing to cover.
8. Distorted coupling slot in rack.
9. Bent actuator rod.
10. Ignition switch mounting bracket bent.

Will Stick in Start

1. Actuator rod deformed.
2. Any high effort condition.
3. Ignition switch defective.

Key Cannot be Removed in Off-Lock

1. Ignition switch is not adjusted correctly.
2. Defective lock cylinder.

Lock Cylinder Can be Removed Without Depressing Retainer

1. Lock cylinder with defective retainer.
2. Lock cylinder without retainer.
3. Burr over retainer slot in housing cover.

Electrical System Will Not Function

1. Poor battery connection.
2. Connector body loose or defective.
3. Defective wiring.
4. Defective ignition switch.
5. Ignition switch not adjusted properly.

Switch Will Not Actuate Mechanically

1. Defective ignition switch.

Noise in Column

1. Coupling bolts not tightened.
2. Column not correctly aligned.
3. Coupling pulled apart.
4. Broken steering shaft plastic injected joint.
5. Horn contact ring not lubricated.
6. Lack of grease on bearings or bearing surfaces.
7. Loose tilt lever opening shields.
8. Lower shaft bearing worn or broken.
9. Upper shaft bearing worn or broken.
10. One click when in off-lock position and the steering wheel is moved.

High Steering Shaft Effort

1. Column assembly misaligned.
2. Improperly installed or deformed dust seal.
3. Defective upper or lower bearing.
4. Flashing on instrument panel of shift tube from plastic joint.
5. Tight steering universal joint. Eldorado only.

High Shift Effort

1. Column not aligned correctly in car.
2. Wave washer with burrs.
3. Improperly installed dust seal.
4. Lack of grease on seal or bearing.
5. Improper screws used for ignition switch, neutral start switch or mounting bracket.
6. Burr on upper or lower end of shift tube.

Improper Transmission Shifting

1. Sheared shift tube joint or lower shift lever weld.
2. Improper transmission linkage adjustment.

Lash in Mounted Column Assembly

1. Instrument panel to dash mounting bolts loose.
2. Broken weld nuts on jacket.
3. Instrument panel bracket capsule sheared.
4. Loose shoes in housing.
5. Loose tilt head pivot pins.
6. Loose shoe lock pin in support.
7. Loose support screws.

Housing Scraping on Bowl

1. Bowl bent or not concentric with hub.

Steering Wheel Loose

1. Wheel loose on shaft.
2. Defective or missing anti-lash spring in spheres.
3. Upper bearing not seating in bearing race.
4. Upper bearing inner race seat missing.
5. Improperly adjusted T & T locking lever.
6. Loose support screws.
7. Bearing preload spring missing or broken.

Steering Wheel Loose—Every Other Tilt Position

1. Loose fit between shoe and shoe pivot pin.

Steering Column Not Locking in Any Tilt Position

1. Shoe seized on its pivot pin.
2. Shoe grooves may have burrs or dirt.
3. Shoe lock spring weak or broken.

Steering Wheel Fails to Return to Top Tilt Position

1. Pivot pins are bound up.
2. Wheel tilt spring is defective.
3. Turn signal switch wires too tight.

Noise When Tilting Column

1. Upper tilt bumpers worn.
2. Tilt spring rubbing in housing.

Accessory Problems

POWER TOP, WINDOW AND SEAT PROBLEMS

Hydro-lectric Type

Top Will Not Operate

1. Mechanical interference due to luggage or other objects.
2. Hold down strap not removed.
3. Top not free from windshield header studs.
4. Electrical shorts or loose connections in control switch circuit.
5. Dirty control switch contacts.
6. Inoperative power unit motor.

7. Hydraulic fluid low.
8. Power unit pump inoperative.
9. Stoppage in fluid pipes.
10. Faulty hydraulic control valve.
11. Broken port plate in hydraulic pump.

Top Operates in One Direction Only

1. Mechanical interference due to luggage or other objects.
2. Hold down strap not removed.
3. Top not free from windshield header studs.
4. Electrical shorts or loose connections in control switch circuit.
5. Dirty control switch contact.
6. Improperly adjusted control rod.
7. Hydraulic power cylinder faulty.
8. Stoppage in fluid pipes.
9. Faulty hydraulic control valve.

Window Lift Inoperative

1. Mechanical interference from door arm rest screw.
2. Misaligned glass run channel or window guide.
3. Window lift not connected to lower sash channel.
4. Electrical short or loose connection in battery, motor or cylinder circuit.
5. Cylinder solenoid inoperative.
6. Power unit motor inoperative.
7. Hydraulic fluid low.
8. Hydraulic hoses crimped.
9. Stoppage in fluid pipes.
10. Pump pressure relief valve stuck.
11. Cylinder piston rod disconnected.
12. Broken port plate in pump.

Windows Operate Slowly Upward

1. Mechanical binding due to misalignment.
2. Glass run channels excessively wet.
3. If window does not fully close, stops are improperly adjusted or there is insufficient hydraulic fluid.

4. Electrical failure due to low battery.
5. Hydraulic failure due to stuck pump pressure relief valve.
6. Top control rod improperly adjusted so that control valve is held partially open to allow fluid to enter top lines.

Windows Operate Slowly Downward

1. If a window moves slowly downward when control switch is in neutral position, the solenoid valve in window lift cylinder is leaking.
2. Mechanical binding due to misalignment.
3. Glass run channels excessively wet.
4. Window lift return spring broken.
5. Hydraulic fluid old, congealed or too heavy for prevailing temperatures.
6. Pump pressure relief valve stuck.

Window Raises When Top or Seat is Operated

1. Electrical control circuit crossed due to switch CYL terminal touching BAT terminal.
2. Hydraulic pressure too high if more than one window raises.
3. Solenoid valve in window cylinder leaking.

Two Windows Operate from One Switch

1. Electrical control circuit crossed due to switch CYL terminals touching.
2. Hydraulic pressure too high.
3. Solenoid valve in window cylinder leaking.

Seat Adjuster Inoperative

1. Mechanical interference from object under seat.
2. Seat adjuster misaligned.
3. Seat adjuster not attached to seat frame or floor.
4. Electrical short or loose connection in battery, motor or cylinder circuit.
5. Cylinder solenoid inoperative.

6. Power unit motor inoperative.
7. Hydraulic fluid low.
8. Hydraulic hoses crimped.
9. Stoppage in fluid pipes.
10. Pump pressure relief valve stuck.
11. Cylinder piston rod disconnected.
12. Broken port plate in pump.

Seat Operates Slowly

NOTE: Same as windows operating slowly upward or downward.

All Units Operate Slowly

1. Mechanical interference due to misalignment.
2. Electrical fault due to low battery.
3. Hydraulic fluid too heavy.
4. Pump pressure relief valve stuck.
5. Crimped fluid hoses.
6. Stoppage in fluid pipes.

Power Unit Inoperative on Any Control Switch

NOTE: When running, the power unit has a clearly audible whirring sound.
1. Battery low.
2. Wiring connections between ignition switch and solenoid relay switch loose, dirty or disconnected.
3. Circuit breaker inoperative.
4. Solenoid relay switch inoperative.
5. Power unit motor inoperative.

ELECTRIC TYPE FOR WINDOWS AND SEATS

NOTE: In addition to the electrical troubles listed below, look for the same mechanical troubles given under the *Hydro-Lectric Type*.

Window Won't Operate from Main Switch Only

1. Broken wire between relay and remote switch.
2. Defective switch in master switch group.
3. Break in wire where it enters door opening.

Window Won't Operate from Main or Door Switch

1. Burned out motor or relay.
2. Defective circuit breaker.
3. Break in battery feed wire from starter solenoid to circuit breaker.

Window Operates in One Direction Only from Main or Door Switch

1. Defective relay.
2. Defective switch.
3. Broken ground wires.
4. Burned out motor.
5. Broken control wire.

Circuit Breaker in Door Clicks On and Off Continuously and Window Won't Operate

1. Control wire grounded.
2. Defective switch.
3. Relay points stuck.

Main or Door Switch Operates Window in Wrong Direction

1. Lead wires are not connected to proper terminals.

Window Operates Sluggishly

1. Binding window regulator.
2. Broken wires or loose connections.
3. Worn motor brushes.

All Windows Do Not Operate

1. Circuit breaker open in control circuit.
2. Circuit breaker open in power circuit.

Seat Regulators Inoperative

1. Circuit breaker open in control circuit.
2. Circuit breaker open in power circuit.

One Seat Regulator Inoperative

1. Defective wiring between relay and circuit breaker.
2. Defective motor.
3. Defective wiring between switch and circuit breaker.
4. Defective relay.

Seat Regulator Operates in One Direction Only

1. Defective wiring between switch and relay that applies to direction of travel desired.
2. Defective toggle switch.

Seat Regulator Operates Sluggishly

1. Binding mechanism.
2. Defective wiring.
3. Loose connectors or poor ground.
4. Worn or dirty brushes in motor.

WINDSHIELD WIPER PROBLEMS

General Inspection

Before deciding that a windshield wiper needs servicing, it might be well to consider some of the external factors which affect their operation.

It must be remembered that windshield wipers will operate more slowly when they do their own work on dry glass. This is specially true on cars with curved windshields. You will also find that wiper blades may chatter or fail to travel a complete arc on dry glass. It is therefore obvious that any testing of windshield wiper operation should be done after the windshield has been sprayed with water.

Windshield wipers that chatter or do not wipe the glass clean under normal operating conditions (wet windshield) may need only replacement of the wiper arms or blades instead of more extensive service. This can be determined by visual inspection and most replacements can be made simply without the aid of any special tools.

Uneven movement of the wiper arms with respect to one another is usually caused by cables, pivots or cranks that are out of adjustment in the windshield wiper transmission system.

Electric Type

All passenger car electric windshield wiper circuits, regardless of manufacturer, include a control switch, a small shunt wound motor, and the wiring connecting these units to the battery. A circuit breaker or fuse may be mounted as a separate unit or incorporated in the control switch itself. A worm gear on the motor armature shaft drives one or two gears mounted on crankshafts for wiper operation.

A parking switch is mounted on the motor and actuated by a cam on one of the cranks. The parking switch, connected to the battery through a control switch, keeps the motor in operation for a brief period after the control switch has been shut off, allowing the wiper blades to return to the parked position.

Both single and multiple speed motors are used, the latter incorporating one or several resistors in the field circuit. The resistors may be located either in the parking switch housing or in the control switch.

In the following text you will find a list of the conditions you are likely to encounter when faced with a repair job on electric wipers. By consulting these possibilities you will simplify the job of locating the source of trouble. But a few words of caution are in order: After you have made your diagnosis and are ready to make repairs, disconnect the battery to avoid damage under the dash or possible personal injury from accidental shorts. Also, on models which use off-glass parking windshield wipers, never remove or disassemble the motor while in Park position.

Vacuum Type

For satisfactory windshield wiper operation, it is necessary to have an adequate supply of vacuum. On some cars the vacuum is made available by tapping directly into the intake manifold. With this type of arrangement it is considered normal for the wipers to slow down or stop entirely while going up a hill or during acceleration, since under those conditions the manifold vacuum would drop below the 8-10 inches needed to operate the wipers. These conditions are almost completely eliminated on cars equipped with a vacuum booster pump. The purpose of this pump is to maintain enough vacuum to work the wipers under any driving conditions.

Some of the conditions which prevent satisfactory windshield wiper operation are listed in the following text and may be used as a guide to help you locate the source of trouble. Always disconnect the battery when working under the dash.

Wipers Won't Operate

1. No vacuum supply to motor due to pinch, restriction or leak in the windshield wiper hose. A vacuum leak or a disconnected hose can easily be located because a hissing sound will be heard whenever the engine is running.
2. Faulty vacuum booster pump.
3. Wiper control switch inoperative or disconnected at motor.
4. Faulty wiper motor.
5. Frozen or binding pivots and linkages.
6. Linkages or cables improperly installed.

Wipers Operate Slowly

1. Low vacuum due to pinch or partial restriction in the wiper hose.
2. Loss of vacuum due to leaks at joints, fittings or in the wiper hose itself.
3. Faulty vacuum booster pump.
4. Faulty wiper motor.
5. Wiper control switch does not move operating valve on the motor to full ON position due to improper adjustment.

6. Air intake on motor (breather port) clogged.
7. Binding pivots, cranks, linkages or binding or frozen idler pulleys on cable tensioners.
8. Cables adjusted too tight.

Wipers Won't Park

1. Faulty parking valve on motor.
2. Wiper control switch out of adjustment.
3. Wiper arms not positioned properly on pivots.

Pressure Wiper

The windshield wiper is hydraulically operated. The hydraulic power for the motor is obtained from the power steering unit. Hydraulic fluid flows from the pump, through the steering gear to the wiper motor, and then to the fluid reservoir. During wiper operation, a part of the fluid is bypassed through the motor by a valve.

Checks and Adjustments: The only adjustment required is the control cable adjustment. To do this, remove the seal plate mounting screws and position the plate and seal out of the way. Adjust the cable so that the control knob on the instrument panel moves the valve control lever on the motor from off to full on.

If the motor operates sluggishly, check the cable adjustment. If this is not at fault, check the hydraulic fluid pressure. If the power steering gear operates satisfactorily, it may be assumed that the fluid pressure is adequate. Check for binding wiper pivot shafts and arms. Repair or replace wiper motor and valves if necessary.

1969-75 Chrysler Models

Wiper Fails to Operate

1. Binding linkage.
2. Faulty instrument panel switch.
3. Linkage disconnected.
4. Faulty motor.
5. Open or grounded wiring.

Wiper Blades not Parking Properly

1. Arm set at incorrect position.
2. Motor park switch timing incorrect.

Blades Slap Against Windshield Mouldings

1. Improperly adjusted wiper arm.
2. Looseness of the motor crank or other drive parts.

Blades Chatter

1. Twisted arm holds blade at wrong angle to glass.
2. Bent or damaged blades.
3. Foreign substances such as body polish on glass.

Motor Will Not Stop When Instrument Panel Switch is Turned Off

1. Motor park switch failure in the closed position.

Motor Stops in any Position When Instrument Panel Switch is Turned Off

1. Motor park switch failure in the open position.
2. Open parking circuit.
3. Open field circuit.

No Speed Control

1. Open circuit in red or green wiring (variable or 3-speed only); brown or red wiring (2-speed only).
2. Defective control switch.

Motor Draws Excessive Current

1. Jammed gearbox mechanism.
2. Shorted park switch.
3. Shorted motor.
4. Gearbox unlatched (variable and 3-speed only).

Motor Overheated

1. Binding linkage.

Motor Stops Intermittently in Any Position When Instrument Switch is Turned Off (variable and 3-speed only)

1. Gearbox unlatched.
2. Intermittent park switch continuity.

Motor Runs But Output Crank Does Not Turn

1. Stripped intermediate gear (2-speed).
2. Stripped output gear.
3. Output gear slips on output shaft (2-speed).
4. Crank not fastened properly to output gear shaft.
5. Broken latch slips on output shaft.

Motor Will Not Run at Any Speed

1. Common brush stuck.
2. Open circuit in armature at commutator.
3. Spring off common brush (2-speed).
4. Open in brown, lead circuit (3-speed).
5. Open green lead circuit (2-speed concealed).
6. Open solder terminal on park switch (3-speed).

No Speed Control—Motor Runs at One Speed Only

1. Open circuit in red or green wiring (3-speed); red or brown wiring (2-speed).
2. Defective control switch.
3. Brush sticking in holder (2-speed).

279

4. No brush spring (2-speed).
5. Broken brush holder (2-speed).
6. Low speed torque limiting resistor open (2-speed).

Motor Runs Slower at High Instrument Panel Switch Position Than at Medium

1. Faulty instrument panel switch.
2. Medium speed field circuit open.

Motor Will Not Stop When Instrument Panel Switch is Turned Off

1. Broken island on gear.
2. Lead not soldered properly at park switch (3-speed).
3. Rocker arm outside outer cam (3-speed).
4. Motor housing not grounded (2-speed with concealed wipers).
5. Defective armature brake switch (2-speed).
6. Broken brush holder (2-speed).

Motor Draws Excessive Current

1. Shorted brush lead or field winding (3-speed).
2. Shorted or burned armature.
3. Seized armature bearing (2-speed).
4. Bearings loose in housing (2-speed).
5. Loose or chipped magnets and loose clips or chips interfering with armature (2-speed).
6. Broken brush holder (2-speed).
7. Binding linkage.

Ford and 1974-75 American Motors

Windshield Wiper Inoperative—Hydraulic

1. Control cable not properly adjusted.
2. Control cable broken.

Inoperative or Slow Wiper

1. Binding linkage.
2. Defective switch.
3. Defective wiper motor(s).
4. Defective wiring or circuit breaker.

Continuous Wiper Action with Selector At Intermittent Position

1. Loose, broken, or plugged vacuum hose from engine to control to governor.
2. Ruptured governor or governor switch diaphragm.
3. Defective control selector switch.

Excessive Dwell Time During Intermittent Operation

1. Pinched hose from lower governor fitting to control switch rear fitting.
2. Plugged orifice in control selector dwell regulator.

Wipers Will Not Stop or Will Not Stop in Park Position

1. Open or broken wire.
2. Defective wiper motor.
3. Defective park switch.
4. Defective wiper switch.

Noisy Wiper System

1. Loose or misaligned wiper motor mounting.
2. Improper wiper arms or blades.
3. Loose or worn linkage.

General Motors 2 Speed-Rectangular Wiper on Car, Fig. 34

Wiper Inoperative or Intermittent

1. Blown fuse.
2. Open circuit in feed wire (No. 2 terminal on wiper motor).
3. Loose mounting of wiper switch.
4. Open circuit in wire to wiper switch (No. 1 terminal on wiper motor).
5. Defective wiper switch.

Wiper Will Not Shut Off

Wiper has both Low and High Speeds

1. Grounded wire (No. 1 terminal on wiper motor) to wiper switch.

Wiper has Low Speed Only

1. Defective wiper switch.
2. Grounded wire (No. 3 terminal on wiper motor to wiper switch).

Wiper Has High Speed Only

1. Defective wiper switch.
2. Open circuit in wire (No. 3 terminal on wiper motor) to wiper switch.

Wiper has High Speed Only

1. Open circuit in wire (No. 3 terminal on wiper motor to wiper switch).
2. Defective wiper switch.

Wiper has Low Speed Only

1. Grounded wire (No. 3 terminal on wiper motor to wiper switch).
2. Defective wiper switch.

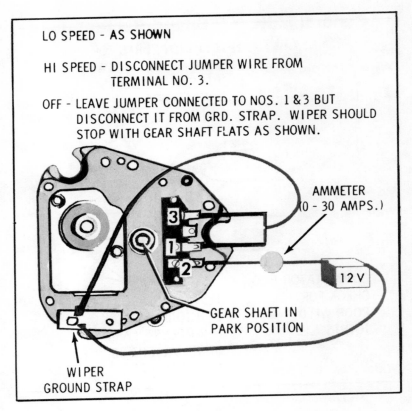

LO SPEED - AS SHOWN

HI SPEED - DISCONNECT JUMPER WIRE FROM
TERMINAL NO. 3.

OFF - LEAVE JUMPER CONNECTED TO NOS. 1 & 3 BUT
DISCONNECT IT FROM GRD. STRAP. WIPER SHOULD
STOP WITH GEAR SHAFT FLATS AS SHOWN.

AMMETER
(0 - 30 AMPS.)

12 V

GEAR SHAFT IN
PARK POSITION

WIPER
GROUND STRAP

Fig. 34.

Blades do not Return to Full Park Position

    1. Loose wiper motor ground strap connection.

Wiper Off Car (Refer to Figs. 35, 36, & 37)

Wiper Inoperative or Intermittent

    1. Broken or damaged gear train (only if inoperative).

283

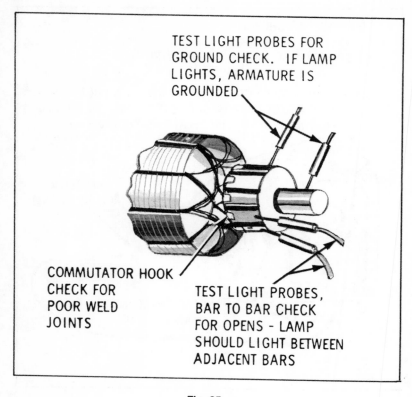

TEST LIGHT PROBES FOR
GROUND CHECK. IF LAMP
LIGHTS, ARMATURE IS
GROUNDED

COMMUTATOR HOOK
CHECK FOR
POOR WELD
JOINTS

TEST LIGHT PROBES,
BAR TO BAR CHECK
FOR OPENS - LAMP
SHOULD LIGHT BETWEEN
ADJACENT BARS

Fig. 35.

2. Poor solder connections at terminal board.
3. Loose splice joints at brush plate.
4. Brushes binding in brush holder.
5. Open circuit in armature.

Wiper will not Shut Off
Wiper has Normal High and Low Speed

1. Defective park switch.
2. Grounded red wire.

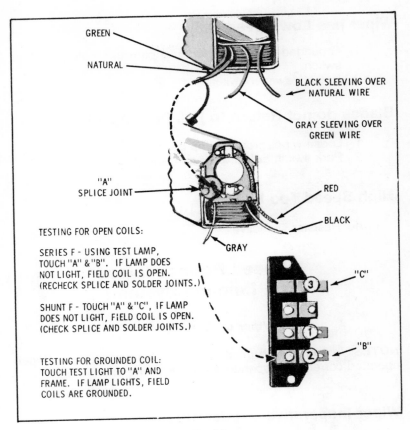

GREEN

NATURAL

BLACK SLEEVING OVER
NATURAL WIRE

GRAY SLEEVING OVER
GREEN WIRE

"A"
SPLICE JOINT

RED

BLACK

TESTING FOR OPEN COILS:

GRAY

SERIES F - USING TEST LAMP,
TOUCH "A" & "B". IF LAMP DOES
NOT LIGHT, FIELD COIL IS OPEN.
(RECHECK SPLICE AND SOLDER JOINTS.)

SHUNT F - TOUCH "A" & "C", IF LAMP
DOES NOT LIGHT, FIELD COIL IS OPEN.
(CHECK SPLICE AND SOLDER JOINTS.)

TESTING FOR GROUNDED COIL:
TOUCH TEST LIGHT TO "A" AND
FRAME. IF LAMP LIGHTS, FIELD
COILS ARE GROUNDED.

"C"

"B"

Fig. 36.

Wiper will not Shut Off
Wiper has Low Speed Only

1. Grounded shunt field coil, Fig. 53.
2. Grounded black wire.

Wiper will not Shut Off
Wiper has High Speed Only

1. Open circuit in shunt field coil.
2. Open circuit in black wire.

285

Wiper has Low Speed Only

1. Grounded wire (No. 3 terminal on wiper motor) to wiper switch.
2. Defective wiper switch.

Blades do not Return to Full Park Position

1. Loose wiper ground strap connection.
2. Park switch defective or contacts dirty.

High Speed Too Fast

1. Resistor Defective.

2-Speed Round Motor
(Exc. Demand System)

Wiper on Car, Fig. 37

NOTES: Ignition switch must be on for all electrical tests. Wiper operated correctly independently of car wiring and switch.

Wiper Inoperative or Intermittent

1. Open lead wire from wiper terminal No. 1 to wiper switch.
2. Wiper switch not securely mounted.
3. Wiper switch defective.

Wiper will not Shut Off—Blades Make Full Wipe Stroke

1. Grounded lead wire from wiper terminal No. 1 to wiper switch.
2. Corroded wiper terminals.
3. Defective wiper switch.

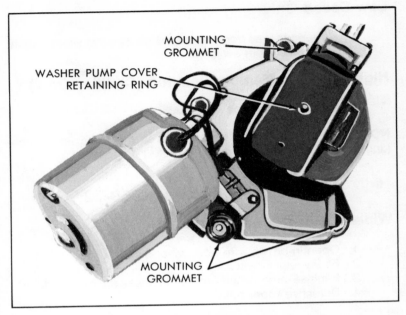

Fig. 37.

Wiper will not Shut Off—Blades Move up and Down About 15 Degrees from Park Position

1. Open in lead wire from wiper terminal No. 3 to wiper switch.
2. Wiper switch mounting loose.
3. Wiper switch defective.

High Speed Only

1. Open lead wire from wiper terminal No. 3 to wiper switch.
2. Wiper switch defective.

Low Speed Only

1. Grounded lead from wiper terminal No. 3 to wiper switch.
2. Defective wiper switch.

High Speed in Medium Position (Cadillac Only)

1. Open medium speed resistor.

NOTE: The following checking procedures should be used in conjunction with *Wiper Off Car* (round motor) diagnosis.

American Motors, 1969-72

Wiper Motor Does Not Operate

1. Open in brown wire from wiper switch.
2. Faulty wiper switch.
3. Faulty 6-amp circuit breaker in wiper motor circuit.
4. Defective wiper motor.

No High Speed Operation

1. Open in black wire circuit of wiring harness.
2. Faulty wiper switch.
3. Defective wiper motor.

No Low Speed Operation

1. Faulty wiper switch.
2. Open in red or black wire of wiring harness.
3. Defective wiper motor.

Wipers Will Not Park

1. Open in yellow, black, blue or red wire of wiring harness.
2. Defective park switch.
3. Defective cam drive plate.
4. Defective wiper switch.

1971-72

Incorrect Wiper Blade Position

1. Transmission linkage incorrectly installed, incorrectly adjusted or damaged.
2. Actuator cam incorrectly installed. The cam must be installed with the stamped letter R facing away from the motor.
3. Contact plate incorrectly installed.

1973-74

Incorrect Wiper Motor Park Position

1. Open in white or black wire of wiring harness.
2. Defective wiper switch.

Incorrect Intermittent Wipe Cycle

1. Defective wiper switch.
2. Open in one or more wires of wiper wiring harness.
3. Defective intermittent governor.
4. Defective wiper motor.

AIR CONDITIONING PROBLEMS

NOTE 1: When a unit must be removed from the system for replacement or repairs, the dehydrator must also be replaced, and the system must be purged, evacuated and recharged to remove excess moisture.

NOTE 2: The evaporator regulator includes the suction throttling valve (STV) used on Ford cars; the Pilot-Operated Absolute (POA) valve used on General Motors cars, and the Chrysler Evaporator Pressure Regulator (EPR) or Evaporator Temperature Regulator (ETR) valve. When any of these devices is used in a system, it can be assumed that the system contains no thermostat control.

System Operates Only on Maximum Cooling

1. A short circuit in the ambient or in-car sensor.

2. A short circuit in the comfort control potentiometer.
3. Defective amplifier.
4. Defective servo.

System Operates on Air Conditioning Mode at All Times with Controlled Air Temperature

1. Vacuum not supplied to pot side of mode actuator.

System Operates Only on Maximum Heating and High Blower

1. An open circuit in the ambient or in-car sensor.
2. An open circuit in the comfort control potentiometer.
3. Defective servo assembly.
4. Defective amplifier.

System Controls in Heat Mode for Most Ambient Temperatures

1. Partially open ambient sensor.
2. Defective amplifier.

System Operates on Heat Mode at All Times

1. Vacuum not supplied to rod side of mode actuator.
2. Partially open ambient sensor.

System Puts Out Only Hot Air in All Modes at All Times

1. Blend air door link off the servo arm and stuck in heat.

System Puts Out Only Cold Air in All Modes at All Times

1. Blend air door link off the servo arm and stuck in A/C.
2. Kinked water hose.
3. Defective water valve.
4. Defective pushbutton switch, and/or crossed vacuum line.

Blower and Compressor Will Not Operate and System Will Not Go Into Selected Mode

1. A failed (open) circuit.
2. A vacuum leak at engine fitting source or reservoir tank in engine compartment.
3. A loose connection between harness and push button switch.
4. A defective (leaking) vacuum harness connector at push

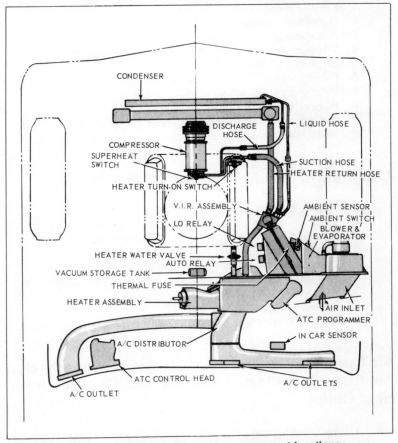

Fig. 37A. Typical air conditioner component locations.

button switch.
5. A defective (leaking) push button switch.
6. Vacuum hose leak in vacuum circuit.
7. Crossed vacuum lines at vacuum reservoir.
8. Pinched vacuum circuit.
9. Defective (leaking) actuator.

Blower Will Not Operate in Any Mode

1. Blower motor wiring disconnected.
2. Defective blower motor.
3. A/C-heater fuse blown.
4. Vacuum operated master on-off switch defective.
5. Leak in vacuum circuit.
6. Resistor block burned out.
7. Pinched vacuum line to master switch.
8. Blower motor not grounded.
9. Defective wiring at the Hi-blower relay insulator.
10. Hi-blower relay failed (open).

Compressor Will Not Operate at Any Time

1. Clutch wire disconnected.
2. Vacuum operated compressor switch, defective.
3. Ambient temperature is below 32 degrees F.
4. Pinched vacuum line to compressor switch.
5. Low pressure cut-off switch defective.
6. System pressure below low pressure cut-off switch limits.
7. Accessory fuse blown.
8. Defective pushbutton switch.
9. Defective wiring or improper connection.

Air Conditioning and Heat Modes Reversed—Hot Air from Conditioning Outlets and Cold Air from Heat Outlets

1. Air conditioning and heat mode actuator vacuum hoses reversed.

Air Coming Out of Air Conditioning Outlets When System is in the Defrost or Hi-Defrost Position

1. Vacuum hoses to mode actuator and defrost actuator reversed.
2. Defective pushbutton switch assembly.

Most of the Air Coming Out of Defrosters When System Should be on Heat Mode

1. Vacuum hoses to shaft and pot side of defrost actuator reversed.

Air Comes Out of the Defrosters When the System Should be in Heat Mode, and Air Comes Out of Heater Outlets When System Should be in Air Conditioning

1. All vacuum lines to mode and defrost actuators completely crossed.
2. Mode door stuck in heat position.

Air Comes Out of All Outlets When the System Should be in Defrost or Air Conditioning. Air Comes Out of Air Conditioning Outlets When the System Should be in Heat Mode

1. All vacuum lines to mode and defrost actuators completely crossed.

System Will Not Change Mode in Auto or Hi-Auto Even with Tester Operating Control Unit

1. Doors binding.
2. Vacuum hose off.
3. Pinched hose to actuator.

System Does Not Achieve a Comfortable Condition. Blower Speed Cycles; Temperature Unstable

1. Defective servo assembly.
2. Aspirator not operating properly (pinched or disconnected tube).
3. Defective engine thermostat.
4. Aspirator scoop missing.

System Does Not Achieve a Comfortable Condition. Temperature Slowly Drifts Up and Down

1. Aspirator not operating properly (pinched or disconnected tube).
2. Frayed or bare sections in sensor leads.
3. Defective amplifier.
4. Defective radiator pressure cap.
5. Defective engine thermostat.

Blower Does Not Shut Off When Off Button is Pushed

1. Check valve 2 failed closed or installed backwards. (Only when engine is cold).
2. Defective pushbutton switch.
3. Pinched vacuum hose.

Blower Does Not Come On in Defrost or Hi-Defrost When the Engine is Cold

1. Check valve 1 failed closed or installed backwards.
2. Blower relay failed open.
3. Master switch failed open.

Blower Speed Changes with Changes in Car Voltage (Car is Accelerated or Accessories are Turned On or Off)

1. Defective amplifier.

System Comes On in Air Conditioning Mode and M2 Blower in Hot Weather When Hi Blower Air Conditioning is Required. (Hi-Auto)

1. No defect.

Air Coming Out of Defroster When System Should be in the Air Conditioning Mode

1. Air conditioning/heat and heat-defroster mode actuator hoses reversed on actuators.
2. Defrost button may be depressed.

Insufficient Air Flow

1. Air distribution ducts disconnected from air conditioning outlets or distribution center.
2. Failing blower motor.
3. Defective resistor block.
4. Freeze-up condition.

Blower Speed Always Too Great on Lo-Auto

1. Resistor block, faulty (resistors shorted.)
2. Connections at resistor block loose or disconnected.

Blower Speeds Always Too Great on Hi-Auto

1. Lower speeds not provided for Hi-Auto.

System Blows Cold Air at the Start During Cold Weather Operation

1. Cold engine lockout switch faulty.
2. Blower master switch inoperative in closed position.
3. Vacuum bleed plugged.
4. Check valve 2 failed open or reversed.

Insufficient Heat When Maximum Heating is Required

1. Defective Servo assembly.
2. Heater core, faulty or plugged.
3. Defective engine thermostat.
4. Blend air door not adjusted properly or binding.

Erratic Temperature Control

1. Heater hoses reversed at core inlet and outlet tubes.
2. Radiator water level low.
3. Defective radiator cap.
4. Loose vacuum or electrical connection at control unit assembly.
5. Defective engine thermostat.
6. Faulty servo assembly.
7. Intermittent sensor or temperature control potentiometer.
8. Erratic amplifier.

Insufficient Cooling When Maximum Cooling is Required

1. EPR valve faulty.
2. Refrigeration system low on refrigerant.
3. H-valve defective.
4. Faulty push button switch.
5. Clutch not running (pinched vacuum line to compressor switch, wires not connected or high resistance compressor switch or ambient switch or low pressure cut out switch.).
6. Outside air door stuck in 100% outside air position (broken return spring or defective vacuum transfer switch.)
7. Faulty clutch.

Discharge Air too Cold at Times

1. EPR valve failed (open).

After Approximately One Hour of Sustained Driving Airflow Drops Off to Practically None, While Blower Can Be Heard Operating at a High Speed

1. Evaporator coil freeze-up, same causes as in *Discharge Air Too Cold At Times*.

Air Comes Out of Air Conditioning Outlets or Heat Outlets While Driving in the Off Position

1. Recirculating door in outside air position (vacuum hoses on recirculation door actuator reversed).
2. Blower master switch (failed in closed position).
3. Recirculating door not sealing properly.
4. Check valve 2 reversed or failed closed.

Objectionable Odors Being Discharged Through the Air Conditioning or Heat Outlets

1. Recirculating door in recirculating air position (vacuum hoses on recirculating air door actuator reversed).

System Quits on Acceleration

1. Defective vacuum-reservoir tank check valve.
2. Vacuum leak.
3. Check valve 1 reversed or failed open.

System Will Not Go to Maximum Heat on Hi-Defrost

1. Defrost override circuit in amplifier.
2. Hi-Defrost feed from pushbutton switch to amplifier not connected at switch.
3. Pushbutton actuated Hi-Defrost feed switch in control head, faulty.
4. Defective servo.

297

System Does Not Achieve a Comfortable Condition —System Leveled Out

1. Comfort control potentiometer out of calibration.
2. Amplifier out of calibration.
3. Air conditioning outlets not directed properly.
4. Aspirator not operating properly (pinched or disconnected tube).

System Does Not Achieve a Comfortable Condition—Erratic Changes of Temperature and Possible Blower Speed

1. Loose electrical connection at sensors, amplifier or servo assembly.
2. Defective amplifier.
3. Defective servo assembly.
4. Aspirator and scoop assembly defective.
5. Blend air door link not connected to servo.

Blower Speeds Not in Sequence

1. Wiring harness error at servo, or resistor block.

System Will Not Park (Center)

1. Defective amplifier.
2. Defective servo.
3. Blown in-line fuse.
4. System battery feed disconnected.
5. System battery feed connected to fuse block accessory terminal.

System Comes On in M1-A/C or Low Heat and Remains There

1. Partially connected main harness connector.

2. Accessory fuse.
3. Defective compressor switch.
4. Vacuum hose (yellow) to compressor switch off.
5. Vacuum hose to compressor switch pinched.

System Comes On in A/C Mode During Hot Weather and Heat Mode During Cold Weather

1. No defect.

System Noise After Engine is Shut Down

1. No defect.

Hi-Blower Inoperative in Both the Air Conditioning and Heat Modes

1. Faulty motor.
2. Faulty Hi-Blower relay.
3. Faulty relay switch in the servo assembly.
4. Faulty wiring.

Clutch Engaged in Vent Mode

1. Faulty pushbutton switch.
2. Faulty wiring.

System Operates in Super Hi-Blower Speed in Lo-Auto Mode

1. ATC diode has failed (short).
2. Faulty wiring.

System Operates in Air Conditioning Mode and M2 Speed Only

1. Faulty vent relay.
2. Faulty pushbutton switch.

299

System Goes to Maximum Heat or Maximum Air Conditioning Position While in Vent Position

1. Vent resistor in servo failed (open or short).

System Operates Only in Hi-Blower and Hi-Auto with Temperature Control

1. Faulty Hi-Blower relay.
2. Faulty relay switch in servo.

System Operates in M2 and Hi Speed While in A/C or Heat Mode and Hi-Auto

1. Faulty wiring.
2. Open diode.
3. Faulty servo.

Low Side Low—High Side Low

1. System refrigerant low.
2. Expansion valve clogged.
3. Restriction in liquid line.

Low Side High—High Side Low

1. Internal leak in compressor—worn.
2. Head gasket leaking.
3. Expansion valve.
4. Drive belt slipping.

Low Side High—High Side High

1. Clogged condenser fins.
2. Air in system.
3. Expansion valve.
4. Loose or worn fan belts.

Low Side Low—High Side High

1. Expansion valve.
2. Restriction in liquid line.
3. Restriction in receiver.
4. Restriction in condenser.

Low Side and High Side Normal (Inadequate Cooling)

1. Air in system.
2. Moisture in system.

Compressor Noise

1. Broken valves.
2. Overcharged.
3. Incorrect oil level.
4. Piston slap.
5. Broken rings.

Excessive Vibration

1. Incorrect belt tension.
2. Clutch loose.
3. Overcharged.
4. Pulley misaligned.

Condensation Dripping in Passenger Compartment

1. Drain hose plugged or improperly positioned.
2. Insulation removed or improperly installed.

A/C Airflow Stops on Acceleration

1. Defective vacuum storage tank.
2. Vacuum line separated or defective.
3. Vacuum switch defective.
4. Vacuum leak.

301

Frozen Evaporator Coil

1. Faulty thermostat.
2. Thermostat capillary tube improperly installed.

Clutch Slippage

1. Head pressure too high.
2. Pulley wobbles.
3. Low clutch voltage.

Velocity of Air at Discharge Nozzles Too Low

1. Restricted evaporator core in evaporator assembly.
2. Restricted air distribution hoses.
3. Defective blower motor. Poor ground connection.
4. Defective switches.

Evaporator Pressure Too Low

1. Insufficient Refrigerant charge.
2. Possible defective P.O.A. valve.
3. Possible defective expansion valve.

Water Blowing Out Air Discharge Nozzle

1. Plugged or kinked evaporator drain hose.

Inoperative Controls

1. Inadequate vacuum.
2. Temperature cable improperly adjusted.

Evaporator Pressure Too High

1. Possible defective P.O.A. valve.
2. Restriction in suction line.
3. Loose compressor drive belt.
4. Defective clutch or coil.
5. Possible defective expansions valve.
6. Clutch slipping.

Nozzle Discharge Air Too Warm (With Other Readings OK)

1. Temperature Control Cable misadjusted.
2. Low refrigerant charge.
3. Too much oil in compressor.
4. Check evaporator seal for hot air bypassing core.

Clutch Slippage

1. Head pressure too high.
2. Pulley wobbles.
3. Low clutch voltage.

Velocity of Air at Discharge—Nozzles Too Low

1. Restricted evaporator core in evaporator assembly.
2. Restricted air distribution hoses.
3. Defective blower motor. Poor ground connection.
4. Defective switches.

Evaporator Pressure Too Low

1. Insufficient refrigerant charge.
2. Possible defective P.O.A. valve.
3. Possible defective expansion valve.

Water Blowing Out of Air Discharge Nozzle

1. Plugged or kinked evaporator drain hose.

Inoperative Controls

1. Inadequate vacuum.
2. Temperature cable improperly adjusted.

Evaporator Pressure Too High

1. Possible defective P.O.A. valve.
2. Restriction in suction line.
3. Loose compressor drive belt.
4. Defective clutch or coil.
5. Possible defective expansion valve.
6. Clutch slipping.

Nozzle Discharge Air Too Warm—With Other Readings OK

1. Temperature Control Cable maladjusted.
2. Low refrigerant charge.
3. Too much oil in compressor.
4. Check evaporator seal for hot air bypassing core.

AUTOMATIC LEVEL CONTROL PROBLEMS

General Motors

Car Loaded, Will Not Rise

1. External damage or breakage.
2. Line leak.
3. Linkage to overtravel lever in wrong hole.
4. Control valve setting incorrect.
5. Defective component.

Car Loaded, Raises to Level, Then Leaks Down

1. Line leak.
2. Control valve exhaust leak.
3. Superlift leak.
4. Control valve leak.

Car Loaded, Raises Partially

1. Load excessive (over 500 lbs. at axle) on cars with special springs.

2. Control valve setting incorrect.
3. Low supply pressure.

Car Unloaded, Rides too High, Will Not Come Down

1. Control valve setting incorrect.
2. Improper springs.
3. External damage or breakage.
4. Linkage to overtravel in wrong hole.
5. Defective control valve.

Car Rises When Loaded but Leaks Down While Driving

1. Time delay mechanism not functioning properly.

Ford Motor Company

Vehicle Loaded, Will Not Raise

1. External damage or breakage.
2. Line or cylinder leak.
3. Pump inoperative or output inadequate.
4. Control valve setting incorrect.
5. Inadequate time delay.

Vehicle Loaded, Raises Partially

1. Load excessive (over 250 lbs.) at axle.
2. Height control valve setting incorrect.
3. Low supply pressure.

Vehicle Unloaded, Rides too High, Won't Come Down

1. Control valve setting incorrect.
2. External damage or breakage.
3. Defective control valve.

Compressor Cycles Continuously

1. Line leak.
2. Air cylinder ruptured.
3. Inadequate time; may take five minutes to balance at idle.

Compressor Does Not Cycle

1. Vacuum hose off or leaking.
2. Pump internal failure.
3. Lines or hoses restricted.
4. Pump filter clogged.

Vehicle Loaded, Raises to Level and Then Leaks Down

1. Line leak.
2. Control valve exhaust leak.
3. Air cylinder leak.
4. If leak down while driving, check for control valve time delay less than one second.

SPEED CONTROL PROBLEMS

American Motors Cruise Command and General Motors Cruise Master (exc. AC Electro-Cruise 1969-76)

Fuse Blows Repeatedly

1. Short or ground in wiring circuit.

Does Not Engage

1. Blown fuse.
2. Brake switch misadjusted.
3. No current to No. 2 terminal (Cruise Master).
4. No current to brown wire (Cruise Command).
5. Bad ground.
6. Vacuum leak.
7. Brake light fuse burned (Cruise Command).
8. Brake lamp bulb burned (Cruise Command).

9. Faulty connections.
10. Inoperative engaging switch.
11. Faulty valve body and magnet assembly.
12. Faulty low speed switch.

Does Not Disengage When Brake Is Applied.

1. Improper brake release adjustment.
2. Defective brake release switch.
3. Faulty valve body and magnet assembly.
4. Collapsed hose from servo to regulator.

Re-engages When Brake Is Released

1. Faulty engaging switch.
2. No. 1 terminal grounded (Cruise Master).
3. Improperly installed electrical connectors (Cruise Command).

Engine Does Not Return To Normal Idle

1. Faulty linkage cable (Cruise Master).
2. Improper accelerator linkage adjustment.
3. Weak or disconnected throttle return spring.

Pulsating Accelerator Pedal

1. Speedometer cable drive cable kinked.

Does Not Maintain Selected Speed

1. Faulty vacuum servo or vacuum hose.
2. Faulty governor assembly.

Controlled Speed Three Or More Mph Above Selected Speed

1. Centering spring improperly adjusted.

Controlled Speed One Or More Mph Below Selected Speed

1. Centering spring improperly adjusted.

Speedometer Inoperative, Cruise Command Operates

1. Speedometer cable not driving speedometer.
2. Faulty regulator.

Engine Accelerates When Started—Cruise Command

1. Vacuum hoses reversed at regulator.

Disengages On Level Road Without Applying Brakes

1. Loose wiring connections or poor ground.
2. Loose vacuum hoses.
3. Brake switch adjusted too tight.

General Motors AC Electro-Cruise

No Action When Engagement Switch Knob is Depressed

1. Broken connection.
2. Blown fuses.
3. Brake release switch out of adjustment.
4. Vacuum leak.
5. Power unit coil open.
6. Defective transistor amplifier.

Cruise Lamp Lights When Knob is Depressed with No Response

1. Harness to speedometer unplugged or loose.
2. Defective contacts on speed transducer.

Cruise Lamp Lights When Knob is Depressed Below 3 Mph of Set Speed

1. Harness to speedometer loose.
2. Defective contacts on speed transducer.

System Remains Engaged When Brake Pedal is Depressed.

1. Brake release switch out of adjustment.
2. Shorted brake release switch.
3. Shorted wire harness in cruise release line.

Blows Fuses

1. Shorted wiring.
2. Shorted differential relay, cruise telltale light or power unit coil.
3. Shorted transistor amplifier.

Engine Races When Started When Engage Button is Not Pushed

1. Shorted wiring harness.
2. Shorted engage switch.
3. Shorted differential relay.
4. Vacuum orifice leak in power unit.
5. Accelerator linkage bound up.

Will Not Lock In After Set Speed is Attained

1. Defective differential relay.

Keeps Accelerating Up Past Set Speed

1. Shorted wire harness.
2. Shorted contacts on Cruise speedometer.
3. Defective differential relay.

System Automatically Locks In on Rough Roads

1. Defective differential relay.
2. Loose connection.
3. Brake release switch set too tight.

System Drops Out Over Rough Roads

1. Defective differential relay.
2. Loose connection.
3. Brake release switch set too tight.

Erratic Cruise Speed.

1. Loose connection.
2. Defective contacts on Cruise speedometer.
3. Armature in power unit hanging up.
4. Vacuum leak.

Slow Response

1. Vacuum leak.

Hunts at Slow Speeds

1. Erratic Cruise speedometer.
2. Excessive slack in ball chain.
3. Stiff accelerator linkage.
4. Vacuum leak.
5. Dragging brakes.

Does Not Disengage When Knob is Pulled

1. Shorted wire harness.
2. Shorted engagement switch.
3. Defective differential relay.

Hissing Noise When Engine is Running

1. Vacuum leak.

Indicator Lamp Does Not Light

1. Lamp socket not plugged in.
2. Burned out tell-tale lamp.
3. Defective differential relay.
4. Broken wire harness.

Car Won't Idle When System is Not Engaged

1. Vacuum leak.
2. Ball chain adjusted too tightly.

Will Not Reach High Cruise Speeds

1. Excessive slack in ball chain.
2. Beyond capabilities of engine due to extremely high altitude and/or excessive road grades.
3. Defective speedometer.

Pointer and Odometer Does Not Record

1. Broken flexible shaft.
2. Defective speedometer.

Cruise Pointer and Speedometer Do Not Coincide When in Cruise

1. Stiff throttle linkage.
2. Cruise speedometer out of calibration.
3. Wrong throttle return spring.
4. Vacuum leak.

Excessive Power Unit Noise

1. Wrong or no sound dampening cushion between power unit and fire wall.
2. Worn or defective power unit armature.
3. Power unit mounting screws too tight.

Pedal Noise When in Cruise

1. Worn accelerator linkage or pedal.
2. Accelerator pedal hinge stiff or worn.

Excessive Overshoot Condition

1. Defective speed transducer.
2. Tight throttle linkage.
3. Vacuum leak.
4. Dragging brakes.

Whistling Noise When Brake or Clutch Pedal is Touched

1. Dirty or worn brake release switch.
2. Foreign matter in cruise release line.

Chrysler Corporation Speed Control 1968-76

No Speed Control When Button Pressed

1. Control ring in Off position.
2. Fuse blown.
3. Vacuum leak.
4. Speed control throttle cable disconnected.
5. Improper stop lamp and speed control switch adjustment.
6. Faulty electrical circuit.

No Resume When Control Ring is Rotated

1. Insufficient rotation of control ring.
2. Faulty electrical circuit.

No System Disengagement When Brake Pedal is Depressed

1. Speed control cable kinked or damaged.
2. Improper adjustment of stop lamp and speed control switch.
3. Faulty electrical circuit.

Speed Control Engages Without Actuating the Switch

1. Faulty electrical circuit.

Carburetor Does Not Return to Normal Idle

1. Speed control throttle cable kinked or damaged.
2. Speed control throttle cable maladjusted.
3. Standard throttle linkage faulty.

Speedometer Noise, Excessive Needle Waiver or Erratic Servo Lock-In Performance

1. Speedometer cable kinked or damaged.
2. Cable core bent or too long.
3. Cable ferrule nut loose at speedometer head, transmission or speed control servo.
4. No lubricant on speedometer cable core.
5. Noisy speedometer head assembly.

Speed Setting After Lock-In, Too High or Too Low

1. Improper adjustment of speed control throttle cable.
2. Vacuum leak.
3. Improper speed control servo lock-in adjustment.

Unit Disengages on Rough Road

1. Improper adjustment of stop lamp and speed control.

Resume Speed is Possible Below 29 Mph

1. Faulty low speed inhibit switch in servo unit.
2. Faulty electrical circuit.

Speed Control Engages When Engine is Started, or Does Not Disengage When Brake Pedal is Depressed

1. Faulty electrical circuit.

Slide Switch Type

Speedometer Noise

1. Cables bent or kinked.

2. Lack of cable lubrication.
3. Noisy speedometer head.

Fuses Blow Repeatedly

1. Short or ground in wiring circuit.
2. Defective motor.
3. Lacked drive screw.

No Speed Control Response

1. Accelerator linkage broken or disconnected.
2. Drive cables broken or disconnected.
3. Blown fuse.
4. Loose connection or broken wires (internal or external).

No Automatic Control When Unit is Set for Automatic Lock-In

1. Driver riding brake pedal or does not accelerate to selected speed.
2. No current at No. 2 terminal.
3. Improper throttle switch adjustment.
4. Improper brake release switch adjustment.

Constant Pressure on Accelerator Pedal Regardless of Dial Setting

1. Blown fuse.
2. No current at No. 1 terminal.
3. Control cable improperly adjusted.
4. Control cable defective.
5. Inoperative motor or locked drive screw.
6. Improper limit switch adjustment.

Automatic Control Engages at Selected Speed Without Unit Set for Automatic Lock-In

1. Improper brake release switch adjustment or defective switch.

Unit Does Not Remain Inoperative in Off Position

1. Limit switch not properly adjusted.

Pulsating Accelerator Pedal

1. Speedometer cable or drive cable kinked or lack lubrication.
2. Improper accelerator linkage adjustment.
3. Improper motor feed points adjustment.

Carburetor Does Not Return to Normal Idle

1. Improper carburetor or accelerator linkage adjustment.
2. Weak or disconnected throttle return spring.

Unit Does Not Control at Selected Speed

1. Improper control cable adjustment.
2. Improper selector dial adjustment.
3. Improper accelerator linkage adjustment.

Unit Controls at Low Speed Regardless of Selector Setting

1. Control cable not secured to selector coupling.

Speedometer Does Not Register

1. Transmission drive gear in transmission defective.
2. Broken drive cable from transmission to power unit.
3. Damaged drive gear or nylon gear in power unit.
4. Broken speedometer cable.

Ford Marquette System
(exc. 1966-67 T-Bird)

Engine Won't Return to Normal Idle

1. Throttle linkage not properly adjusted.
2. Speed control accelerator linkage improperly adjusted.

315

Vehicle Over-Speeds Speed Setting

1. Pressure hose between sensor pump and metering valve leaking.
2. Defective metering valve diaphragm.
3. Vacuum hoses to metering valve reversed.

Increase in Minimum Controllable Speed

1. Loss of fluid from sensor pump.

Dial Speed Setting Does Not Correspond to Speedometer Reading

1. Improper control cable adjustment.

High Engagement Speed Over Set Speed

1. Contact points in metering valve too far apart.

System Resumes Speed After Depressing and Releasing Brake Pedal or Resumes Speed Well Below Set Speed

1. Metering valve contact points too close or fused together.
2. Shorted resume-speed button or wiring.

Control Button Won't Stay Out, System Inoperative

1. Blown fuse.
2. Wire off back of switch or ignition, or wiring is defective.
3. Switch button burned out.

Control Button Stays Out, System Inoperative

1. Any of system components.

Control Engages Below Desired Speed

1. Resume-speed switch shorted.
2. Metering valve points shorted.
3. Wiring shorted.

Control Won't Resume when Resume Switch is Activated

1. Resume-speed switch defective.
2. Switch not properly grounded.
3. Wire off back of switch or defective wiring.

Control Will Not Disengage when Brake Pedal is Depressed

1. Brake switch not properly adjusted or defective.

Control Inoperative, Speedometer Does Not Register

1. Broken speedometer cable between transmission and sensor pump.

Control Operates but Speedometer Does Not Register

1. Broken speedometer cable between sensor pump and speedometer.
2. Inoperative speedometer mechanism.

Speed Continuously Changes Up and Down

1. Vacuum hose split between intake manifold of engine and vacuum valve, between vacuum valve and metering valve or between metering valve and vacuum bellows.
2. Ruptured vacuum bellows.
3. Defective metering valve.
4. Sticky carburetor or accelerator linkage.

System Sluggish, Won't Hold Speed on Hills

1. Ball chain between vacuum bellows and accelerator not properly adjusted.
2. Defective sensor pump.
3. Sticky carburetor or accelerator linkage.
4. Vacuum leak in hoses.
5. Leak in vacuum bellows.

Ford Marquette System
1966-67 T-Bird

Switch Button Won't Stay Out, System Inoperative

1. Fuse blown.
2. Wire on back of switch button off or defective wiring.
3. Switch button burned out.

Switch Button Stays Out, System Inoperative

1. Defective electrical circuit.
2. Rubber tube between sensor pump and metering valve or inhibitor switch off or leaking.
3. Fluid low or gone from sensor pump.
4. Ruptured vacuum bellows.
5. Vacuum bellows disconnected from accelerator linkage.
6. Brake release relay or wiring defective.
7. Defective lock-in valve.

Speed Continuously Changes Up and Down

1. Vacuum hose split between engine intake manifold and vacuum valve, between vacuum valve and metering valve, or between metering valve and vacuum bellows.
2. Ruptured vacuum bellows.
3. Defective metering valve.
4. Sticky carburetor or accelerator linkage.

System Does Not Retard With Retard Switch Pressed

1. Defective retard switch in steering wheel.
2. Wire disconnected or defective at brake retard vacuum valve.
3. Defective brake retard valve.
4. Vacuum line split or off between vacuum reservoir and brake retard vacuum valve or brake retard vacuum valve and vacuum motor.
5. Ruptured brake retard vacuum motor.
6. Brake retard vacuum motor disconnected from brake pedal bracket.

7. Ball chain not adjusted properly.

System Sluggish, Won't Hold Speed on Hills

1. Defective sensor pump.
2. Sticky carburetor or accelerator linkage.
3. Vacuum leak in hoses, vacuum bellows or kinked vacuum hoses.

Low Speed Setting Too High

1. Rubber tube between sensor pump and inhibitor switch or metering valve leaking.

System Retains Memory After Engine is Turned Off and then Restarted

1. Defective or disconnected wiring between starter relay and control relay.

Speed Control Remains Engaged when Brake is Depressed or Retard Switch is Pressed

1. Defective brake pedal pad switch.
2. Defective vacuum switch.
3. Vacuum leak in retard system.

System Inoperative, Speedometer Does Not Register

1. Speedometer cable broken between transmission and sensor pump.
2. Defective speedometer drive or driven gear.

System Operative but Speedometer Does Not Register

1. Speedometer cable between sensor pump and speedometer broken.
2. Defective speedometer head.

SPEEDOMETER AND CABLE SERVICE PROBLEMS

Inaccurate Speedo

1. Damaged or improperly installed cable silencing sleeve on upper core tip (if used).
2. Speedo improperly calibrated.
3. Incorrect speedo drive pinion gear.
4. Damaged speedo drive pinion gear.
5. Cable improperly installed to speedometer.

Ticking Noise

1. Damaged or improperly installed cable silencing sleeve on upper core tip (if used).
2. Damaged or improperly routed cable assembly.
3. Defective speedometer head.
4. Casing connector loose on speedometer case.

Squealing Noise

1. Damaged or worn bearings in speedometer.

NOTE: In extremely cold weather, a slight squeal on initial running of the vehicle does not indicate a malfunction.

Whirling Noise, Inoperative

1. Cable damaged.
2. Broken cable core.
3. Damaged odometer gears in speedometer.
4. Cable disconnected.
5. No drive through EGR Maintenance Switch on Chrysler models.

Speedometer Pointer Flutter or Waiver

1. Cable core malfunction.
2. Cable improperly routed.
3. Cable improperly installed in speedometer.

Handling Emergency Situations

A highway emergency might be nothing more than a stalled car and a long annoying walk to get help. Or it might be worse. It might be a traffic accident. No one likes to think about such things. But let's face it. They do happen. And when they do, knowing what to do to control the situation could go a long way in preventing a bad situation from becoming worse. Here, then, are some possible emergencies and the right way to meet them:

If your car stalls on the highway

Get completely off a busy road as fast as you can, even if you have to ruin a tire to do so.

Turn your 4-way turn signal flasher on. If you don't have one, flash the headlights on and off as the car is moving. Your taillights, if on and not flashing, may cause another motorist to ram into the rear of your car. At night, keep your headlights on with beams lowered. Also switch on the dome light. If you're in a dangerous traffic situation, get everyone out of the car to a safe spot. Day or night, set a flare not less than 300 feet behind the car. If you have no lights, wave a light-colored cloth or paper, (even newspaper) to warn oncoming traffic.

If you need help, raise the hood of your car or attach a handkerchief to your radio antenna. A woman alone at night should stay in the car, with the doors locked, and wait until help arrives.

In case of brake failure

If your brakes suddenly fail, quickly pump the brake pedal to try to build up pressure in the system. Put the transmission in a lower gear (standard transmission into an intermediate gear) and apply the parking brake with a pumping action. At the same time, look for an escape route into which you can turn.

If you are on a steep grade and you are heading for a busy intersection, this downshifting technique may not be enough. In this event, move onto the right shoulder of the road, scraping the bank or guard rail if necessary, or turn into a field if one is handy. Even mowing down small trees is preferable to collision with another car.

If you're running low on gas

If you notice your gas gauge reads low, drive with your foot as steady as possible, at about 30 mph until you reach a gas station. A car that normally gives 12 miles per gallon at 50 will usually give about 20 miles at 30. This will save you quite a walk.

321

If headlights go out

Apply your brakes and get off the road as quickly as possible. If everything else electrical has gone off, a battery cable has probably loosened. Tap the cable lightly at the battery post with a rock or your shoe. Try the headlights. If they work, drive carefully to the first service station and have the cables cleaned and tightened.

If everything electrical is OK, but the headlights are out, probably a fuse has blown. If you don't have a replacement, try using the radio or heater fuse. If the lights flash off and on intermittently, you have a short and the circuit breaker is cutting on and off. Try locating the short by lightly jiggling the wires leading to the headlights. A spark will pinpoint where the insulation on the wire has worn off and rubbed the body, causing a short. If you don't have insulating tape handy, make temporary repairs by wrapping the worn wire with a non-conductive material such as paper or cloth.

If your engine catches fire

Stop the car and turn the ignition off. Get everybody out of the car as quickly as possible. If you have a fire extinguisher, raise the hood up only part way, so as to minimize the draft. Keep your back to the wind if possible. Aim your fire extinguisher stream at the base of the flames. If the flames are not too large, a wool blanket or jacket will also smother them.

If you see that it's only insulation burning on electrical wires, try cutting the wire or disconnecting the battery.

If an animal jumps in front of you

Try to steer around the animal if at all possible, taking into account other vehicles around you. If there is no time for an evasive maneuver, apply your brakes as hard as you can without locking them. Locking the brakes could cause a dangerous skid. The slower you are traveling at the time of impact with the animal, the easier the impact will be. If you hit an animal, report it to the owner or the police as soon as possible.

If the hood flies up

Quickly check the traffic to your rear. Slow down and pull to the side of the road. If you cannot pull right over because of traffic, quickly put the window down so you can put your head out of the window just far enough to see what's ahead.

If your accelerator sticks

Throw the gear shift in neutral and turn off the ignition key. If traffic allows, coast over to the shoulder of the road, using the foot brake to stop. A quick check of the throttle and pedal linkage will reveal what's wrong. Often a few drops of oil is all that is needed to unloosen a sticking throttle.

If your horn won't stop blowing

Lift the hood, find the horn relay switch, and tap it several times (it may be short circuited). If this fails, remove the lead wires to each horn, or as a last resort, simply cut the wires.

If you lock bumpers

One way to untangle cars with locked bumpers is for one or two people to stand on the end of the car with the lower bumper, while the other driver tries to back away. Lifting the upper bumper may also work, but be careful that arms or legs aren't caught in the process. If this doesn't work, you may have to jack up one of the cars in order to slip free.

If you lose your driver's license, money and all identification while traveling

Report it immediately to the local police. Next, contact the driver's license division of your state and request a duplicate driver's license. If you have lost travelers checks, stop payment immediately at the nearest bank. If you have lost credit cards, wire the various companies to cancel them immediately and issue replacements.

Usually the quickest way to obtain emergency money is to contact a relative, friend or your local bank and request that they wire you what you need. Ask the sender to "waive identification" and include a "test question" (no extra charge) in the money wire.

If you have to travel over flooded roads

If your car has to cross deep puddles after a heavy rain, drive slowly in low gear. If your engine sputters or stops, dry the spark plugs and the distributor with a dry cloth. Another warning: When water covers the exhaust pipe, engines stop. It can mean a tow job to get you out.

If your door lock freezes in winter

For a frozen lock, simply heat the key with a match or cigarette lighter and insert it. You may have to repeat the process several times, but it usually will thaw a frozen lock.

If you lose your keys or you lock yourself out of your car

If you are near the dealer from whom you bought your car, he can probably supply you with the key. If not, call the police. They will either refer you to someone who has master keys or will know how to employ the same break-in method used by car thieves. As a last resort for a lost ignition key the ignition lock can be bypassed with a jumper cable. An easy job for a mechanic.

It is always a wise idea to carry a spare key (other than in your key case) on your person for such emergencies. Another solution is to keep a key hidden under the car or hood. But remember, unless it's concealed cleverly, it's an open invitation for car theft.

If a tire blows out

Resist the urge to slam on the brakes. Don't panic. Pump the brakes gently so that you do not lose control. Keep a firm hand on the steering wheel and try to steer in a straight line. After your speed is reduced, ease the car onto a shoulder.

If you are the first one at the scene of an accident

Park your car off the road a safe distance away from the wreck (in case of fire). Don't start dragging the victims away from the wreckage, as an injured person can be killed as a result of improper handling. Move them only if traffic, fire or excessive bleeding requires it. Turn off the ignition of badly damaged cars. If other people arrive at the scene, send one to call the police and station the rest up and down the road to warn oncoming cars. Do not administer first aid unless you are qualified. Try to make the victims comfortable by loosening tight clothing and covering them if they are cold. Slow the flow of blood by pressing a clean cloth over the wounds. If you know what you're doing, apply pressure on the correct artery.

If your car suddenly goes into a skid

The best thing to know about a skid is how to avoid it. So keep your eyes peeled for wet leaves, mud slicks, and wet or icy spots on the pavement. In the event of a skid, do not panic and hit the brakes. Instead, let up on the accelerator gradually while turning the front wheels in the same direction as the skid. That is, if your rear wheels skid to the right, turn the front wheels to the right. Avoid over-correcting the skid and keep your car in gear. Once you're tracking again, lift your foot off the gas and pump the brakes lightly to slow down.

If you have to drive through fog

Turn on your lights, even during the daytime. But don't use your bright lights. The fog will reflect the beam back into your eyes and cut down on your vision. If necessary, turn on the defroster and wipers to keep the windshield clear. Reduce speed, of course.

If an oncoming car neglects to dim his lights

Don't look at oncoming lights. To avoid being blinded, keep your eyes directed to the right side of the road when passing. Dim your own lights. Chances are the other driver will dim his. If he doesn't, dim yours anyway. It's better to have one blinded driver instead of two. Most drivers find night driving easier if they keep their dash light on low.

If you have to drive in a bad electrical storm

One of the safest places for people during an electrical storm is inside a car because the rubber tires keep the car from being grounded. If a severe storm causes an electrical wire to fall across your car, avoid touching any metal parts inside the car. To summon help, use a plastic object or dry cloth or a piece of wood to depress your car's horn button or ring. Avoid parking under overhead power lines strung along the roadside.

If your vision is suddenly obstructed, as by mud, a water splash or paper blowing across the windshield

Slow down and hold the wheel in a straight line. Usually the windshield wiper will clear the obstruction. If there's water or mud around, don't jam the brakes. This may cause a skid.

If you see a car coming at you head on

If you have any steering room, try to steer out of the way! Remember, if two cars traveling at 50 mph meet head-on, it is similar to one of them hitting a solid wall at 100 mph.

If your right wheels go off the pavement onto a soft shoulder

Don't panic and try to make a quick correction. Instead, grip the wheel firmly and slow down as you guide the car back on the road.

CARRY THIS EMERGENCY EQUIPMENT IN YOUR CAR

Here's a list of tools and safety devices that you should keep in your car packed handily for quick use:

1. A supply of red flares for maximum protection against a night time "sitting duck" accident.
2. Fire extinguisher (multi-purpose dry chemical is best).
3. Electric lantern or flashlight. (Check batteries.)
4. Jack, lug wrench and jack support.
5. Supply of fuses.
6. Screwdrivers (blade and phillips), pliers, a set of wrenches, tape and any other car tools you know how to use.
7. Battery jumper cables.
8. A first-aid kit and manual.
9. Accident report forms and a list of your insurance company's offices.

325

10. Tow strap or chain.
11. A pair of work gloves and some clean rags.
12. A distress sign. You can make or buy an inexpensive sign with letters four to six inches high which says "Need Gas" on one side and "Send Help" on the other.
13. Safe container for gas.
14. Block and tackle.
15. Tow rope.
16. Tire pump.
17. Wooden blocks or chocks.
18. Siphon hose.
19. Fan belt.
20. Radiator hoses and clamps.
21. Engine oil.
22. Transmission fluid.
23. Ignition points.
24. Spark plugs.
25. Tire/tube repair kit.
26. Spare keys.
27. This book for quick reference.

What To Do If You Have A Traffic Accident

Unfortunate as it is, there are hundreds of thousands of traffic accidents in this country every year. And despite how good a driver you are or how well maintained your car is, the chances are still good that you may be involved in an auto accident sometime in the next 12 months.

Of course, let's hope that it doesn't happen. But should it happen, it will be to your advantage to know what to do. Besides the tragedy of any physical injuries that may occur, there is the other problem of possible litigation against you which could cause you great financial hardship.

So, here is what to do during those first critical moments after a traffic accident occurs.

Regardless of who's at fault,

1. Stop. It's unlawful to leave the scene of an accident.
2. Turn off the ignition switch. Don't smoke.
3. Secure medical help for anyone injured. Don't move them unless it's necessary to protect them from traffic or fire.
4. To prevent further accidents, arrange to warn oncoming traffic especially at night. If the cars are in the way of oncoming traffic, move them if you can.
5. Get the names of all witnesses at the scene, whether they actually saw the crash or not. Often witnesses won't want to get involved or even give their names. But if you can get their license number or house address, you may later be able to subpoena their testimony.
6. Exchange name, address, phone number, license information and insurance information with the other driver. Study the other driver's license. If the license makes a reference to eye glasses, note whether or not he has them on.
7. Do not discuss the accident. And do not argue about who was at fault. Watch what you say. It may be repeated in court. Don't promise restitution and don't sign anything! Actually, try not to say anything. If the other party presses, tell him you'd rather not discuss it now.
8. Note the physical condition of the other driver. Is he dazed? Does he smell of alcohol? Don't assume that a person is not injured because he says he isn't. It's wise in most instances to insist on a medical examination to avoid future complications.
9. Report the accident to the police (unless it's only a slight scratch). Be sure you get the names and badge numbers of the policemen who arrive on the scene. Your insurance company may want to have their testimony or want to see their official reports. Answer all police questions accurately and briefly. If you feel you are not at fault and the consequences of the accident are serious, you can refuse

to answer questions until a lawyer is with you. However, you must show the police your driver's license.

10. If passengers were in the other car, get their names and addresses. Often passengers involved in an accident are not always friendly toward their driver, so note any comments they may make. For example, one of them may complain that the driver was going too fast.

11. Get the name and address on the registration certificate on the other car. Note the license number, make, model, year, color and general condition. Examine the damage suffered by the other car, and look for evidence of prior damage (nicks and dents). If you should have to pay the repair bills, there is no point in paying for previous damage.

12. Record all details of the crash scene. It's always advisable to keep copies of your state accident report form in your glove compartment at all times. If you don't have a copy, record date, time, place, speed, position and direction of cars on a diagram.

13. Look for the unusual. Were road signs in place and traffic signals operating? Was the street or road under repair? Perhaps another car forced the other driver to swing wide. These facts could help your insurance investigator considerably in establishing blame or negligence for the accident. If a case is a toss-up in court, it usually goes to the side which can build up the clearest, most convincing picture through detail.

14. Report the accident promptly. Most states require that you file an official report within 24 hours. Also get in touch with your insurance agent or representative as soon as you can get to a telephone. Ask him for help in filling out official reports.

15. Regardless of who is at fault in the accident, you have the right to safeguard your car and its contents. It is the obligation of the police to give you this protection. No one can remove the car from the scene without your approval (except that the police can move it out of the way of traffic.)

Witness reliability

According to the American Automobile Association, witnesses rarely get called to court. Usually, the mere knowledge that a reliable witness saw an accident results in settlement out of court and protects the innocent party.

If anyone sees an accident occur, it is his moral duty to offer his name and address to the drivers. He should cooperate fully with the police in describing the accident, including what he believes to be the cause. A statement, called a deposition, is usually the extent of his involvement.

If necessary consult an attorney

While most auto accident claims are paid off without lawyers, a good lawyer can possibly boost the settlement you'd otherwise get. If you need a lawyer, try to get one of the top accident men in your area. An expert negligence attorney will cost no more than a kid just out of law school. Instead of charging you a flat fee, he'll probably take a percentage of what he can collect.

If there are any criminal charges against you as a result of the accident, then you must consult an attorney to defend you at the trial. Be honest with your attorney. Give him all the facts and details as they actually happened. Remember, he is on your side.

The towing racket

Because he monitors police calls by way of mobile radio, the tow car racketeer often arrives at an accident even before an ambulance. Avoid signing any papers, especially if offered by a tow truck operator who just "happens" to arrive. You may find, to your dismay, that you have not only authorized him to tow the car away at as much as $40 a mile, but completely repair it as well. This could void your right to reimbursement from the insurance company. Sign nothing until every increment of cost is spelled out.

An honest towing outfit will (a) move the car out of traffic as ordered by police, as a courtesy, (b) tow the car anywhere you direct, charging by the mile, (c) store the car in its own garage if you so direct, (d) make an estimate of repairs at no charge, just as a way of promoting business.

Before you say "tow it," ask to see the tow truck operator's credentials. Some city and highway authorities (particularly eastern expressways) closely regulate and license tow services.

Always get the name and address of the garage where your car will be towed. A lot of accident victims don't. Don't expect them to phone you. The worst of them will be glad to let your car pile up a big storage charge.

How To Plan A Successful Auto Trip

A family car trip should be a happy occasion. It's probably vacation time (90% of all vacations are car trips) and everyone in the family is looking forward to a good time, not a 4-wheeled nightmare that keeps getting worse as the trip progresses.

Like anything else in life, a happy, safe trip is more likely if you take the time beforehand to plan the trip. If you're planning a long trip by car—and most vacation trips average more than 1000 miles according to recent surveys—then advance planning is all the more necessary to insure that your family will be safe and comfortable for the duration of the trip.

Have a trip plan

Your first item of business should be a trip plan. Simply loading the car and roaring off is the best way to wind up in the middle of that nightmare we spoke of earlier.

Your local automobile club and most oil companies will be glad to map a route for you and provide you with up-to-the-minute information on new interstate highways and detours you may encounter. They can also recommend restaurants and lodgings.

Try to plan your trip and nightly stops according to how far you can comfortably go in one day. The amount of mileage you can roll up in one day will depend on the driver, whether there are any relief drivers, how often you stop, and the kind of roads you travel. On older roads, 300 miles a day may be a safe maximum (that's six hours on the road at a 50 mph average). Unless roads are exceptionally good, more daily mileage can be both tiring and dangerous.

We've all heard those slightly tired stories about how Bill's friend down at the lodge made it from New York to Miami Beach in one flat-out blast of 18 hours. But do you really want that kind of fatiguing trip? Or are you looking forward to more than just making time? Most Americans consider getting there by car part of the vacation. It's a more sensible attitude than simply trying to pile up mileage at the expense of all else.

Of course, with today's superhighways and modern cars, it's not unusual for a good driver in a good car to cover 500 miles in a day and not feel that he pushed too hard. However, this is one decision you have to make considering your own circumstances and your family's comfort as well.

A budget for travel

Your budget is an important item that should come into the planning picture early. Vacation expenditures will, of course, depend to a great extent on personal preferences, tastes and means. But like everything else these days, the cost of traveling by car has been caught in the inflationary spiral. The cost of gasoline alone has gone up about 80% in the past two years. But on the average, a couple should budget at least $46 a day to cover necessary spending such as meals, a night's lodging, gas, oil and normal car maintenance, plus a contingency fund to cover emergencies. Camping of course, will cut these daily expenditures greatly. Going the other route, that is, staying at luxury motels and eating gourmet meals, will, of course, increase your expenses enormously.

Based on a $46 daily average for two, the motorist's vacation dollar is divided approximately as follows: 36% for food; 30% for gas and oil; 26% for lodging; and 8% for tips and miscellaneous.

If possible, plan your trip for the spring or autumn. This way you avoid peak travel seasons when roads and overnight accommodations are crowded and prices high.

Try to visit travel attractions that offer you something worthwhile for your money. Avoid the usual tourist traps.

Drive during the early part of the day, and stop in the late afternoon so that you have plenty of time to find the type of accommodations you want at a price you can afford to pay.

Checklist of take-alongs

A few weeks before you start, begin making a list of things to take along and things to do. When you're ready to leave, check the list to see that you have all the luggage, driver's license, car title, auto insurance identification card, hospitalization card and other traveling papers. Be sure you have enough money. The best way to carry it is in traveler's checks which can be cashed anywhere—but only by you. Before leaving, be sure to check that you have sufficient auto insurance coverage. A few adjustments may be necessary if you plan to travel out of state or out of the country.

Credit cards can also save you the worry of carrying large sums of cash. This will give you an accurate record of your expenses during the trip, and payment will be delayed for about a month after your purchase is made. In some cases, gas credit cards are issued free of charge and are honored at various motel chains. These cards can save you an annual membership fee.

If you wear glasses, carry an extra pair of prescription glasses or carry the prescription with you.

Wear comfortable, loose clothing. Permanent-press clothing can be washed nightly, thereby saving you the trouble of carrying extras.

Check your car

Before starting on a long trip, be sure your car is ready for hard driving. A tuneup before starting out may save a dangerous stall or towing expense later. Tell your serviceman that you're going to take a trip. Here is a check list of things that should be inspected— brakes, steering, lights, horn, windshield wipers, mirrors, exhaust system, cooling system, and all hoses and belts. In addition, be sure that all fluid levels are checked, including battery, water, oil, transmission, differential, power steering reservoir and master brake cylinder.

Loading the car

Remember, a heavy load changes the handling characteristics of your car. So you may find increased sway on curves. Acceleration will also be more sluggish and stopping distances will be greater. You will have to allow more room for passing and stopping.

Try to distribute your load so that the steering and headlight aim won't be affected. Never load the car so you block the rear corner vision or the rear view mirror.

Never keep heavy, hard or pointed objects on the rear shelf. They can become lethal missiles should you have a minor collision or even a sudden stop.

You can often save an hour or so every day in loading and unloading if you store your luggage on the roof of your car. A lot of approved carriers are available at almost any auto accessory house. A top carrier can distribute the heavy load better.

If roof racks aren't practical, then try to pack the luggage you'll need for the night as one of the last items to go in. This way, it will be near the top and won't require the whole trunk to be unloaded when you want to get it out.

Because of the extra weight from passengers and luggage, tires must be in good shape to withstand the punishment. Make sure your tires are the right size for the load.

Additional air pressure is needed, too, when you travel at high speeds and/or in a fully loaded car. The extra air pressure in the tires helps stabilize the sidewalls and gives the tires extra carrying capacity to help support the load. The rule of thumb is four to six extra pounds of pressure for heavy loads and high speeds. But check your owner's manual for your manufacturer's specific recommendation.

Never *never* reduce the air pressure after the tires are hot. Taking the air pressure out of a hot tire will give a false reading. You may think the tire is overinflated. It's not. Always take tire pressure readings with the tire cold.

On the road

Remember, you may cover as many miles in one day of touring as you would in weeks of normal around town driving. So allow for routine maintenance more often. For example, the need for lubrication may come due once a week instead of every two months.

Set a definite time to service your car each day so you won't forget to take care of these chores. Before starting out in the morning, perhaps while the family is having breakfast, or on the first rest stop after breakfast are all good choices. When on the road, try to tie in gasoline stops with food and sightseeing stops. This saves time and is a good precaution against running low on fuel in thinly populated areas or where stations are closed on Sunday.

Besides filling the gas tank, remember to have the oil and battery checked each time you refuel. The coolant level should be checked only with the engine cold. So do it before starting out each morning. Check the tire pressure first thing each morning, too, when the tires are cold.

While driving, glance regularly at the dash instruments or warning lights, as well as the scenery. They are there to warn of trouble in the making.

Tailor your speed to the condition of the road, the traffic, the weather and your own fatigue point.

Know the law

Before taking a trip, check the speed limits for vehicles pulling trailers in the states you plan to travel through. These laws vary from state to state.

What To Do If You Are Getting Poor Gas Mileage

If you complain of excessive fuel consumption, a careful investigation of your driving habits and operating conditions, as well as the mechanical condition of the engine and fuel system are required. Otherwise, much needless work may be done in an attempt to increase fuel economy.

Driving habits which negatively affect fuel economy are high speed driving, frequent and rapid acceleration, driving too long in low and second gear when getting underway and excessive idling while standing.

Operating conditions which adversely affect fuel economy are excessive acceleration, frequent starts and stops, congested traffic, poor roads, hills and mountains, high winds and low tire pressures.

Driving at high speeds is the greatest contributor to low gas mileage. Air resistance increases as the square of speed. For instance, a car going 60 miles an hour must overcome air resistance four times as great as when going 30 miles an hour. At 80 miles an hour the resistance is over seven times as great as when going 30 miles an hour. Over 75% of the power required to drive a car 80 miles an hour is used in overcoming air resistance, while at 30 miles an hour only 30% of the power required is used to overcome air resistance.

Gas mileage records made by car owners never give a true picture of the efficiency of the engine fuel system since they include the effects of driving habits and operating conditions. Because these conditions vary widely, it is impossible to give average mileage figures for cars in general use. Therefore, any investigation of a mileage complaint must be based on an accurate measurement of gasoline consumption per mile under proper test conditions.

Gasoline Mileage Test

There are a number of gasoline mileage testers commercially available that measure fuel consumption precisely. Manufacturers of these devices furnish full instructions for their use. However, you can make an inexpensive tester with a quart oil can, suitable fittings

334

and a tube to connect the can to the carburetor.

Drill or punch a hole in the bottom of the can and solder a fitting to the hole. The fitting at the carburetor end should be the same as the existing fitting at the carburetor inlet. Arrange a suitable handle or wire hook to the can so it can be mounted either under the hood or in the driver's compartment.

Before making the test, disconnect the fuel pipe at the carburetor and plug the pipe opening with a small cork so that the fuel will not spurt out during the test. Run the engine until all the fuel in the carburetor is used up. Then connect the tester tube to the carburetor.

With the can mounted at a higher level than the carburetor so the fuel will flow into the carburetor by gravity, pour exactly one quart of gasoline into the can.

Make the test on a reasonably level road, at fixed speeds, without acceleration or deceleration. Test runs should be made in both directions over the same stretch of road to average the effect of grade and wind resistance. Test runs made at 30, 50, and 70 miles an hour will indicate the approximate efficiency of the low speed, high speed and power systems of the carburetor and show whether fuel consumption is actually abnormal. Under the conditions given, the fuel consumption in miles per gallon, based on the normal economy of a car capable of giving 20 miles per gallon at 20 miles per hour, should be approximately as follows:

Constant Speed	Miles per Gallon
20	20.0
30	19.7
50	15.9
70	8.0

If it takes five miles to empty the can, it means that the fuel consumption is 20 miles per gallon, since there are four quarts to the gallon.

If the test indicates that the fuel consumption is above normal, go over the following list before deciding to take the carburetor apart:

1. Check all gasoline pipe connections, fuel pump bowl gasket, gasoline filter gasket, and carburetor bowl gasket.
2. Check for low tire pressures.
3. Check for dragging brakes.
4. Late ignition timing causes loss of power and increases

fuel consumption. Dirty or worn out spark plugs are wasteful of fuel.

5. Use of gasoline of such low grade that ignition timing must be retarded to avoid excessive detonation will give very poor fuel economy.

6. Check for sticking manifold heater valve or improper setting of the thermostat.

7. Check for dirty or clogged air cleaner element and for excessive oil in the crankcase.

8. Check for sticking choke valve and improper setting of the automatic choke thermostat.

9. Check for insufficient valve operating clearance or sticking valve.

10. Check for excessive fuel pump pressure.

11. Check for carburetor idle adjustment. On Carter carburetors, the metering rod setting may be checked without removing the carburetor. For all other corrections to high speed and power systems on all carburetors, the carburetor must be removed and disassembled.

Changing Carburetor Jets

Under no circumstances should leaner than standard jet sizes, metering rods and other calibrations of a carburetor be changed from factory specifications. The specified calibrations must be adhered to unless these are later changed by a bulletin issued by the carburetor manufacturer.

Carburetor calibrations have been determined by exhaustive tests with laboratory equipment and instruments which accurately measure overall performance and economy. Besides, the leanest possible mixture obtainable by the use of smaller jets, etc., will not increase mileage as much as 10%, and will often impair engine performance.